wiat-ii

Wechsler Individual Achievement Test®
Second Edition

Examiner's Manual

THE
PSYCHOLOGICAL
CORPORATION®

A Harcourt Assessment Company

Acknowledgments

The development of the *Wechsler Individual Achievement Test–Second Edition* (WIAT–II) began in 1996. In the past five years, literally hundreds of people have made significant contributions to this publication, and it is impossible to thank each of them by name. Nonetheless, several individuals deserve recognition and gratitude.

A noteworthy group of consultants in the field provided invaluable guidance throughout the project. Drs. Robert Abbott, Steve Graham, Betty Gridley, Nancy Robinson, Gale Roid, Don Saklofske, Richard Venezsky, and Susan Vogel generously shared their expertise and ideas. A special thanks is due Dr. Virginia Berninger, who spent many days and nights reviewing test items and manuals, and unselfishly shared her time and expertise with the research director. Her commitment to the co-development of the *Process Assessment of the Learner for Reading and Writing* (PAL–RW) and WIAT–II ensures that cutting-edge research can be used to improve assessment and intervention practices.

Dr. Aurelio Prifitera, President of The Psychological Corporation, began the journey with the development staff and his support, encouragement, and advice have been unwavering. His commitment to excellence set the standard that everyone working on the project aspired to meet. Dr. Larry Weiss, Director of the Psychological Measurement Group, kept the project on track and provided assistance, especially with data analysis, during the last year of the project.

Several Research Directors made significant contributions to test development. Dr. Kathleen Matula assisted with the development of the blueprint and provided guidance through the pilot phase. Dr. Denise Hildebrand contributed to several aspects of tryout and provided content expertise for the development of the various scoring assistants and report writers. Drs. Elizabeth Stanczak and Marites Piñon diligently assisted with analysis of the standardization data and the development of the final test kit components. Dr. Piñon also took the lead in the data analysis for the college and adult samples and prepared the *WIAT–II Supplement for College Students and Adults*.

The development team tackled the difficult task of improving the WIAT. Both Victoria Locke, Research Analyst, and Sandy Grossman, Research Associate, worked diligently throughout the project and deserve special thanks. Victoria did everything from developing test items to recruiting test examiners and sites and preparing a monthly examiner's newsletter. Sandy's commitment and dedication to the project was exceptional as she meticulously maintained the case databases through each testing phase, served as the liaison between development and the examiners, and solved a multitude of day-to-day problems which allowed the research director to stay focused and on task. Dianna Carrizales, Research Associate, developed the standardization scoring manual and trained the hand scoring staff. Her assistance with data preparation, the coordination of the clinical case studies, and the review of kit components was invaluable. Sharon Primeaux, Research Associate, ensured that the tables for the Supplements were formatted correctly and helped with the quality assurance process. Alanna McCormick, Research Assistant, assisted with the development of the final record form, response booklet, and stimulus booklets. Jeff Gatlin, project employee, worked on several aspects of the project and helped coordinate the development activities of the PAL–RW with WIAT–II. Six interns from Trinity University, Beth Abrahamson, Judith Longfellow, Amy Cassata, Kerri Siefkin, Monica Feuerborn, and Lew Huck helped test cases, reviewed manuscripts, and provided invaluable support along the way.

Dr. Christina Wynings, Manager of Clinical Sampling, supervised case collection. Several members of her team deserve special recognition. The outstanding efforts of Peggy Castro, Sunny Henson, Patsy Morris, and Ruth Mendez enabled us to meet the sampling plan for tryout and standardization. Scoring activities were accomplished under the direction of David Quintero with data preparation support from Fred Casillas, Glen Larson, and Robert Streckfus. The Computer Products Group, directed by Dr. Jim Segapeli, undertook the development of a case tracking system.

Appreciation is extended to members of the psychometrics team, under the leadership of Dr. Charles Wilkins, for their hard work throughout the project phases. Drs. Larry Price and Agnes Stephenson, along with Cleopatra DeLeon, Research Analyst, and Cindy Kreiman, helped with the analysis for the tryout and standardization phases. A special thanks is due to Dr. Jianjun Zhu, Senior Research Director, for his unselfish assistance at the eleventh hour. Three consultants, Dr. Gale Roid, Tom Trippel, and Dr. Hsin-Yi Chen, provided invaluable assistance in the development of the norms and in conducting the ability–achievement analysis.

The preparation of the test components and the administration manual and supplements has been a complex task, requiring many hours of design, editing, and proofreading. Senior Editor Elizabeth Manclark worked tirelessly to make sure that the components met high standards and were completed in a timely manner. Other staff members who assisted with the editorial tasks include Kathy Overstreet, Supervising Editor, Janice Miller, Pam Parmer, Cynthia Woerner, Harriett Wiygul, Margaret Cooley, Michelle Girard, and Dawn Dunleavy. Many members of the Production Department also contributed to the overall appearance and design of the test kit. Marian Zahora, Designer, and Javier Flores worked tirelessly to design an effective record form and a design for this manual. David Mellott is to be commended for his hard work in typesetting and managing the contents of the stimulus booklets and manual. Production and Manufacturing activities were kept on track by Cyndi Sweet, Production Specialist, Pat Malec, Design and Composition Manager, Robin Espiritu, Production Coordinator, and Stephanie Adams, Production Manager. Jeffrey Heinke excelled in his cover designs, and Eric Fonseca managed specifications and artists.

Thanks to Project Managers Daniel Hunt and Dr. Tommie Cayton for their efforts in keeping the team focused as we moved from standardization into the final phase. Their ability to "muster the troops" enabled us to meet the publishing timeline.

Finally, a heartfelt thanks to the many examiners and examinees who devoted significant time and energy to the collection of research data. Without their participation, there would be no WIAT–II.

Donna Rury Smith, Ed.D.
Research Director

Contents

Chapter 3. Testing Considerations

Chapter 4. Administration and Scoring

Chapter 5. Development and Standardization

Chapter 6. Reliability and Validity

Chapter 7. Interpretation

WIAT–II Examiners, Reviewers, and Participating Schools and Districts

References

Figures

Tables

1 Introduction

The *Wechsler Individual Achievement Test–Second Edition* (WIAT–II) is a comprehensive, individually administered test for assessing the achievement of children, adolescents, college students, and adults who are in Grades Pre-kindergarten (PreK) through 16 or who are aged 4 through adulthood. The WIAT–II is a revision of the *Wechsler Individual Achievement Test* (WIAT; The Psychological Corporation, 1992). While the WIAT–II retains the basic content domains of reading, writing, mathematics, and oral language, the depth of each subtest has increased to include new items, and the content updated to reflect current curriculum standards. The WIAT–II (see Figure 1.1) can be used to comprehensively assess a broad range of academic skills or to test only in the area of need. Administration time varies depending on the age of the examinee and the number of subtests administered.

The WIAT–II was nationally standardized on 5,586 individuals and features comprehensive normative information including age- and grade-based standard scores, percentiles, stanines, normal curve equivalents (NCEs), and age and grade equivalents for each of the subtests. Additionally, a subset of the WIAT–II standardization sample was administered the *Wechsler Intelligence Scales*. The *Wechsler Preschool and Primary Scale of Intelligence–Revised* (WPPSI–R; Wechsler, 1989) was administered to 199 children, the *Wechsler Intelligence Scale for Children– Third Edition* (WISC–III; Wechsler, 1991) was given to 775 students, and the *Wechsler Adult Intelligence Scale–Third Edition* (WAIS–III; Wechsler, 1997) was administered to 95 students aged 16–19. For a description of the college and adult WAIS–III linking sample, see the *WIAT–II Supplement for College Students and Adults*.

Scale Antecedents

The first edition of the WIAT was designed as a norm-referenced measure of academic achievement of students in Grades Kindergarten (K) through 12 and was the only individually administered achievement test directly linked with the Wechsler scales. Experts emphasize the importance of using co-normed or linked data from achievement and ability tests as a way to reduce measurement error when conducting a discrepancy analysis (Berk, 1984; Reynolds, 1990; Shepard, 1980). The WIAT was also unique in its comprehensive coverage of the areas of learning disability specified in the Education for All Handicapped Children Act of 1975 (Public Law 94-142): oral expression, listening comprehension, written expression, basic reading skill, reading comprehension, mathematics calculation, and mathematics reasoning.

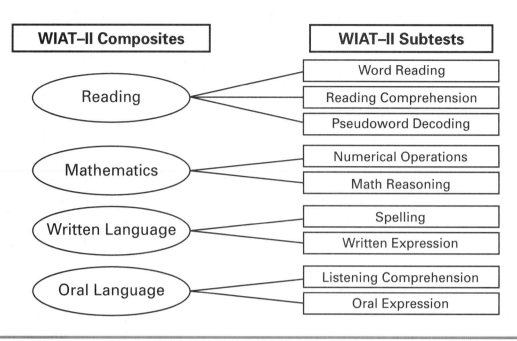

Figure 1.1.
WIAT–II Composites and Subtests

Development of the WIAT–II

One of the principal goals of the WIAT–II was to develop norms based on a contemporary sample of individuals. Although the basic structure of the revision retains specific features from the first edition of the WIAT, including linkage with the Wechsler scales and domain coverage consistent with areas specified by law to assess learning disability, the WIAT–II incorporates the following modifications.

- **Modification of Subtests.** The WIAT subtests were updated and modified to strengthen the WIAT–II theoretical base and to reflect changes in curriculum standards and classroom instructional practices. The Listening Comprehension and Oral Expression subtests were revised to be more representative of the language skills that are required for success in the classroom. The Reading Comprehension subtest was modified to include higher-order comprehension questions and to assess oral reading and reading rate. A measure of phonological decoding was added to evaluate word attack skills, and the single prompt format for the Written Expression subtest was revised to provide the examinee multiple opportunities to demonstrate writing skills. Refer to Chapter 2 for a detailed summary of the subtest modifications. A description of the WIAT–II composites and subtests can be found in Table 1.1.

- **Strengthening of the Link Between Assessment and Instruction/Intervention.** The link between assessment and instruction/intervention was strengthened by expanding the skill analysis feature and by evaluating both the product (e.g., writing sample) and the process (e.g., word fluency) that contribute to skill acquisition. Qualitative Observations checklists were added to the record form to provide additional information that can guide the development of effective instructional plans.

- **Extension of the Age Range.** To fully assess pre-academic skills and facilitate early identification and intervention for young children at-risk for academic failure, the age range of the

WIAT–II was lowered to include children aged 4 years and 0 months. To assess the academic achievement of college adults who are experiencing academic difficulties and to include adults in the general population who need a comprehensive evaluation of academic skills, the age range was extended to include adults aged up to 85 years.

- **Improved Scoring.** The scoring systems for the Reading Comprehension, Written Expression, and Oral Expression subtests were improved by introducing scoring rules consistent with instructional practice and by providing additional scoring examples for the examiner.

- **Inclusion of Ability–Achievement Discrepancy Tables Using Verbal IQ, Performance IQ, and Factor Scores.** The WIAT–II features ability–achievement discrepancy (predicted achievement and simple difference) tables based on Full Scale, Verbal, and Performance IQs from the WPPSI–R, WISC–III, and WAIS–III and, the Verbal Comprehension Index (VCI), and the Perceptual Organization Index (POI) factor scores from the WISC–III and the WAIS–III.

- **Statistical Linkage to a Process Instrument.** The WIAT–II was linked to the *Process Assessment of the Learner–Test Battery for Reading and Writing* (PAL–RW; Berninger, 2001), a process instrument used for diagnostic and prescriptive purposes.

Using the WIAT–II Examiner's Manual and Supplements

The WIAT–II is organized into a general manual and two supplements. The *WIAT–II Examiner's Manual* includes a description of test development and provides general administration, scoring, reliability, validity, interpretation, and intervention information. Scoring guidelines and samples and normative data are provided in the companion supplements, the *WIAT–II Scoring and Normative Supplement for Grades PreK–12* and the *WIAT–II Supplement for College Students and Adults.* The *WIAT–II Supplement for College Students and Adults* also includes information specific to using the WIAT–II with college and adult examinees.

WIAT–II Examiner's Manual

The WIAT–II materials are designed so that once familiar with administration procedures as detailed in the *Examiner's Manual,* the examiner will not need to use this manual during the assessment session. This chapter provides an introduction to the WIAT–II, a description of the subtests, the context of assessment, applications, test limitations, and user responsibilities. Chapter 2 details the theoretical framework and research findings that formed the development of the subtests and composites. General testing considerations, which include start points, reverse and discontinue rules, stop points, and an overview of recording and scoring procedures, including instructions on using the record form are located in Chapter 3. Chapter 4 includes specific administration details, and recording and scoring procedures for each subtest. Detailed information regarding the process of scale revision, scale development and standardization, and the technical attributes of the test are presented in Chapter 5. Evidence for test reliability and validity is located in Chapter 6. Chapter 7 provides information about using the WIAT–II in conjunction with the WPPSI–R, the WISC–III, and the WAIS–III to calculate ability–achievement discrepancies. Chapter 7 also provides interpretation guidelines including the use of the Qualitative Observations checklists and item-level error analysis, and intervention recommendations based on test results. This manual also includes a list of the examiners, reviewers, participating schools and districts, and references.

Table 1.1.

Description of the WIAT–II Composites and Subtests

Composite	Subtest	Description
Reading	Word Reading	Assess pre-reading (phonological awareness) and decoding skills. • Name the letters of the alphabet • Identify and generate rhyming words • Identify the beginning and ending sounds of words • Match sounds with letters and letter blends • Read aloud from a graded word list
	Reading Comprehension	Reflect reading instruction in the classroom. • Match a written word with its representative picture • Read passages and answer content questions • Read short sentences aloud, and respond to comprehension questions
	Pseudoword Decoding	Assess the ability to apply phonetic decoding skills. • Read aloud a list of nonsense words designed to mimic the phonetic structure of words in the English language
Mathematics	Numerical Operations	Evaluate the ability to identify and write numbers. • Count using 1:1 correspondence • Solve written calculation problems • Solve simple equations involving all basic operations (addition, subtraction, multiplication, and division)
	Math Reasoning	Assess the ability to reason mathematically. • Count • Identify geometric shapes • Solve single- and multi-step word problems • Interpret graphs • Identify mathematical patterns • Solve problems related to statistics and probability
Written Language	Spelling	Evaluate the ability to spell. • Write dictated letters, letter blends, and words
	Written Expression	Measure the examinee's writing skills at all levels of language. • Write the alphabet (timed) • Demonstrate written word fluency • Combine and generate sentences • Produce a rough-draft paragraph (Grades 3–6) or a persuasive essay (Grades 7–16)
Oral Language	Listening Comprehension	Measure the ability to listen for details. • Select the picture that matches a word or sentence • Generate a word that matches a picture and oral description
	Oral Expression	Reflect a broad range of oral language activities. • Demonstrate verbal word fluency • Repeat sentences verbatim • Generate stories from visual cues • Generate directions from visual or verbal cues

WIAT–II Scoring and Normative Supplement for Grades PreK–12

The *WIAT–II Scoring and Normative Supplement for Grades PreK–12* includes scoring guidelines and additional scoring examples for the Reading Comprehension, Written Expression, and Oral Expression subtests in Appendix A. Conversion tables for the supplemental scores are located in Appendices B (grade-based) and E (age-based). Appendices C (grade-based) and F (age-based) contain all of the normative tables for determining the subtest standard scores. Additional grade-based normative information, such as confidence intervals, percentile ranks, stanines, NCEs and grade equivalents, is included in Appendix D. The same information for age-based scores is found in Appendix G. Table 1.2 presents the types of derived scores for the WIAT–II composites and subtests. Appendix H contains the WIAT–II composite and subtest scores predicted from the WPPSI–R, WISC–III, and WAIS–III. Appendix I provides information on the differences required for statistical significance and the differences obtained by the standardization linking sample when using the predicted-achievement method for ability-achievement analysis. Appendix J presents data on the differences required for statistical significance and the differences obtained by the standardization linking sample when using the simple-difference method. Appendix K contains the ipsative information about differences in standard scores and differences in composite scores required for statistical significance and the cumulative percentages of the standardization sample obtaining various discrepancies. Intersubtest scatter for the cumulative percentages of the standardization sample and intercorrelations of WIAT–II subtest and composite standard scores and the Wechsler IQ scores are also included in Appendix K.

Table 1.2.
Derived Scores for the WIAT–II Composites and Subtests

Score Type	Description
Standard Score	By age ($M = 100$, $SD = 15$), with a range of 40 to 160.
	By grade ($M = 100$, $SD = 15$), with a range of 40 to 160, with separate Fall, Winter and Spring tables for Grades PreK–8 and yearly tables after Grade 8.
Percentile Rank	By age or grade, indicating the percentage of individuals of the same age or grade who scored the same or lower than the examinee.
Age or Grade Equivalent	By age or grade, providing the age or grade which the individual's raw score is the median score of all scores in that age group or grade.
Normal Curve Equivalent	A normalized transformation of age- and grade-based standard score information ($M = 50$, $SD = 21.06$).
Stanine	A transformation of age- and grade-based standard score information to a 9-point scale.
Quartile Score	Each quartile score represents the corresponding quarter of a distribution of scores. The quartile score of 1 is the first quarter (the bottom 25%) of the distribution, etc. In certain subtests, there is a finer categorization than quarters so that the bottom 5% can be identified. In these cases, the bottom 5% are given a quartile score of 0.
Decile Score	Each decile score represents the corresponding tenth of a distribution of scores. A decile score of 1 represents the first tenth (the bottom 10%) of the distribution, etc.

WIAT–II Supplement for College Students and Adults

The *WIAT–II Supplement for College Students and Adults* provides information specific to using the WIAT–II with college and adult examinees. General information about the test and how to administer it can be found in the Examiner's Manual. The supplement includes an introduction to the WIAT–II, information about the process of scale development and standardization, the technical attributes of the test, and evidence for test reliability and validity. Appendix A includes scoring guidelines and additional scoring examples for the Reading Comprehension, Written Expression, and Oral Expression subtests. Conversion tables for the supplemental scores are located in Appendices B (grade-based) and E (age-based). Appendices C (grade-based) and F (age-based) contain all of the normative tables for determining the subtest standard scores. Additional grade-based normative information, such as confidence intervals, percentile ranks, stanines, NCEs and grade equivalents, is included in Appendix D. The same information for age-based scores is found in Appendix G. Refer to Table 1.2 for the types of derived scores for the WIAT–II composites and subtests. Appendix H contains the WIAT–II composite and subtest scores predicted from the WAIS–III. Appendix I provides information on the differences required for statistical significance and the differences obtained by the standardization linking sample when using the predicted-achievement method for ability–achievement analysis. Appendix J presents data on the differences required for statistical significance and the differences obtained by the standardization linking sample when using the simple-difference method. Appendix K contains the ipsative information about differences in standard scores and differences in composite scores required for statistical significance and the cumulative percentages of the standardization sample obtaining various discrepancies. Intersubtest scatter for the cumulative percentages of the standardization sample and intercorrelations of WIAT–II subtest and composite standard scores and the WAIS–III IQ scores are also included in Appendix K.

WIAT–II Applications Within the Context of Assessment

An individually administered achievement test such as the WIAT–II can be used in a variety of settings including schools, clinics, private practices, and residential treatment facilities. The WIAT–II can provide meaningful information to assist with diagnostic, eligibility, placement, and intervention decisions. WIAT–II users have a significant responsibility to ensure the accuracy and thoroughness of test administration and interpretation in order to protect the social and legal rights of the individual whose achievement is assessed. Kamphaus (1993) stresses an integrative method of assessment interpretation that includes the collection and integration of data from numerous sources. Matarazzo (1990) highlights the distinction between testing and assessment, emphasizing the need to collect information in addition to test results. He recommends that test results be integrated with information gained from direct observation; background information from the family, adolescent, or young adult; information from school records; and information from additional sources. Salvia and Ysseldyke (1991) suggest that it is important to view learning difficulties within the context of the individual's instructional environment and history. Therefore, the results obtained from the WIAT–II should never be interpreted in isolation but in combination with a thorough evaluation and review of the individual's background, personality, current emotional functioning, and attention and motivation levels.

Limitations of the WIAT–II

Like all assessment instruments, the WIAT–II has certain limitations. Academic achievement can be conceptualized and assessed in many different ways. As a result, it is impossible to develop an instrument that assesses all components of achievement within the constraints of a typical standardized assessment situation. The WIAT–II measures aspects of the learning process that take place in the traditional academic setting in the areas of reading, writing, mathematics, and oral language. Although the WIAT–II item content encompasses a wide range of skills and concepts, it was not designed as a measure of academic giftedness in older adolescents or adults.

User Qualifications and Test Security

In general, professionals who are involved in psychological or educational testing and who have training in the use of individually administered assessment instruments are qualified to administer and interpret the WIAT–II. In all cases, examiners should have training in the fundamental principles of assessment procedures, including how to: establish and maintain rapport, elicit optimum performance, follow standardized administration procedures, understand the psychometric statistics, score and interpret tests, and maintain test security. The examiner should have experience in testing individuals whose ages and linguistic backgrounds, as well as their clinical, cultural, or educational histories, are similar to those of the individuals they will assess with the WIAT–II. Experienced professionals should supervise examiners who do not have formal training in assessment and must ensure best clinical practice so that test results are reliable and valid. *Only individuals who have received professional training in educational or psychological assessment should interpret the WIAT–II results.*

It is the responsibility of the test user to ensure the security of the test materials. Test materials, record forms, and interpretative reports should be released only to professionals who will safeguard their proper use. Although reviewing the test results with parents, the examinee, and appropriate school personnel is appropriate and encouraged as proper assessment practice, this review should not include disclosure or copying of test items, record forms, or other test materials that would compromise the security, validity, or value of the test as a measurement tool. Because all test items, norms, and other testing materials are copyrighted, the Rights and Permissions Department of The Psychological Corporation must approve *in writing* the copying or reproduction of any test materials. The only exception to this requirement is the copying of a completed record form to convey an individual's records to another qualified professional. These user qualifications, the test security policy, and the copyright restrictions are consistent with the guidelines set forth in the *Standards for Educational and Psychological Testing* (1999).

Revisions of the Scale

Although the basic structure of the WIAT–II is the same as that of the WIAT, the modifications to the second edition were determined by an extensive review of the research literature and on data collected during the tryout and standardization phases. Changes include the addition of a new reading subtest; changes in the items, administration, and scoring of some subtests; and an expansion of the error analysis as a guide to instructional planning. The most significant modification is the extension of the age range from 5 through 19 years to 4 years through adulthood with the inclusion of preschoolers, college students, and adults.

Revisions Guided by Research, Standards, and Mandates

The WIAT subtest content was reviewed according to the current research, state standards, government reports, and legislative actions. Nationally based focus groups and surveys explored content-related issues, and a test-users panel provided valuable input about the functionality of the test components. After each recommendation was considered, modifications were incorporated into the second edition.

Reading Subtests

The revision of the reading subtests was strongly influenced by the work of Virginia Berninger from the University of Washington. Berninger conducts reading and writing assessment and intervention research funded by the National Institute of Child Health and Human Development (NICHHD). According to Berninger's research, instruction and assessment should be aimed at both low-level (word recognition) and high-level (comprehension) skills, and at all levels of language (subword, word, and text).

Another strong influence in the revision of the reading subtests was the report of the National Reading Panel (2000). Specifically, letter identification and phonological awareness tasks were added to the Word Reading subtest because correlational studies identified phonological awareness and letter knowledge as excellent school-entry predictors of how well children learn to read during the first 2 years of instruction (National Reading Panel). Delays in the development of phonological awareness are frequently found in children with developmental reading disabilities (Alexander, Andersen, Heilman, Voeller, & Torgesen, 1991; Bradley & Bryant, 1978; Gough & Tunmer, 1986), and early assessment of these skills prior to formal reading instruction is a reliable predictor of later reading achievement (Torgesen, Wagner, & Rashotte, 1994). Other studies (Adams, 1990; Lennon & Slesinski, 1999) suggest that letter naming is also an appropriate measure for selecting examinees for differing levels of intervention.

Phonological awareness is also measured by the Pseudoword Decoding subtest. This subtest was created to measure a different skill set than that measured in the Word Reading subtest. The examinee is not able to use sight-word knowledge to decode the nonwords and must rely on phonological abilities to do so. Specifically, the nonwords can be decoded on the basis of spelling–phoneme relationships, but not by retrieval of word-specific representations in long-term memory. Pseudoword decoding is widely used to evaluate if the phonological decoding mechanism is developing according to expectations based on developmental trends. Gough and Tunmer (1986) suggested that the purest measure of spelling–sound correspondence rules of the English language is the ability to pronounce pseudowords. Rack, Snowling, and Olson (1992) note that difficulty in reading aloud well-spelled nonsense words is a singularly powerful indicator of a specific reading disability. However, it is imperative that the pseudowords include not only nonwords that are visually similar to real words, but also include more complex nonwords that place increased demands on phonological processing. Nonwords that are visually similar to real words allow individuals to read by analogy (e.g., *ched, broan, pragment*), but complex nonwords require the reader to blend multiple units to achieve the correct pronunciation (e.g., *unfrodding, retashment, tomingly*). If the pseudoword list includes complex nonwords, research indicates that phonologically unskilled readers will demonstrate a nonword reading deficit that may not be apparent if the individual reads only from a real word list (Manis, Szeszulski, Holt, & Graves, 1988; Olson, Wise, Conners, Rack, & Fulker, 1989; Snowling, 1981).

The Reading Comprehension subtest was revised to measure not only comprehension of short passages, but also reading rate, oral reading prosody, and the ability to read target words in the context of a sentence. According to Pressley and Wharton-McDonald (1997), "the most important goal of reading education is to develop readers who can derive meaning from texts" (p. 448). Research has shown that fluency of oral reading appears to be necessary, but is not necessarily sufficient, for many kinds of reading comprehension (Kuhn & Stahl, 2000; Stahl, Heubach, & Cramond, 1997). Because the vast majority of examinees in the WIAT–II standardization sample chose to read passages silently, the reading speed tables are based on the silent reading fluency of passages. The speed of silent reading is an important issue in evaluating if an individual should be allotted extra time in a standardized testing session. Although curriculum-based, oral reading fluency measures evaluate reading speed early in the developing reader, students who have transitioned from oral to silent reading (e.g., in the intermediate grades) may be more appropriately evaluated using a measure of silent reading speed. It is important to assess reading speed in relationship to accuracy (Berninger, 1989). Lovett (1987) identified two subtypes of reading disability: accuracy-disabled and rate-disabled. According to her definition, an individual with an *accuracy disability* has difficulty with both speed and accuracy, but an individual with a *rate disability* has age-appropriate word recognition (accuracy) but demonstrates slower reading speed when compared to his or her age-group peers. On the WIAT–II, the Reading Rate score identifies the slow and accurate, slow and inaccurate, fast and accurate, and fast and inaccurate reader.

Mathematics Subtests

One of the major goals in updating the WIAT math subtests was to respond to issues raised by the National Council of Teachers of Mathematics (NCTM) in the *Principles and Standards for School Mathematics* (2000). Many states have formulated their own standards for math instruction based on the NCTM recommendations. These standards include the mathematical domains of: number and operations, algebra, geometry, measurement, data analysis and probability, problem solving, reasoning and proof, communication, and connections and representation. The NCTM report is intended to set forth a comprehensive and coherent set of mathematical goals that will orient curricular, teaching, and assessment efforts for the future. According to the report:

"math assessment should support the learning of important mathematics and furnish useful information to both teachers and students . . . When teachers have useful information about what students are learning, they can support their students' progress toward significant mathematical goals. The instructional decisions made by teachers—such as how and when to review prerequisite material, how to revisit a difficult concept, or how to adapt tasks for students who are struggling or for those who need enrichment—are based on inferences about what students know and what they need to learn. Assessment is a primary source of the evidence on which these inferences are based, and the decisions that teachers make will be only as good as that evidence." (p. 21–22)

The Numerical Operations and Math Reasoning subtests include several new items directed at the young student because, according to the NCTM (2000) document, even young children are interested in mathematical ideas and are developing "a rather complex set of informal ideas about numbers, patterns, shapes, quantities, data, and size" (p. 21). Further, Gelman and Gallistel (1978) and Resnick (1987) have noted that many of these ideas are learned naturally, before children begin school. Because math assessment should focus on examinees' understanding, as well as their procedural skills, the math subtests encourage error analysis. Additionally, you may want to readminister specific items after test administration and invite the examinee to "think aloud" during problem solution. Since individuals can solve problems using multiple approaches, thinking aloud can provide a complete representation of the procedures employed and allow the individual to demonstrate his or her best strengths. The NCTM notes that the instructional value of assessment is maximized when teachers move beyond the "right or wrong" analysis of tasks to focus on how a student is thinking about the tasks. Gaining this insight helps teachers evaluate a student's progress toward instructional goals, and also aids in making decisions about the content of instruction.

Pure memorization of math facts or procedural steps produces learning that is often tenuous (Bransford, Brown, & Cocking, 1999) and difficult to generalize; math makes more sense and is easier to remember and apply if the individual is able to connect new knowledge to old in meaningful ways (Schoenfeld, 1988). A recently published study by Bryant, Bryant, and Hammill (2000) notes that individuals diagnosed with math learning disabilities most often have trouble with multi-step problem solving, regrouping and renaming, and recalling number facts automatically. The Byrant et al. research concludes that having difficulty with "multi-step problems is the single most important behavior for predicting math weaknesses," (p. 175). When an individual demonstrates this difficulty, paired with an inability to regroup and rename, these behaviors signify potentially serious learning problems. The skill analysis for the Math Reasoning subtest identifies the items that require a multi-step solution.

Written Language Subtests

The revision of the Spelling and Written Expression subtests was guided by current research as reported by Moats (1995), Berninger (1998), Graham, Berninger, Abbott, Abbott, and Whitaker (1997), and Berninger (2001). Specifically, the Spelling subtest words were revised to include words representing different levels of morphological knowledge. For example, the words include inflectional suffixes that mark past tense (e.g., *closed*), derivational suffixes that mark a part of speech (e.g., *carefully*), and prefixes (e.g., *infamous*). The Spelling subtest also contains words from the Anglo-Saxon layer of language (e.g., *you, the*), which is the word origin for most primary grade reading materials, words from the Romance layer of language (e.g., *flexible, ridicule*), and the Greek layer of language (e.g., *phonograph, scholar, topography*). Starting with Grade 4, literacy materials contain many words from the Romance and Greek layers of language (Balmuth, 1992; Henry, 1990).

Spelling tasks require both phonological skills (e.g., accurate representation of spoken words in memory), orthographic skills (e.g., expressive production of letters), and the knowledge of phoneme–spelling correspondence. The inclusion of high frequency homonyms in the Spelling subtest measures the examinee's lexical access, that is, the ability to identify spelling based on the contextual meaning provided in the dictated sentence. Thus, spelling requires the coordination of subword-, word-, and sentence-level processes that draw upon the phonological, orthographical, semantic, and syntactic knowledge of language, and the morphological knowledge of inflectional suffixes, derivational suffixes, and prefixes (Nagy, Winsor, Osborne, & O'Flahavan, 1994).

The Written Expression subtest also allows for identification of an individual's difficulty with both low-level writing tasks (e.g., transcription and handwriting) and high-level composition. The timed Alphabet Writing section is a strong predictor of reading, spelling, and writing skills acquisition for primary-grade students (Berninger et al, 1992; Berninger, Cartwright, Yates, Swanson, & Abbott, 1994). Development of written communication follows a predictable, ordered pattern from random scribbling to the formation of true letters, then words, sequences of related words, and finally, sentences (Traweek & Berninger, 1997). Therefore, timed Alphabet Writing, sentence combining and generation, and written word fluency are evaluated in the Written Expression subtest.

Just as dissociation can occur in reading, individuals can vary within themselves in their relative ability to produce written language. As a result, some individuals who are experiencing difficulty with composition (a high-level skill) are actually having trouble with the low-level skills of handwriting and spelling. Intra-individual differences in levels of written language (e.g., subword, word, and sentence) affect the text-generation process. Nonetheless, an individual's word writing skill does not predict the individual's sentence writing or text writing skills; and the individual's sentence writing skills do not predict text writing skills (Berninger, Cartwright, et al., 1994; Whitaker, Berninger, Johnston, & Swanson, 1994). The WIAT–II evaluates writing at each level; namely, at the subword, word, sentence, and text levels.

The writing samples of individuals with writing disabilities demonstrate different productivity, syntactic maturity, vocabulary, and/or mechanics than the writing samples of their normally-achieving peers (Barenbaum, Newcomer, & Nodine, 1987; Houck & Billingsley, 1989; Moran, 1981; Thomas, Englert, & Gregg, 1987). Specifically, the Houck and Billingsley study found that normally achieving students in Grades 4, 8, and 11 outperformed their peers with learning disabilities in the number of words written ($M = 140.9$ vs. 112.3), the number of sentences ($M = 9.0$ vs. 6.4), the use of correct capitalization ($M = 93\%$ vs. 82%), and correct spellings ($M = 97\%$ vs. 90%). Houck and Billingsley also noted that 75% of all word omissions across groups were made by the group with writing disorders. Therefore, the Written Expression subtest revision employs a scoring rubric that evaluates written text based on organization, vocabulary, theme development, and mechanics.

Oral Language Subtests

The revisions to the Oral Language subtests were determined by three goals: (a) to design a tool that evaluates the types of oral language activities as they occur in a classroom setting, at all levels of language (see Berninger, 1998), (b) to identify individuals that need a more comprehensive speech and language evaluation, and (c) to link language more closely to reading activities. In many instances of reading difficulty, individuals have problems that are language-based. Many poor readers may be delayed in their development of certain language skills (Mann, Cowin, & Shoenheimer, 1989). For example, poor beginning readers make more errors than good beginning readers of the same age in repeating spoken sentences (Holmes & McKeever, 1979; Jorm, 1979, 1983; Mann, Liberman, & Shankweiler, 1980). Poor beginning readers tend to comprehend certain types of spoken sentences less accurately than good beginning readers (Mann, Shankweiler, & Smith, 1984; Smith, Mann, & Shankweiler, 1986). According to Mann, et al. (1989), "the inferior performance of the poorer readers cannot be attributed to basic auditory deficits, attentional deficits, deficient intelligence, a general memory impairment, and so forth, so much as to some type of language impairment" (p. 77). This research suggests that measures of spoken language tend to be strongly associated with early reading skill.

The verbal communication skills of listening, speaking, reading, and writing are interrelated and are frequently taught in an integrated fashion through language-arts instruction. Moreover, as an individual enters school, his or her listening and speaking vocabulary expands and listening comprehension skills develop. These skills form the foundation for reading in the early grades. For this reason, skill deficits in the acquisition of receptive and expressive vocabulary or in the comprehension of spoken language can have a significant impact on learning.

Changes in the Subtests

The following sections describe the key changes in the content, administration, and scoring of each subtest. Several of the WIAT–II subtests have more items; however, the number of items actually administered to the majority of examinees does not differ significantly from that in WIAT, with the exception of the Written Language and Oral Language subtests. Table 2.1 summarizes the subtest changes in the WIAT and the WIAT–II.

Table 2.1.
Summary of Subtest Changes From the WIAT to the WIAT–II

WIAT Subtest	Measures	WIAT–II Subtest	Measures
Basic Reading	• Accuracy of word recognition	**Word Reading**	• Letter identification • Phonological awareness • Alphabet principle (letter-sound awareness) • Accuracy of word recognition • Automaticity of word recognition
Reading Comprehension	• Literal comprehension • Inferential comprehension	**Reading Comprehension**	• Literal comprehension • Inferential comprehension • Lexical comprehension • Reading rate • Oral reading accuracy • Oral reading fluency • Oral reading comprehension • Word recognition in context
		Pseudoword Decoding	• Phonological decoding • Accuracy of word attack

Table 2.1.

Summary of Subtest Changes From the WIAT to the WIAT–II *(continued)*

WIAT Subtest	Measures	WIAT–II Subtest	Measures
Spelling	• Alphabet principle (sound-letter awareness) • Written spelling of regular and irregular words • Written spelling of homonyms (integration of spelling and lexical comprehension)	**Spelling**	• Alphabet principle (sound-letter awareness) • Written spelling of regular and irregular words • Written spelling of homonyms (integration of spelling and lexical comprehension)
Written Expression	• Descriptive writing (evaluated on extension and elaboration, grammar and usage, ideas and development, organization, unity and coherence, and sentence structure and variety) • Narrative writing (evaluated on the same criteria as descriptive)	**Written Expression**	• Timed alphabet writing • Word fluency (written) • Sentence combining • Sentence generation • Written responses to verbal and visual clues • Descriptive writing (evaluated on organization, vocabulary, and mechanics) • Persuasive writing (evaluated on organization, vocabulary, theme development, and mechanics) • Writing fluency (based on word count)
Numerical Operations	• Numerical writing • Calculation (addition, subtraction, multiplication, division) • Fractions, decimals, algebra	**Numerical Operations**	• Counting • One to one correspondence • Numerical identification and writing • Calculation (addition, subtraction, multiplication, division) • Fractions, decimals, algebra
Mathematics Reasoning	• Quantitative concepts • Problem solving • Money, time, and measurement • Geometry • Reading and interpreting charts and graphs • Statistics	**Mathematics Reasoning**	• Quantitative concepts • Multi-step problem solving • Money, time, and measurement • Geometry • Reading and interpreting charts and graphs • Statistics and probability • Estimation • Identifying patterns
Listening Comprehension	• Receptive vocabulary • Listening–literal comprehension • Listening–inferential comprehension	**Listening Comprehension**	• Receptive vocabulary • Expressive vocabulary • Listening–inferential comprehension
Oral Expression	• Expressive vocabulary • Giving directions • Explain steps in sequential tasks	**Oral Expression**	• Word fluency (oral) • Auditory short-term recall for contextual information • Story generation • Giving directions • Explaining steps in sequential tasks

Changes in the Reading Subtests

Word Reading

Content: The WIAT Basic Reading subtest was renamed the Word Reading subtest to provide a more precise representation of the subtest task demands. The item content has been modified and expanded to assess phonological awareness and letter identification skills in children. Examinees identify and generate rhyming words, identify beginning and ending sounds, and match sounds with visually presented letter blends. Beginning with Grade 3, examinees read aloud as quickly as possible from a list of words.

Administration and Scoring: The examinee reads a list of words from the Word Card. The subtest has been expanded to nine start points, which reflects the extension of the age and grade range. The reverse rule has changed from a requirement of 5 consecutive correct responses to establish a basal level, to a requirement of 3 consecutive correct responses. Items are scored dichotomously and self-corrections, automaticity, and word errors are recorded.

Reading Comprehension

Content: The Reading Comprehension subtest contains significant modifications. The expanded content includes reading sentences aloud and reading slightly longer narrative, informative, and functional passages. The subtest measures higher-order critical thinking skills, such as summarizing the main idea, recognizing stated details, predicting events and outcomes, recognizing stated and implied cause and effect, and using context to determine word meaning. Initial items measure the ability to select the picture that matches a written word, phrase, or short sentence. On later items, the examinee reads short sentences aloud and reads short passages silently, then answers comprehension questions about what has been read. Oral reading of sentences provides an added opportunity to identify word recognition errors. Reading rate is calculated by comparing reading comprehension (accuracy) to reading speed to differentiate between accuracy and speed deficits.

Administration and Scoring: Administration of the Reading Comprehension subtest has changed substantially. Children in Grades PreK–K are not administered the subtest. Examinees are administered a predetermined number of items based upon grade. The reverse rules and stop points are grade-specific. Grade-specific reverse rules allow for optimal testing of those individuals whose reading is significantly below grade placement. Responses are scored 0, 1, or 2 points based on accuracy and quality of the response.

Pseudoword Decoding

Content: The Pseudoword Decoding subtest is a new subtest in the WIAT–II. Pseudoword Decoding assesses the examinee's ability to pronounce unfamiliar words correctly while reading from a list of nonsense words that are phonetically correct. These words mimic the phonological structure of words in the English language.

Administration and Scoring: The examinee reads aloud from the Pseudoword Card and the items are scored dichotomously. To measure the full range of phonological decoding knowledge, all examinees begin at the same starting point. The discontinue rule requires 7 consecutive scores of 0. Examiners are encouraged to record errors for the purpose of error analysis.

Changes in the Mathematics Subtests

Numerical Operations

Content: The Numerical Operations subtest has been expanded to include items that assess early math calculation skills, such as number recognition and number counting, and higher math calculation skills, such as the solution of equations with one and two unknowns.

Administration and Scoring: The Numerical Operations subtest retains four starting points, but the reverse rule has been changed from reversing if an examinee earns a zero on any of the items in the item set to reversing when a score of 0 is earned on any of the first 3 items administered. Thus, the basal level is established when a score of 1 is earned on 3 consecutive items. The discontinue rule has also been changed from 4 consecutive errors in a set to 6 consecutive scores of 0.

Math Reasoning

Content: The Math Reasoning subtest has been expanded to include items designed to assess early math reasoning concepts such as counting, concepts of quantity (more and less), and identification of geometric shapes. New items assess single- and multi-step word problem-solving skills, the interpretation of graphs, telling time, money concepts, and the usage of fractions, decimals, and percentages. Examinees also solve problems that require knowledge of statistics and probability.

Administration and Scoring: The subtest includes nine start points to address the expanded age and grade range. The reverse rule has changed from reversing after a score of 0 on any of the first 5 items administered to reversing when an examinee scores a 0 on any of the first 3 items administered. The discontinue rule applies after 6 consecutive scores of 0.

Changes in the Written Language Subtests

Spelling

Content: The expanded Spelling subtest includes items that assess early spelling concepts such as sound to letter correspondence for vowels, consonants, and consonant blends. Additions include words that vary in spelling-phoneme predictability, high-frequency homonyms, and contractions.

Administration and Scoring: The Spelling subtest includes six start points to address the expanded grade and age range. The reverse rule applies when the examinee scores a 0 on any of the first 3 items given, rather than on any of the first 5 items administered.

Written Expression

Content: The Written Expression subtest revision offers the examiner more approaches to identifying writing deficits. A new section, Alphabet Writing, measures the ability to remember and produce in writing the ordered set of alphabet symbols. Other new items reflect the writing requirements typically encountered in a classroom setting such as a measure of written word fluency, the generation of sentences in response to verbal and visual cues, and sentence combining. Examinees in Grades 3–6 compose a paragraph; older examinees write a persuasive essay.

Administration and Scoring: The revision tailors the test to grade-level writing expectancies. A scoring rubric is used to evaluate the organization, vocabulary, theme development, and writing mechanics of the paragraph or essay response.

Changes in the Oral Language Subtests

Listening Comprehension

Content: The Listening Comprehension subtest has been significantly modified and expanded. The majority of the items are new. Since new items were introduced, exploratory factor analysis was conducted to examine the factor structure of the subtest. Next, confirmatory factor analysis was conducted using a structural equation modeling approach. The results of the confirmatory factor analysis provide evidence that listening comprehension is assessed through one-word receptive and expressive vocabulary items and through sentence comprehension items.

Administration and Scoring: The items require the examinee to process incoming verbal information and to demonstrate understanding by providing an appropriate verbal or motor response. Sentence Comprehension items require the examinee to select one picture from a set of four that exactly matches a sentence that has been read aloud.

Oral Expression

Content: The Oral Expression subtest has been significantly modified and expanded. Four different types of skills are measured: verbal word fluency, sentence repetition, story generation, and giving directions.

Administration and Scoring: The Word Fluency section requires the examinee to generate nouns or verbs in response to a verbal prompt. Examinees in Grades PreK–3 repeat short sentences (Sentence Repetition). All examinees create stories based on visually presented, cartoon-like passages (Visual Passage Retell), and give verbal directions both with and without visual cueing (Giving Directions). Responses must either be written verbatim by the examiner or captured using a tape recorder. Scoring of Visual Passage Retell and Giving Directions is based on requirements that are identified in a scoring rubric on the record form. The Visual Passage Retell scoring rubric includes elements such as the main idea, details, names, setting, plot, sequencing, conclusion, prediction, and comparison. The Giving Directions scoring criteria include discussion of each step involved in a set of directions. Score ranges on these two sections are based on a 3-point scale (0 points indicates *no evidence* of the skill, 1 point indicates *evidence* of the skill, and 2 points indicate *skilled* elaboration).

3 Testing Considerations

This chapter presents basic assessment techniques and introduces the WIAT–II administration and scoring procedures. More detailed procedural information can be found in Chapter 4 and the stimulus booklets. Additional scoring guidelines and examples of scored responses are located in the supplements. Closely review Chapter 3 before administering the subtests; it contains administration principles that apply to all or to some of the subtests.

Suitability

The WIAT–II is designed to assess the academic achievement of individuals aged 4 through adulthood, a range that encompasses school-aged children, adolescents, and adults. For children who are not yet enrolled in kindergarten, the WIAT–II assesses pre-academic skills. Determine the appropriate subtests to administer by reviewing the content of each subtest and the curriculum material that has been presented to the examinee. Note that although the WIAT–II item content encompasses a wide range of skills and concepts, the instrument is not designed to be used as a measure of academic giftedness in adolescents. Numerical Operations, for example, does not contain advanced algebra, trigonometry, or calculus problems.

Standard Procedures

The norms on the WIAT–II were established on the basis of standard administration and scoring procedures under uniform testing conditions. To obtain results that are interpretable according to national norms, the WIAT–II should be administered according to the administration and scoring procedures as well as the recommended testing conditions. Deviation from the standard procedures, such as changes in the phrasing or presentation of a test item, could reduce the reliability and validity of test results (*Standards for Educational and Psychological Testing*, 1999).

Adherence to standardized procedures does not mean that the battery must be administered in a rigid or unnatural manner. You can create a pleasant assessment environment by using a friendly, conversational tone of voice, encouraging interest in the tasks, and reinforcing the examinee's efforts.

Administration Time

The WIAT–II can be used to comprehensively assess a broad range of academic skills or to test only in the area of need. Administration time varies depending on the age of the examinee and the number of subtests administered. Testing time for the entire battery is approximately 45 minutes for Grades PreK–K, approximately 90 minutes for Grades 1–6, and $1\frac{1}{2}$ to 2 hours for Grades

7–16. Variables including test familiarity, specific academic strengths and weaknesses of the examinee, and test-session behavior may result in a longer or shorter testing time.

Make every effort to give all of the selected subtests in one session. However, if the examinee becomes fatigued, inattentive, overly restless, or uncooperative, stop testing and allow him or her to rest. Breaks, if necessary, should take place at the end of a subtest. Try to complete testing after a short break. Do not stop the assessment before the completion of an individual subtest.

Physical Conditions

The physical setting can affect the examinee's performance. To prevent distractions and interference, conduct the testing in a quiet, adequately lit, well-ventilated room. If you are testing younger examinees (Grades PreK through 2), use a room that does not have the alphabet displayed. As a rule, no one other than you and the examinee should be in the room during the testing. On rare occasions, however, you may find that allowing the accompanying adult to remain in the room facilitates testing. He or she should remain silent and out of the examinee's view during the test session.

Seating arrangements are important for efficient test administration. The furniture should be comfortable and appropriately sized for the examinee. The desk or table should have a smooth surface. You and the examinee should sit at one corner of the desk or table so that you are sitting at one side and the examinee at the other. Figure 3.1 illustrates this arrangement and also denotes correct stimulus booklet position. Keep in mind, however, that several subtests contain items requiring you or the examinee to point to pictures or text in the stimulus booklet. Also, an examinee can effectively convey a correct response for some oral-response items by pointing. Therefore, you may find it necessary to lean to one side, forward, or both in order to see the examinee's response.

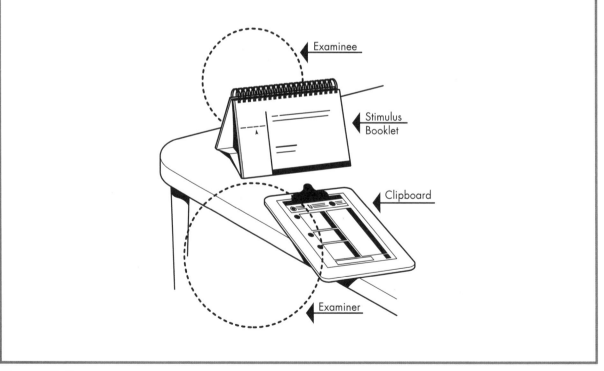

Figure 3.1.
Suggested Seating Arrangement

Materials

Figure 3.2 presents the materials included in the WIAT–II kit. You will need to provide blank, white paper for the Numerical Operations, Math Reasoning, and Written Expression subtests, and a pencil without an eraser for the Numerical Operations, Spelling, Math Reasoning, and Written Expression subtests. If you are testing examinees in Grades K or 1, you will need to provide 8 pennies for the Numerical Operations subtest. You will also have to either provide a stopwatch for timing or conduct the testing in a room with a clock that has a second hand. The stopwatch should operate quietly and be used as unobtrusively as possible. The record form and stimulus booklets contain a stopwatch icon to identify items that require precise timing. It is also recommended that you use a tape recorder to facilitate recording and scoring of verbatim responses. The tape recorder should run quietly and the examinee should be informed of its use.

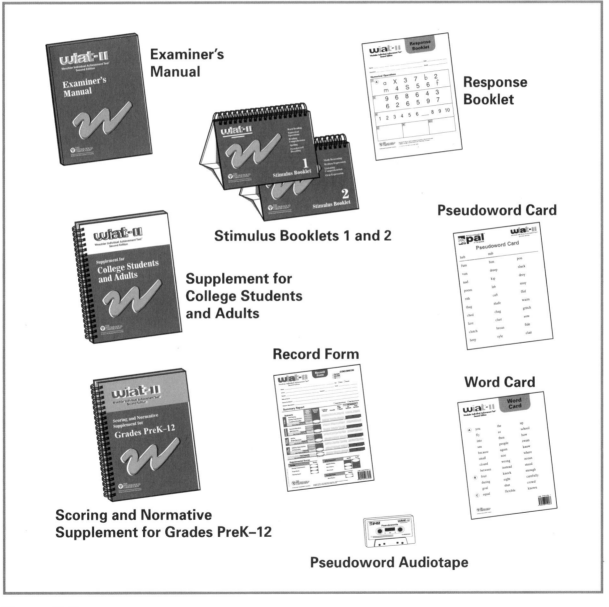

Figure 3.2.
Materials Included in the WIAT–II Kit

The stimulus booklets have an easel back that allows the books to stand freely (see Figure 3.2). The stimulus booklets contain pages for the examiner and the examinee. To correctly arrange a stimulus booklet, make sure the front cover faces you. The examiner's pages contain instructions for administering the subtests as well as correct responses for many of the items. The record form, stimulus booklets, and supplements contain all necessary administration and response information; therefore, you do not need to use the *Examiner's Manual* during administration.

The Pseudoword Audiotape is included to assist in scoring by presenting the correct pronunciations for the Pseudoword Decoding subtest. Listen to the tape prior to administering the subtest. The tape is not intended for use during the testing session.

The Word Card and the Pseudoword Card are given to the examinee during administration of the Word Reading and Pseudoword Decoding subtests. The examinee will determine the position of the card while reading.

The following is a list of guidelines for setting up test materials and managing them during the test session.

- Prior to the test session, arrange the materials so that you will have easy access to them during testing. Materials not being used should be out of the examinee's sight but within easy reach for you.

- Use a clipboard to ensure the examinee does not see the record form because some of the pages contain correct responses. However, you should avoid any self-conscious efforts to conceal the materials, because such behavior may make the examinee apprehensive or suspicious.

- Use similar caution with the stimulus booklets; most of the subtest instructions also list correct responses.

Establishing and Maintaining Rapport

A cooperative relationship between the examinee and the examiner is essential to all assessment situations. As in all interactions with examinees, an accepting, non-threatening tone promotes rapport. You can also develop and maintain rapport in other ways. A thorough understanding of the fundamental mechanics of the administration, timing, recording, and scoring procedures enables you to interact with the examinee without interrupting the test pace. Mastering, though not completely memorizing, the details of administration and scoring will enable you to read from the stimulus booklets and record responses without awkward pauses.

At the beginning of the test session, put the examinee at ease by engaging in a brief conversation regarding his or her activities or interests. The time devoted to building rapport depends on the examinee's age and temperament. Use your experience to determine the most effective way to establish rapport with each examinee.

Introduce the WIAT–II in language appropriate for the examinee's age. Mention that he or she will be asked to engage in tasks that most examinees enjoy. Indicate that some of the tasks may be easy, while others may be more difficult. Encourage the examinee *to try his or her best* and stress that he or she is not expected to answer all the questions correctly. If the examinee expresses misconceptions or concerns regarding testing or asks why the assessment is necessary, address these concerns in a truthful and understanding manner.

Once testing begins, maintain a steady pace but always be alert for changes in the examinee's mood, activity level, and cooperativeness. If the examinee appears inattentive, bored, or fatigued, brief conversations between subtests may reduce general test apprehension and rekindle interest in the next subtest. However, as mentioned earlier, the examinee may need a short break. With some younger examinees or individuals with attention or concentration difficulties, multiple short breaks may be required. Breaks should only be taken after the completion of a subtest.

To sustain rapport throughout the test, convey your sincere enthusiasm and interest in what the examinee is doing. Praise and encourage the examinee for the effort made except when specified otherwise in the administration directions (e.g., when administering items used for teaching and prompting). Do not, however, indicate whether a particular response is correct or incorrect unless prompted to do so. Avoid feedback such as *Good* or *That's right.* If an examinee does poorly on an item or an entire subtest and is clearly aware of it, acknowledge the task difficulty. For example, say, *That was a hard task, but let's go on.* If the examinee asks for assistance, say, *I want to see how well you can do it yourself.*

Testing Examinees With Physical or Language Impairments

Individuals with physical or language impairments are frequently referred for evaluation and may require testing accommodation or modification to participate fully in the assessment process. Depending on the nature of the impairment and the subtest administered, the examinee may be at a disadvantage if the test is administered in a standard manner. For example, an individual with a hearing impairment may have difficulty understanding oral instructions.

Before testing an examinee with a physical or language impairment, become familiar with the examinee's limitations and preferred mode of communication, all of which may necessitate deviations from standard procedures. Some flexibility may be necessary to balance the needs of a particular examinee with the need to maintain standard procedures. Consult assessment resources such as *Clinical Assessment of Children's Intelligence: A Handbook for Professional Practice* (Kamphaus, 1993), *WISC–III Clinical Use and Interpretation* (Prifitera and Saklofske, 1998), and *Assessment of Children: Cognitive Applications* (Sattler, 2001) for specific information regarding assessment procedures and modifications for individuals with physical or language impairments.

Although modifications of test procedures may be necessary, the WIAT–II was not standardized with such modifications. For example, if sign-language translation or other visual aids are used to give instructions to an examinee with a hearing impairment, remember that such alterations may have an impact on test scores. Note any modifications on the record form. Later, as you evaluate the examinee's achievement, rely on your professional judgment to evaluate the impact of such modified procedures on the test scores. Also, remember that even though some modifications will invalidate the use of norms, the information obtained through the use of modifications often provides valuable qualitative information regarding the examinee's strengths and weaknesses.

Administration of the WIAT–II

The following are the general rules for administering the WIAT–II. Because these rules and instructions are fundamental for obtaining reliable and valid test results, it is essential that you review them before administering the WIAT–II.

Sequence of Subtests

The WIAT–II subtests should be administered in the sequence indicated by the stimulus booklet and the record form. This was the order used in the standardization of the test. If you are administering only selected subtests, the sequence should also follow the prescribed order. Table 3.1 provides the recommended order of subtest administration.

Starting, Reversing, Discontinuing, and Stopping

The administration rules for the WIAT–II vary according to the age or grade of the examinee. To facilitate administration, the start points, reverse rules, discontinue rules, and stop points of each subtest are provided in the record form and the stimulus booklets. Table 3.1 provides a summary of administration rules for all the WIAT–II subtests. Four symbols are used to help you find this information in the stimulus booklets and record form quickly and easily.

| Start Point | Reverse Rule | Discontinue Rule | Stop Point |

Table 3.1.
Summary of Subtest Start Points, Reverse Rules, Discontinue Rules, and Stop Points

Subtest	Start Points	Reverse Rule	Discontinue Rule	Stop Points
Word Reading	Grades PreK–K: Item 1 Grade 1: Item 22 Grade 2: Item 34 Grade 3: Item 48 Letter A Grade 4: Item 72 Letter B Grade 5: Item 81 Letter C Grade 6: Item 84 Letter D Grades 7–8: Item 93 Letter E Grades 9–16: Item 96 Letter F Adults: Start at last grade completed	Score of 0 on **any** of the first 3 items given, administer the preceding items in reverse order until 3 consecutive scores of 1	After 7 consecutive scores of 0	
Numerical Operations	Grade PreK: Do not administer Grades K–1: Item 1 Letter A Grades 2–4: Item 8 Letter B Grades 5–8: Item 13 Letter C Grades 9–16: Item 15 Letter D Adults: Start at last grade completed	Score of 0 on **any** of the first 3 items given, administer the preceding items in reverse order until 3 consecutive scores of 1	After 6 consecutive scores of 0	
Reading Comprehension	Grades PreK–K: Do not administer Grade 1: Item 1 Grade 2: Item 10 Grade 3: Item 20 Grade 4: Item 34 Grade 5: Item 55 Grade 6: Item 59 Grades 7–8: Item 75 Grades 9–12: Item 94 Grades 13–16: Item 108 Adults: Start at last grade completed	**Grades 1–8:** Score of 0 on **all** of the grade-specific reversal items given, go back three Start Points and continue by following the administration rules of the new grade level **Grades 9–12:** Score of 0 on **all** of the grade-specific reversal items given, administer Items 75–114 **Grades 13–16:** Score of 0 on **all** of the grade-specific reversal items given, administer Items 94–127		Grade 1: After Item 27 Grade 2: After Item 44 Grade 3: After Item 54 Grade 4: After Item 69 Grade 5: After Item 85 Grade 6: After Item 93 Grade 7: After Item 107 Grade 8: After Item 114 Grades 9–12: After Item 127 Grades 13–16: After Item 140

Table 3.1.
Summary of Subtest Start Points, Reverse Rules, Discontinue Rules, and Stop Points *(continued)*

Subtest	Start Points	Reverse Rule	Discontinue Rule	Stop Points
Spelling	Grade PreK: Do not administer Grades K–1: Item 1 Grade 2: Item 13 Grades 3–4: Item 16 Grades 5–7: Item 19 Grades 8–9: Item 23 Grades 10–16: Item 27 Adults: Start at last grade completed	Score of 0 on **any** of the first 3 items given, administer the preceding items in reverse order until 3 consecutive scores of 1	After 6 consecutive scores of 0	
Pseudoword Decoding	Grades PreK–K: Do not administer Grades 1–16: Sample Item 1 (S1) Adults: Sample Item 1 (S1)		After 7 consecutive scores of 0	
Math Reasoning	Grades PreK–K: Item 1 Grade 1: Item 4 Grade 2: Item 16 Grade 3: Item 21 Grade 4: Item 23 Grade 5: Item 28 Grade 6: Item 30 Grades 7–8: Item 35 Grades 9–16: Item 41 Adults: Start at last grade completed	Score of 0 on **any** of the first 3 items given, administer the preceding items in reverse order until 3 consecutive scores of 1	After 6 consecutive scores of 0	
Written Expression				

Alphabet Writing
 	
Word Fluency
Sentences
Paragraph
Essay
	Grades PreK–2: Item 1
	Grades 3–6: Item 2
	Grades 7–16: Item 10
	Adults: Start at last grade completed
				Grades PreK–K:
				  After Item 1
				Grade 1: After Item 5
				Grade 2: After Item 7
				Grades 3-6: After Item 9
				Grades 7–12:
				  After Item 16
				Grades 13–16:
				  After Item 17

Listening Comprehension				
Receptive Vocabulary	Grades PreK–5: Item 1 Grades 6–16: Item 7 Adults: Start at last grade completed	Score of 0 on **any** of the first 3 items given, administer the preceding items in reverse order until 3 consecutive scores of 1	After 6 consecutive scores of 0	
Sentence Comprehension	Grades PreK–5: Item 17 Grades 6–16: Item 21 Adults: Start at last grade completed	Score of 0 on **any** of the first 3 items given, administer the preceding items in reverse order until 3 consecutive scores of 1	After 6 consecutive scores of 0	
Expressive Vocabulary	Grades PreK–5: Item 27 Grades 6–16: Item 31 Adults: Start at last grade completed	Score of 0 on **any** of the first 3 items given, administer the preceding items in reverse order until 3 consecutive scores of 1	After 6 consecutive scores of 0	
Oral Expression				
Sentence Repetition	Grades PreK–K: Item 1 Grades 1–3: Item 5 Grades 4–16: Do not administer Adults: Do not administer	Score of 0 on **any** of the first 3 items given, administer the preceding items in reverse order until 3 consecutive scores of 1	After 6 consecutive scores of 0	
Word Fluency	All Grades: Item 10			
Visual Passage Retell	All Grades: Item 11			
Giving Directions	All Grades: Item 14			

Start Points

The *start points* for children, adolescents, and college students are determined by the examinee's current grade level. The grade level of the last grade completed determines the start points for adults. If you suspect that an individual is functioning at a level lower than his or her current grade assignment, use the start point for the next lower grade.

Reverse Rules

Reverse rules help ensure that the most appropriate items are administered to an examinee. Seven of the WIAT–II subtests have a basal requirement and contain a reverse rule as indicated in Table 3.1. There are two types of reverse rules. The first type of reverse rule requires that if the examinee scores 0 points on any of the first three items administered, you proceed backward from the start point (i.e., reverse order) until you can establish the *basal level.* The basal level occurs when three consecutive items have been answered correctly. Once the examinee establishes a basal level of performance, award 1 point for each preceding, unadministered item and proceed forward with the subtest items until the discontinue criterion is met. This type of reverse rule applies to the following subtests: Word Reading, Numerical Operations, Spelling, Math Reasoning, Listening Comprehension, and the Sentence Repetition section of Oral Expression. Figure 3.3 provides an example of establishing a basal level when the reverse rule procedure is not necessary. Figure 3.4 illustrates establishing a basal level when the reverse rule should be applied.

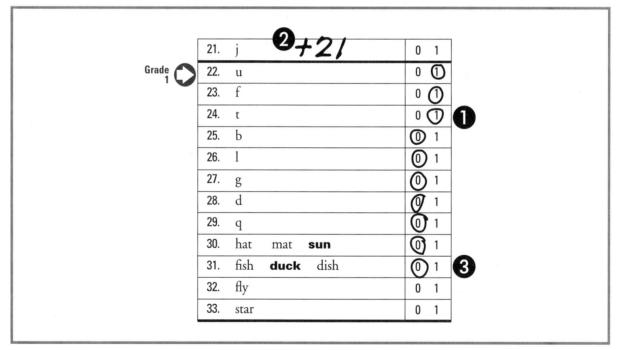

Figure 3.3.
Reverse Rule Example: Reverse Rule Not Applied

In the example in Figure 3.3, the examiner began with Item 22, the appropriate start point for Grade 1. The examinee scored 1 point on each of the first three items administered (see 1). Thus, the examiner did not need to apply the reverse rule. The examiner then gave the examinee 1 point for each of the preceding, unadministered items (Items 1–21; see 2). The examinee scored 0 points on each of the next seven items; therefore, the examiner discontinued administration of the subtest after Item 31 (see 3). The total raw score is 24.

Item	Response		Score			
41.	shell	+41 ④	0	1		❸
42.	a		0	①		
43.	w		0	①		
44.	g		0	①		
45.	st		⓪	1		
46.	dr		0	①		
47.	sh	❷	0	①	>3"	SC
48.	you	❶	⓪	1		
49.	the	❺	0	①		
50.	up		0	①		
51.	fly		⓪	1		
52.	so		⓪	1		
53.	school		⓪	1		
54.	into		⓪	1		
55.	then		⓪	1		
56.	how		⓪	1		
57.	sea	❻	⓪	1		

Grade 3 ⇨ Ⓐ (points to Item 48)

Figure 3.4.
Reverse Rule Example: Reverse Rule Applied and Basal Level of Performance Established

In the example in Figure 3.4, the examiner began with Item 48, the appropriate start point for Grade 3 (see 1). The examinee scored 0 points on Item 48, thus, the reverse rule was applied. The examiner then administered the items preceding the start point in reverse order (see 2). The examinee scored 1 point on Items 47 and 46, but scored 0 points on Item 45. The examiner continued to administer the items in reverse order. The examinee correctly responded to Items 44, 43, and 42 (see 3). The basal level was established and the examiner gave credit for Items 1–41 (see 4) and proceeded with Item 49 (see 5). The examinee answered Items 49 and 50 correctly, but missed Items 51–57, and the subtest was discontinued (see 6). The total raw score is 48.

The second type of reverse rule applies to the Reading Comprehension subtest. The required basal items are called *grade-specific reversal items*. To establish the basal level, the examinee must score at least 1 point on *any* of the grade-specific reversal items. If the examinee scores 0 points on all of the grade-specific reversal items, the reverse rule is applied. To apply the reverse rule, do not administer items in reverse order. Instead, reverse to the specified item and administer in *forward sequence*. On the rare occasion that an examinee does not establish the basal level after the reverse rule is applied, you should reverse to the item that is an additional three start points lower. The grade-specific reversal items are indicated on the record form with a reverse icon in the left margin (see Figure 3.5). If an examinee in Grades 4–8 scores 0 points on all of the grade-specific reversal items, go back to the item that is **three** start points lower and continue by following the administration rules of the new grade level. If examinees in Grades 2–3 score 0 points on all of the grade-specific reversal items, reverse and administer the items for Grade 1. If examinees in Grades 9–12, score 0 points on all of the grade-specific reversal items, reverse and administer Items 75–114; and if Grades 13–16 score 0 points on all of the grade-specific reversal items, reverse and administer Items 94–127. This reverse rule enables you to measure the reading comprehension of an individual who is reading significantly below grade placement. Figure 3.5 shows how the Reading Comprehension reverse rule is applied.

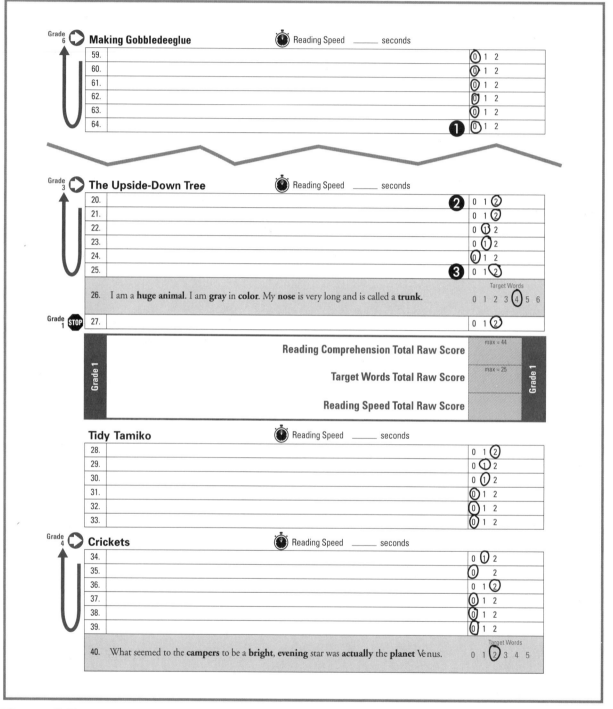

Figure 3.5.
Reverse Rule Example for the Reading Comprehension Subtest

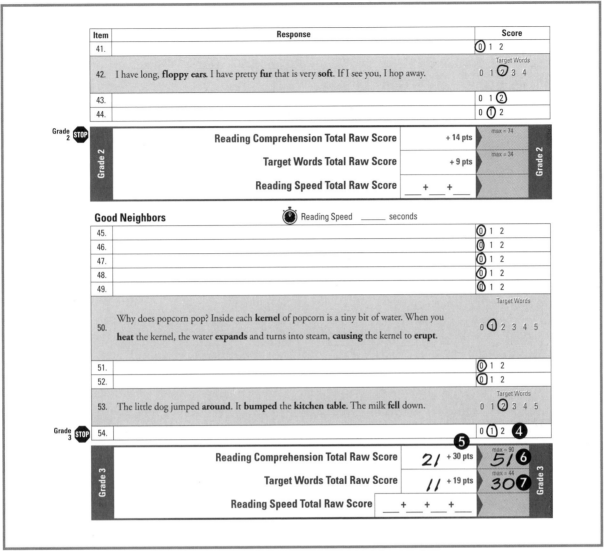

Figure 3.5.
Reverse Rule Example for the Reading Comprehension Subtest *(continued)*

In the example in Figure 3.5, the examiner started with Item 59, the appropriate start point for Grade 6. The examinee scored 0 points on all of the grade-specific reversal items (Items 59–64; see 1). The examiner applied the reverse rule and administered the items for Grade 3 (three start points lower) beginning with Item 20 (see 2). The basal level was established (see 3), and the remaining items for Grade 3 were administered (see 4). In Figure 3.5, if the examinee was unable to score any points on Items 20–25 (i.e., establish the basal level), the examiner should have reversed to Item 1 because that is the lowest item available.

Once the examinee establishes a basal level of performance by correctly responding to any of the grade-specific reversal items, award 1 point for each of the preceding, unadministered items and continue administration to the stop point for that grade. The number of points to be awarded is included on the record form in the scoring section for each grade level. In Figure 3.5, the Reading Comprehension total raw score is the sum of the 21 points scored on the *passage items* and the 30 points awarded for the preceding, unadministered passage items (see 5) for a total of 51 (see 6).

The Target Words total raw score is calculated by adding the 11 scored points for the Grade 3 *sentence items* to the 19 points awarded for preceding, unadministered sentence items for a total of 30 (see 7).

Discontinue Criterion

The administration of a subtest is stopped when the *discontinue criterion* is met. The discontinue criterion applies when the examinee scores 0 points on a specified number of consecutive items. Discontinue rules apply to items administered in forward or reverse order. Refer to Table 3.1 for a summary of the discontinue rules for the WIAT–II subtests. If you are unsure how to score a response and cannot determine quickly whether to discontinue a subtest, administer additional items until you are certain the discontinue criterion has been met. The Reading Comprehension and Written Expression subtests do not have a discontinue rule because all of the items for a grade level must be administered. The Listening Comprehension subtest includes discontinue rules for the Receptive Vocabulary, Sentence Comprehension, and Expressive Vocabulary sections. The Oral Expression subtest includes a discontinue rule for the Sentence Repetition section only.

Stop Points

Two subtests have *stop points* rather than discontinue rules. Administration of the Reading Comprehension and Written Expression subtests should stop when all of the items for a grade have been administered. For example, when administering Reading Comprehension to an examinee in Grade 5, stop after Item 85. Stop points are noted in the record form and stimulus booklets with a stop sign icon. Three sections in the Written Expression subtest (Alphabet Writing, Paragraph, and Essay) have time limits that determine the stop point. When the time limit is reached, stop administration of the section.

Timing

Specific timing information for the WIAT–II subtests is included in the record form, stimulus booklets, and Chapter 4 of this manual. The Written Expression and Oral Expression subtests contain items with strict time limits. The Reading Comprehension subtest requires that the examiner time the examinee as he or she reads passages silently. Administration of these subtests requires a stopwatch or clock with a second hand. On the record form, a stopwatch icon has been included to remind you of this requirement. Because timing should be done discreetly, the stopwatch should not have an audible signal. The directions for each subtest specify when timing is required. Record the elapsed time in seconds. It is important for you to adhere strictly to the time limits and to record time information accurately.

In the Word Reading subtest, timing is optional. If you wish to determine whether the examinee can automatically read words from the word list, you can mark response times that exceed 3 seconds on the record form. This timing enables you to compare word reading automaticity to word reading accuracy by noting the number or percentage of words that the examinee was able to read automatically. You can also use the information to complete the Qualitative Observations. Chapter 7 of this manual contains a discussion of the value of the automaticity information. For the other subtests, the time information is intended only as a guideline. The purpose of including general time guidelines is to assist you with maintaining an even administration pace and to prevent unduly distressing an examinee who obviously cannot perform the task. With the exception of the time-limited subtests, never stop an examinee who is actively engaged in a task because the suggested time limit has expired.

Teaching or Modeling

Many of the WIAT–II subtests provide instructions for teaching or modeling the task, such as sample items. The purpose of these items is to ensure that the examinee understands the task or to provide additional instruction. Teaching or modeling does not change the examinee's score on an item. It simply serves to clarify directions and help the examinee do as well as possible on subsequent items. The Pseudoword Decoding, Written Expression, and Oral Expression subtests include teaching items. Directions for teaching or modeling the task are included in the stimulus booklets for the appropriate subtests. Make sure that you teach or model only on the designated items and that you do so in the manner prescribed. Additional teaching would be inconsistent with the standardized administration procedures and would yield inaccurate scores and a misleading assessment of the examinee's achievement.

Repeating, Prompting, and Querying

Except where specifically prohibited (such as repetition of the Sentence Comprehension items in the Listening Comprehension subtest), you may repeat or paraphrase questions or instructions when the examinee requests it or when the examinee does not seem to understand the task. If an examinee frequently requests that instructions or test items be repeated, you should note the behavior on the front of the record form next to Behavior Observations.

If an examinee refuses to respond to an item or hesitates while responding, prompt him or her by saying,

> **Just try it once more,** or **Try it just a little longer,** or **I think you can do it.**

When relevant and permitted, you may repeat a question after you give encouragement. If the examinee asks for help, say,

> **I want to see how well you can do it yourself.**

If an examinee's response to an item is ambiguous, ask the examinee to clarify his or her response. Say,

> **Explain what you mean** or **Tell me more about that.**

When you query a response, record *Q* followed by the examinee's response to make it clear that the additional response was not spontaneous. If you have queried an otherwise 1-point response, and the examinee is able to clarify his or her response to meet the requirements for a 2-point response, award the higher score. A 0-point response also can earn a higher score following appropriate clarification.

Recording and Scoring

Some of the WIAT–II subtests require you to record responses verbatim because scoring these responses is more subjective, and you will be using the scoring rules and guidelines to evaluate the characteristics and details of the response. You can accomplish this either by writing or tape recording the examinee's responses. Verbatim recordings are required for the Expressive Vocabulary items in the Listening Comprehension subtest, and the Sentence Repetition, Oral Expression Word Fluency, Visual Passage Retell, and Giving Directions items in the Oral Expression subtest. Until you become familiar with the scoring of the Reading Comprehension subtest, you may wish to record verbatim responses that do not appear in the stimulus booklet for scoring after test administration.

For the Numerical Operations, Spelling, and Written Expression subtests the examinee will use a pencil without an eraser to write his or her responses in the response booklet. Explain to the examinee the procedure for changing a response as outlined in the stimulus booklet. It is important to monitor the examinee's responses on the Numerical Operations and Spelling subtests to determine when the basal level has been established. Once the basal level is established, you can allow the examinee to continue without your monitoring.

Recording Qualitative Observations

As you administer the subtests you may notice examinee behaviors that should be recorded because they provide information that will contribute to the qualitative analysis of test performance. You are encouraged to record any general behaviors that you observe (e.g., "frequently asks to have items repeated") on the front of the record form next to Behavior Observations. You should also note if specific behaviors were observed during the Word Reading, Numerical Operations, Reading Comprehension, Spelling, and Math Reasoning subtests by recording the frequency of the behavior on the Qualitative Observations at the end of each subtest. Rate a behavior *Never, Seldom, Often, Always,* or *Not Observed* based on how frequently it occurs during the administration of the subtest. The Qualitative Observations do not yield a standardized score, but are helpful for understanding an examinee's quantitative scores and for planning appropriate intervention or modifications. Figure 3.6 illustrates a completed Word Reading Qualitative Observations. As noted in Figure 3.6, during administration of the Word Reading subtest, the examinee tended to pronounce words automatically, but when he or she responded incorrectly, the errors usually involved the addition, omission, or transposition of syllables. The examinee did not typically "sound out" unfamiliar words, seldom made accent errors when pronouncing words, and did not lose his or her place when reading from the word list.

Word Reading Qualitative Observations Note how frequently a behavior occurred by checking the appropriate box.	Never	Seldom	Often	Always	Not Observed
Substitutes a visually similar letter when identifying letters					✓
Provides nonword responses for rhyming words					✓
Pronounces words automatically			✓		
Laboriously "sounds out" words		✓			
Self corrects errors					
Loses his/her place when reading words	✓				
Makes accent errors		✓			
Adds, omits, or transposes syllables when reading words			✓		

Figure 3.6.
Example of a Completed Word Reading Qualitative Observations

Overview of Subtest Scoring Procedures

All subtests except Written Expression have a reverse rule, a discontinue rule, or both, that necessitate scoring the responses during test administration. If you are unsure how to score any response, record it (verbatim in the case of an oral response) so you can score it later. To prevent discontinuing prematurely, do not count the response when observing the discontinue rule if you are unsure of its score.

The scoring procedures for Word Reading, Numerical Operations, Spelling, Pseudoword Decoding, Math Reasoning, and Listening Comprehension are objective. The responses are scored dichotomously (0 points for an incorrect response, 1 point for a correct response) by using the correct responses that appear on the examiner's pages of the stimulus booklet or on the record form.

The scoring procedures for Reading Comprehension, Written Expression, and Oral Expression are more subjective, and scoring responses for these subtests requires your judgment. The following list outlines the scoring procedures for these subtests.

- Responses to the Reading Comprehension passages are scored 0, 1, or 2 points. The stimulus booklet contains the most common correct and incorrect responses, along with additional criteria in some cases. Additional examples of correct and incorrect responses are in Appendix A.1 of the supplements.

- The Written Expression Sentence items are scored 0, 1, or 2 points. Appendix A.2 of the supplements contains examples and explanations of scored responses for each item.

- The Written Expression Paragraph and Essay can be scored analytically by recording scores on the scoring rubric in the record form. To complete the scoring rubric, refer to the scoring rules and guidelines in Chapter 4 and Appendix A.2 of the supplements. Paragraph scoring for Grades 3–6 evaluates the response on the elements of mechanics, organization, and vocabulary. Essay scoring for Grades 7–16 evaluates the response on the elements of mechanics, organization, theme development, and vocabulary. Paragraph and essay sample responses that have been scored using the scoring rubric are in Appendix A.2 of the supplements.

- The Written Expression Paragraph and Essay can also be scored using a holistic scoring system. The holistic scoring criteria are in Chapter 4 and Appendix A.2 of the supplements. Note that standard scores are not provided for holistic scores. You cannot calculate the Written Expression subtest score or the Written Language composite score using a holistic score. Paragraph and essay sample responses that have been scored using the holistic scoring criteria are in Appendix A.2 of the supplements.

- The Sentence Repetition, Word Fluency, Visual Passage Retell, and Giving Directions sections of the Oral Expression subtest are scored by following the scoring rules in Chapter 4 and Appendix A.3 of the supplements. Visual Passage Retell, and Giving Directions are scored by using the scoring rubric on the record form. The responses are evaluated using a 3-point scale. Sample responses are provided in Appendix A.3 of the supplements.

Required Scoring Using Conversion Tables

Scores for the following require conversion of raw scores to quartile-based scores **prior to calculating the subtest standard scores**. These conversion tables are located in Appendix B (grade-based) and Appendix E (age-based) in the supplements.

Written Expression: Word Fluency

Written Expression: Paragraph Spelling Errors

Written Expression: Paragraph Punctuation Errors

Written Expression: Essay Spelling Errors

Written Expression: Essay Punctuation Errors

Oral Expression: Word Fluency

Optional Scoring Using Conversion Tables

The following optional scores are calculated by converting total raw scores to quartile-based scores. None of these scores are required to calculate a subtest or composite standard score. Transfer the total raw scores from the subtest page to the Supplemental Score Conversion Worksheet in the record form. Then use Appendix B (grade-based) or Appendix E (age-based) of the supplements to look up the quartile-based score. The quartile-based scores for Reading Comprehension and Reading Speed are used to calculate the Reading Rate on the record form.

> Reading Comprehension
>
> Reading Comprehension: Target Words
>
> Reading Comprehension: Reading Speed
>
> Written Expression: Paragraph or Essay Word Count

For students in Grades PreK–K only, the score for Alphabet Writing requires conversion of the total raw score to a decile-based score using the conversion tables in Appendix B (grade-based) and Appendix E (age-based) of the *Scoring and Normative Supplement for Grades PreK–12*.

Scoring Guidelines

When scoring responses, do not penalize an examinee for using slang, informal language, or regional variation in pronunciation. Additionally, if an examinee has an articulation disorder, do not penalize him or her for mispronunciations that are a direct result of the disorder. You must decide, however, if the Pseudoword Decoding subtest, which requires correct pronunciation, is appropriate for such an examinee.

Although the response modes are always indicated to the examinee (as in *Point to the second apple from the bowl*), give credit for a clearly correct response conveyed in a manner other than the one indicated. For example, if an examinee responds to a Math Reasoning item by pointing to a word in the stimulus booklet and that word correctly answers the question, score the response 1 point.

If the examinee spontaneously gives or changes a response for an item administered earlier, and the new response warrants changing the score for that item, change the score accordingly if you are still administering the subtest. Otherwise, do not change the score.

Spoiled Responses

A response is considered *spoiled* when an examinee's elaboration of a correct response indicates a fundamental misconception of the item, question, or passage. For example, refer to the following response for Item 12 of the Reading Comprehension subtest:

> **What will happen if Tim has the best pet for Pet Day?**
>
> *He will get a prize . . . because all the kids get prizes.*

This response is spoiled because the additional information reveals that the examinee had a fundamental misconception of what would happen. It is important to distinguish between a spoiled response and a vague response. Spoiled responses should be considered incorrect; vague responses should be queried, and the resulting response should be scored.

Multiple Responses

Occasionally, an examinee will spontaneously give several responses to an item. Use the following rules as guidelines for scoring multiple responses:

- If a second or third response is intended to replace a previous one, score only the last response.

- If an examinee gives both a correct and an incorrect response, and you are unsure which is the intended response, ask the examinee which one is intended and score that response.

Using the Supplements

The *WIAT–II Scoring and Normative Supplement for Grades PreK–12* and the *WIAT–II Supplement for College Students and Adults* provide the scoring and normative information you will need to score the WIAT–II. Appendix A includes scoring guidelines and additional scoring examples for the Reading Comprehension, Written Expression, and Oral Expression subtests. Conversion tables for the quartile-based and decile-based scores are located in Appendices B (grade-based) and E (age-based). Appendices C (grade-based) and F (age-based) contain the normative tables for determining the subtest standard scores. Additional grade-based normative information, such as confidence intervals, percentile ranks, NCEs, stanines, and grade equivalents, is included in Appendix D. The same information for age-based scores is in Appendix G. Appendix H contains the predicted WIAT–II subtest and composite scores for the WPPSI–R, the WISC–III, and the WAIS–III. Appendix I provides information on the differences required for statistical significance and the differences obtained by the standardization linking sample when using the predicted-achievement method for ability–achievement analysis. Appendix J presents data on the differences required for statistical significance and the differences obtained by the standardization linking sample when using the simple-difference method. Appendix K contains the ipsative information about differences in standard scores, differences in composite scores required for statistical significance, and the cumulative percentages of the standardization sample obtaining various discrepancies. Intersubtest scatter for the cumulative percentages of the standardization sample and intercorrelations of WIAT–II subtest and composite standard scores and the Wechsler IQ scores are also included in Appendix K.

Using the Record Form

The WIAT–II Record Form is designed to facilitate administration and scoring of the test. It also includes optional procedures that can help you interpret test results. The front page of the record form provides space for calculating the examinee's chronological age, recording pertinent demographic information, recording the reason for the referral and general behavior observations, and completing the Summary Report. The Summary Report is designed for recording derived scores and other types of normative information, including Supplemental Scores. The Parent Report is a single, foldout page that can be detached from the rest of the record form. Use the Parent Report to copy test results from the Summary Report. The Parent Report contains a description of each WIAT–II subtest, a brief description of the WIAT–II scores, and a graph, based on the bell curve, to plot the examinee's scores. An example of a completed demographic section of the record form is presented in Figure 3.7, and a completed Parent Report is presented in Figure 3.8.

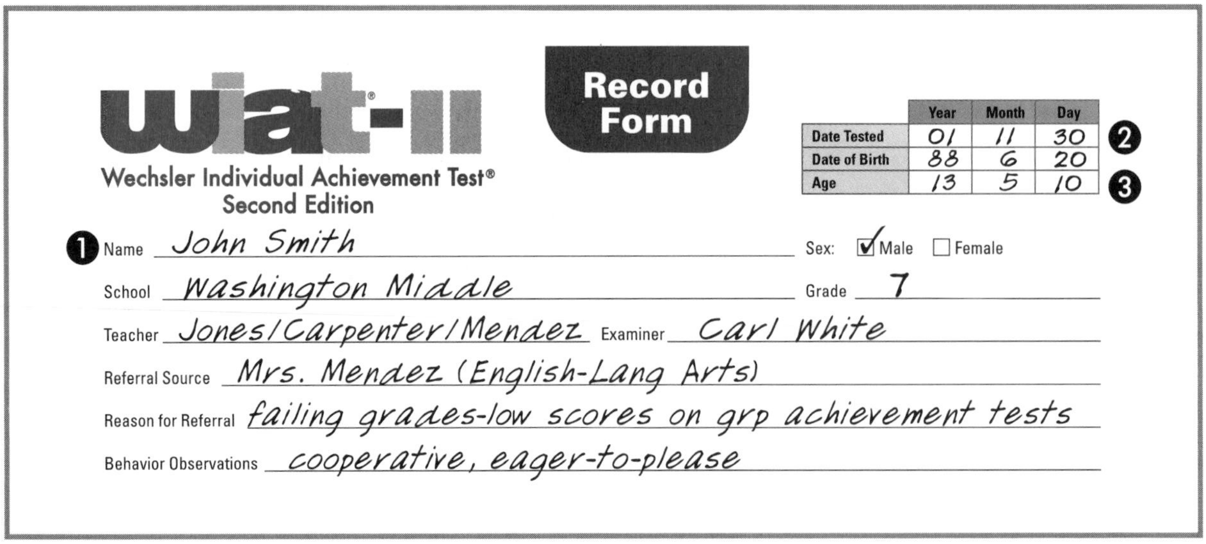

wiat-ii

Record Form

Wechsler Individual Achievement Test®
Second Edition

	Year	Month	Day	
Date Tested	01	11	30	❷
Date of Birth	88	6	20	
Age	13	5	10	❸

❶ Name *John Smith*　　Sex: ☑ Male ☐ Female

School *Washington Middle*　　Grade *7*

Teacher *Jones/Carpenter/Mendez* Examiner *Carl White*

Referral Source *Mrs. Mendez (English-Lang Arts)*

Reason for Referral *failing grades-low scores on grp achievement tests*

Behavior Observations *cooperative, eager-to-please*

Figure 3.7.
Example of a Completed Demographic Section of the Record Form

Before you begin testing, complete the demographic information indicated on the front page of the record form (see 1 in Figure 3.7): the examinee's name, sex, school, grade, and teacher; your name; the name of the person who referred the examinee for testing; and the reason for the referral.

Next, calculate the examinee's chronological age using the following procedure. First, enter the date of testing and the examinee's date of birth in the appropriate spaces (see 2). If the examinee is tested in two sessions and the sessions occur on different days, use only the first date as the date tested. Subtract the date of birth from the date tested and record the difference in the Age spaces provided (see 3). For these computations, assume that all months have 30 days. Do not round days of age upward to the nearest month; for example, if the chronological age is 6 years, 2 months, 20 days, do not round to 6 years, 3 months.

Completing the Parent Report

The Parent Report can be completed easily if you detach the page to copy information from the Summary Report. First, complete the demographic information about the examinee. If your evaluation includes an ability score, especially if you are reporting an ability–achievement discrepancy, identify the source of the ability score (i.e., check the box beside WPPSI–R, WISC–III, WAIS–III, or write the name of the instrument next to *Other*). Report the range of the Full Scale IQ Score by checking the box beside *Extremely Low, Borderline, Low Average, Average, High Average, Superior,* or *Very Superior.* Consult the examiner's manual of the ability test to determine which descriptor is appropriate for a given score. For example, a Full Scale IQ score of 89 on the WISC–III is categorized as *Low Average* (WISC–III manual, p. 32).

Transfer the Subtest Standard Scores from the Summary Report to the Parent Report (see 1 on Figure 3.8). You may include scores for other tests in your report as well (see 2). For instance, you may want to include scores from an earlier administration of another achievement test. Space is also provided for you to include relevant notes.

Standard scores can be plotted on the graph (see 3) at the bottom of the page, to help the parent better understand test results. Use the illustration to compare scores and to describe where scores fall in relation to *Average* performance.

WIAT–II Parent Report

Student _John Smith_   Date _12-4-01_

Grade _7_   School _Washington Middle_

Ability Scores (check one): ☐ WPPSI–R   ☑ WISC–III   ☐ WAIS–III   ☐ Other _____

Full Scale IQ Score (check one):

☐ Extremely Low   ☐ Borderline   ☐ Low Average   ☑ Average   ☐ High Average   ☐ Superior   ☐ Very Superior

WIAT–II Achievement Subtest Standard Scores:

❶

Reading Composite		Mathematics Composite		Written Language Composite		Oral Language Composite	
Word Reading	70	Numerical Operations	101	Spelling	71	Listening Comprehension	93
Reading Comprehension	74	Math Reasoning	90	Written Expression	76	Oral Expression	90
Pseudoword Decoding	68						
Reading Composite	67	Mathematics Composite	94	Written Language Composite	71	Oral Language Composite	88

❷ Other scores: _PPVT-3   90_

Notes _____

_____

_____

_____

_____

❸

Qualitative Description: Extremely Low | Borderline | Low Average | Average | High Average | Superior | Very Superior

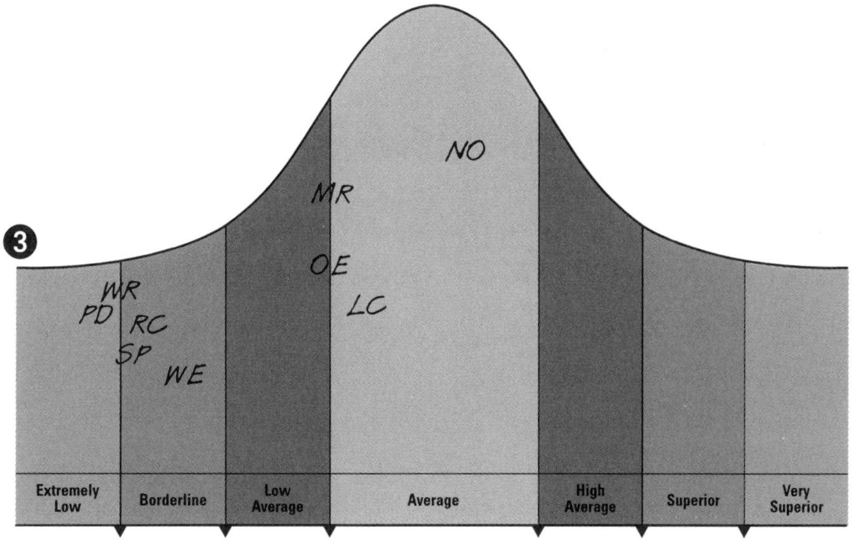

Figure 3.8.
Example of a Completed Parent Report

The back of the Parent Report includes a description of each subtest and information to help the parent understand the WIAT–II scores. We suggest that you spend time with the parent discussing the Parent Report, addressing concerns, and answering questions.

Completing the Subtest Pages

Subtests are presented on the record form in the order of administration. Subtest instructions in the stimulus booklets indicate when responses must be recorded verbatim or when recording only incorrect responses is adequate. If you need additional room to record a response, attach additional pages to the record form.

The WIAT–II record form provides space to record and score the examinee's responses to the test items and also provides start points, reverse rules, discontinue rules, stop points, time limits, and other prompts to facilitate proper test administration. Examinees' written responses are recorded in the response booklet. You do not need to rewrite the responses written by the examinee; however, you may transfer errors verbatim from the response booklet to the record form. Most subtests (i.e., Word Reading, Reading Comprehension, Pseudoword Decoding, Math Reasoning, and the Receptive Vocabulary and Sentence Comprehension sections of Listening Comprehension) are scored on the record form during administration of the subtest. Numerical Operations and Spelling are scored in the response booklet and transferred to the record form after administration. Written Expression and Oral Expression are scored on the record form by consulting the examinee's responses and the subtest scoring rules and guidelines.

The following standard abbreviations may be useful in recording responses.

Q (Query): A query or question was asked to clarify the examinee's response.

DK (Don't Know): The examinee said "I don't know" or otherwise indicated that he or she did not know the correct response.

PC (Pointed Correctly): The examinee pointed to the correct response.

PX (Pointed Incorrectly): The examinee pointed to an incorrect response.

NR (No Response): The examinee gave no response.

To ensure accurate scoring of responses and to create a record that can be used when evaluating test session behavior, it is especially important to note querying and to record any subsequent response. It is also important to record in an unobtrusive manner so that you avoid distracting the examinee.

The record form also enables you to record the frequency of test behaviors, using the Qualitative Observations that appear after the Word Reading, Numerical Operations, Reading Comprehension, Spelling, and Math Reasoning subtests.

Calculating and Recording Raw Scores

After you complete the test administration, calculate the total raw score for each subtest and record it in the appropriate space on the record form. For Word Reading, Numerical Operations, Reading Comprehension, Spelling, Pseudoword Decoding, Math Reasoning, and Listening Comprehension, calculate the total raw scores by summing the item scores. Transfer the total raw scores to the Total Raw Score column on the Total Raw Score Conversion Worksheet in the record form.

For examinees in Grades PreK–K, the total raw score for Written Expression will be the score for Alphabet Writing only. Transfer the total raw score for Alphabet Writing to the Supplemental

Score Conversion Worksheet. Convert the total raw score to a decile-based score using Table B.4 (grade-based) or Table E.4 (age-based) of the supplements. Examinees in Grades PreK–K will *not* have a Written Expression standard score or a Written Language composite score.

For Examinees in Grades 1–16, three scores must be converted to quartile-based scores before calculating the total raw score for the Written Expression subtest. First, use the conversion tables in Appendix B (grade-based) or Appendix E (age-based) of the supplements to convert the Word Fluency score and the Paragraph or Essay Spelling Errors and Punctuation Errors. Note that if the examinee produces 6 or fewer words for the Paragraph item, or 23 or fewer words for the Essay item, the Spelling Error and Punctuation Error quartile scores are 0.

The Word Fluency item in the Oral Expression subtest must be changed to a weighted score using Table B.12 or Table E.12 prior to adding to the other subtotals when calculating the subtest total raw score. This score is quartile-based but is weighted during the conversion process so that the two Word Fluency items are given credit independent of each other.

Converting Total Raw Scores to Standard Scores

To convert subtest total raw scores to standard scores, use the following steps and Appendix C (grade-based) or Appendix F (age-based) of the supplements. Figure 3.9 presents a completed Total Raw Score Conversion Worksheet.

Total Raw Score Conversion Worksheet

	Total Raw Score	Standard Score
Word Reading	90	70
Numerical Operations	35	101
Reading Comprehension	132	74
Spelling	23	71
Pseudoword Decoding	11	68
Math Reasoning	47	90
Written Expression Grades 1–16 only	15	76
Listening Comprehension	28	93
Oral Expression	25	90

Figure 3.9.
Example of a Completed Total Raw Score Conversion Worksheet

1. Use Tables C.1 (grade-based) or F.1 (age-based) in the supplements to convert the subtest total raw score to a standard score. To locate the standard score for a subtest, first turn to the appropriate age or grade page in the supplement.

   The grade-based standard scores in Table C.1 are organized by grade and either fall, winter, or spring (for Grades PreK–8). Use the current grade placement of the examinee to locate the appropriate page of the table. Fall includes the months of August, September, October, and November; winter includes the months of December, January, and February; and spring includes the months of March, April, May, June, and July.

   The age-based standard scores are in Table F.1. Each page provides the standard scores for a particular age span. Four-month age spans are presented for Ages 4–13, one-year age spans are provided for Ages 14–16, and age bands are provided for adults.

2. For each subtest, find the total raw score under the subtest name. Then, reading across from the total raw score to the extreme left or extreme right column, find the equivalent standard score for the subtest.

3. Record the subtest standard score in the oval to the right of the previously recorded total raw score on the Total Raw Score Conversion Worksheet.

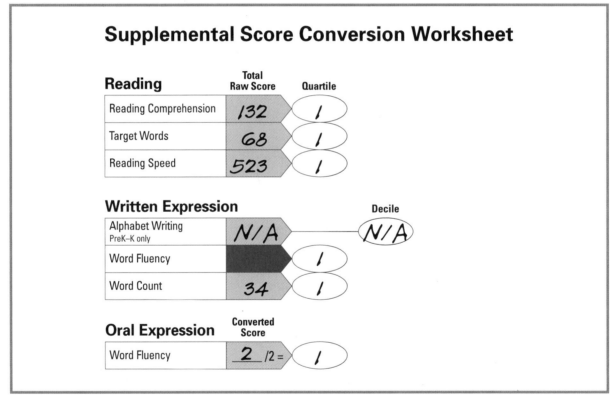

Figure 3.10.
Example of a Completed Supplemental Score Conversion Worksheet

Converting Raw Scores to Supplemental Scores

To calculate the Supplemental Scores for the Reading Comprehension, Written Expression, and Oral Expression subtests, refer to the following steps. Figure 3.10 illustrates a completed Supplemental Score Conversion Worksheet.

1. Transfer the total raw scores for Reading Comprehension, Target Words, Reading Speed, Alphabet Writing (Grades PreK–K only), Word Count, and Oral Expression Word Fluency from the subtest to the Supplemental Score Conversion Worksheet.

2. Convert the total raw scores to quartile-based or decile-based scores using the conversion tables in Appendix B (grade-based) or Appendix E (age-based) of the supplements. The score for Written Expression Word Fluency has already been converted and can simply be transferred from the subtest page to the quartile oval on the conversion worksheet.

3. Calculate the quartile score for Oral Expression Word Fluency by dividing the weighted score by 2 and writing the quotient in the quartile oval. This procedure enables you to compare the word fluency scores from the two subtests.

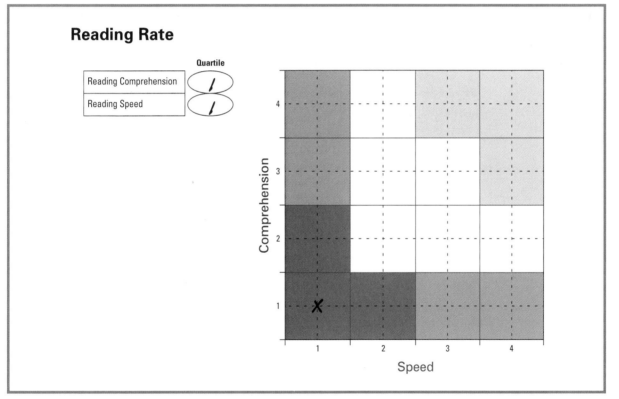

Figure 3.11.
Example of a Completed Reading Rate Page

Calculating Reading Rate

To calculate the Reading Rate for the Reading Comprehension passages, transfer the Reading Speed total raw score and the Reading Comprehension total raw score from the Reading Comprehension subtest to the Supplemental Score Conversion Worksheet. Convert the scores to quartile-based scores using Appendix B (grade-based) or Appendix E (age-based) in the supplements. Transfer the Reading Comprehension quartile and the Reading Speed quartile from the

Supplemental Score Conversion Worksheet to the Reading Rate page in the record form. To plot Reading Rate, place an **X** on the dotted lines that correspond to the intersection of the Reading Comprehension Quartile and the Reading Speed Quartile. Reading Rate can be expressed as the relationship between Reading Comprehension (which can also be referred to as accuracy) and Reading Speed. In general, based on the degree of shading in the graph, you can identify scores that are indicative of different types of reading rates. Figure 3.11 presents a completed Reading Rate page. See Chapter 7 for the interpretative considerations of Reading Rate.

Completing the Summary Report

To complete the Summary Report on the front page of the record form, refer to the following steps. Figure 3.12 presents an example of a completed Summary Report.

1. Indicate whether you used grade-based or age-based standard scores by checking the appropriate box (see 1). Keep in mind that you should use the same type of standard score for subtests and composites, and that you must use age-based standard scores to calculate ability–achievement discrepancies.

2. Fold out the Raw Score Conversion Worksheet so that the worksheet is on the right and the Summary Report is on the left. This layout makes it convenient for transcribing the subtest standard scores to the Summary Report. Transfer the subtest standard scores from the Raw Score Conversion Worksheet to the spaces provided on the Summary Report (see 2).

3. Calculate the composite standard scores. First, add the standard scores for the subtests that contribute to that composite (see 3). For example, add the standard scores for Word Reading, Reading Comprehension, and Pseudoword Decoding for the Reading composite. Then use the grade-based or age-based norms in Tables C.2 or F.2 in the supplements to convert the sums of subtest standard scores to composite standard scores (see 4). If one of the subtests that contribute to a composite is not administered, you cannot calculate the composite standard score. Note that this procedure is different from the WIAT, where subtest *raw scores* rather than *standard scores* were used to calculate composites.

   Note that for examinees in Grade K or age 5, only the composite scores for Mathematics and Oral Language can be calculated. The Reading composite score is not available because Reading Comprehension and Pseudoword Decoding are not administered and the Written Language composite score is not available because only the Alphabet Writing section of Written Expression is administered. For examinees in Grade PreK or age 4, only the composite score for Oral Language can be calculated because Numerical Operations, Reading Comprehension, Spelling, and Pseudoword Decoding are not administered, and only the Alphabet Writing section of Written Expression is administered.

4. To supply the confidence interval information for each subtest and composite standard score, use Tables D.1 or G.1 for subtest standard scores, and Tables D.2 or G.2 for composite standard scores. Select the level of confidence (90% or 95%) and record it in the space provided in the Confidence Interval column (see 5). Then find the age or grade of the examinee and the selected level of confidence in the table and read across to locate the size of the confidence interval for each subtest. Note that each value in Table D.1 is the average of the values obtained separately for the fall and spring standardization samples.

5. To obtain the percentile ranks for the subtest and composite standard scores, use Tables D.3 or G.3 in the supplements to locate the information, and record it in the Percentile

column (see 6). Use the same table to obtain NCEs or stanines. Check the box next to either NCE or Stanine and record the scores in the spaces provided.

6. To obtain grade or age equivalents, use the subtest total raw scores rather than the standard scores. Refer to the Raw Score Conversion Worksheet for the total raw scores. Find the desired equivalents using Table D.4 for grade equivalents and Table G.4 for age equivalents, and record the equivalents in the spaces provided. There are no grade or age equivalent scores for the composite scores.

7. To calculate the total composite score, add the standard scores of all nine subtests. Then use Table C.2 or Table F.2 to convert this sum to a total composite standard score. If you do not administer all of the requisite subtests, do not calculate a total composite score.

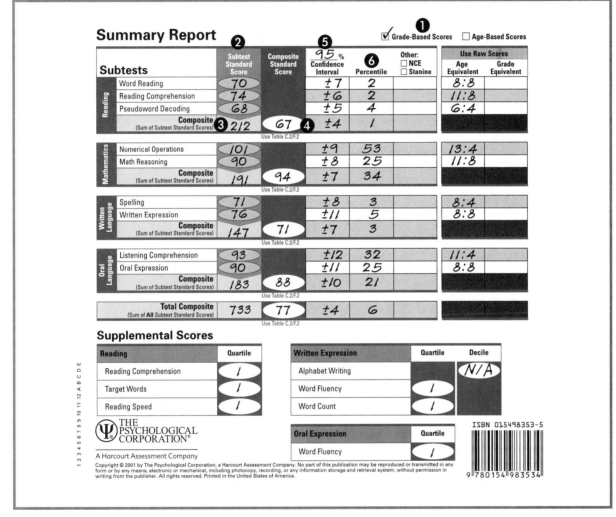

Figure 3.12.
Example of a Completed Summary Report

Completing the Ability–Achievement Discrepancy Analysis

The Ability–Achievement Discrepancy Analysis is located on the back of the record form and is used in conducting the ability–achievement discrepancy analysis using the WIAT–II and a Wechsler ability scale (e.g., WPPSI–R, WISC–III, or WAIS–III). To complete this page, use the following procedures, which are illustrated in Figure 3.13. It is helpful to fold out the record form so that the Summary Report is on the right and the Ability–Achievement Discrepancy Analysis page is on the left.

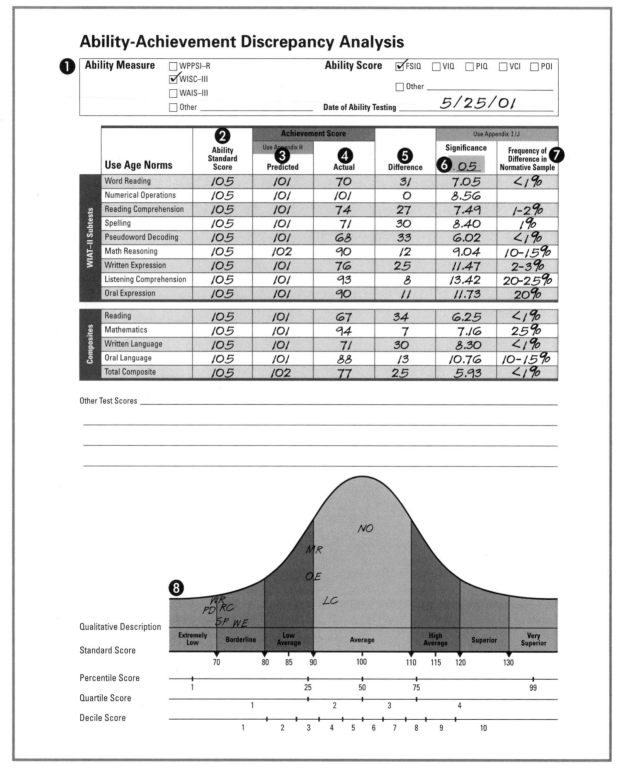

Figure 3.13.
Example of a Completed Ability–Achievement Discrepancy Analysis Page

1. Record the name of the ability test used and the date of ability testing in the spaces provided (see 1).

2. For each ability–achievement discrepancy you wish to calculate, enter the Wechsler score in the Ability Standard Score column (see 2). Except under unusual circumstances (see Chapter 7), it is recommended that you use the Full Scale IQ score. In Figure 3.13, discrepancies are calculated using the WISC–III FSIQ score.

3. Decide whether you want to use the predicted-achievement or the simple-difference method of calculating ability–achievement discrepancies. If you are not required to use a particular method, the predicted-achievement method is recommended (Reynolds, 1985).

4. Calculate the desired ability–achievement discrepancies. To employ the predicted-achievement method, refer to the appropriate table, based on the Wechsler test and the selected ability score, in Appendix H of the supplements. Find the ability score (i.e., FSIQ, VIQ, PIQ, VCI, or POI) in the far left or right column, then read across the row to find the predicted-achievement score for each of the subtests or composites. For each subtest, record the predicted WIAT–II scores in the Predicted column on the Ability–Achievement Discrepancy Analysis page (see 3). Next, transfer the actual WIAT–II subtest and composite standard scores from the Summary Report to the Actual column (see 4). Be sure that you are using age-based standard scores. Then, subtract each actual standard score from the corresponding predicted score and record the difference in the Difference column (see 5).

   To use the simple-difference method of calculating ability–achievement discrepancies, record the WIAT–II age-based standard scores in the Actual column, subtract from the ability score, and enter the difference in the Difference column.

5. Determine whether each ability–achievement discrepancy is statistically significant. Begin by deciding which level of significance you wish to use (.05 or .01) and write this level in the space provided in the Significance column (see 6). Then consult the appropriate Appendix table. Use Appendix I for discrepancies calculated according to the predicted-achievement method and Appendix J for discrepancies calculated according to the simple-difference method. For each subtest and composite standard score, find the selected level of significance and the ability score selected, then read across the row to locate the difference required for significance. Record the number in the Significance column.

6. To determine how frequently a statistically significant difference occurred in the standardization linking sample, consult the appropriate table in Appendix I or Appendix J. For example, Table I.4 reports the various percentages of children in the WPPSI–R linking sample that obtained a similar difference between predicted and actual subtest and composite standard scores. Record each frequency in the last column marked Frequency of Difference in Normative Sample (see 7).

7. To plot a profile displaying the relationship of the ability standard score(s) to the WIAT–II standard scores, use the graph, based on the bell curve, in the lower portion of the page (see 8).

WIAT-II Scoring Assistants

Three different software scoring programs are available for use with the WIAT-II. The first is the WIAT–II Scoring Assistant. When total raw scores are entered, they are converted into various derived scores (e.g., standard scores, quartiles.) If you prefer, you may also enter item-level information and supplemental raw scores. This information will allow you to conduct an error analysis and receive supplemental scores on several of the subtests. The WIAT–II Scoring Assistant can save you time when scoring Reading Comprehension and Written Expression, as it will convert the required raw scores and give you a final standard score. The error analysis and supplemental scores are optional; however, the information will be very helpful when making specific recommendations (e.g., creating an Individual Educational Plan) for the examinee. This scoring program does not include the ability–achievement discrepancy capability.

The second software program, the WISC–III/WIAT–II Scoring Assistant, includes all of the capabilities of the WIAT–II Scoring Assistant but also conducts the ability–achievement discrepancy analysis using the WISC–III. The software program employs the recalibrated WISC–III norms when using the predicted-achievement method.

The third software program, the WAIS–III/WMS–III/WIAT–II Scoring Assistant, includes all of the capabilities of the WIAT–II Scoring Assistant but also conducts the ability–achievement discrepancy analysis using the WAIS–III. Reports are available for WAIS–III/WIAT–II and WAIS–III/WMS–III.

4 Administration and Scoring

Word Reading

Materials

- Stimulus Booklet 1
- Record Form
- Word Card

Start Points

Grades PreK–K:	Item 1	
Grade 1:	Item 22	
Grade 2:	Item 34	
Grade 3:	Item 48	Letter A
Grade 4:	Item 72	Letter B
Grade 5:	Item 81	Letter C
Grade 6:	Item 84	Letter D
Grades 7–8:	Item 93	Letter E
Grades 9–16:	Item 96	Letter F
Adults:	Start at the level of the last grade completed	

Reverse Rule

Score of 0 on **any** of the first 3 items given, administer the preceding items in reverse order until 3 consecutive scores of 1

Discontinue Rule

Discontinue after 7 consecutive scores of 0

Description

Word Reading assesses early reading (phonological awareness) and word recognition and decoding skills. Tasks include the ability to name letters of the alphabet, identify and generate rhyming words, identify beginning and ending sounds of words, blend sounds into words, and match sounds with letters and letter blends. Words are also read aloud from a word list. Word reading accuracy is scored and word reading automaticity and self-corrections are marked for qualitative analysis.

General Directions

To begin, turn to the Administration section for Word Reading in Stimulus Booklet 1. Follow the administration directions and begin the subtest at the grade-appropriate start point. If you have reason to believe that the examinee's word reading skills are below grade level, you may begin the subtest at the start point for the previous grade level.

During administration, the examinee should hold the Word Card. Be sure that the examinee understands that he or she is to read the words going across, not down, the page. If the examinee inadvertently skips a word or row of words, redirect the examinee to the appropriate word or row and make a note on the record form to remind you of this behavior.

Recording and Scoring

If the examinee responds correctly to three consecutive items, award 1 point for each of the preceding, unadministered items. The Word Reading total raw score is the total number of 1-point responses.

To assist you in monitoring the frequency of self-corrections or delayed responses (any response that exceeds the 3" time limit), space is provided for you to place check marks beside the items in columns labeled **SC** (self-corrections) and **>3"**, beginning with Item 48. Record the number of self-corrections and the number of >3" responses in the spaces provided on the record form. This information can be used to rate the frequency of the behaviors using the Word Reading Qualitative Observations.

Figure 4.1 demonstrates how to score Word Reading for an examinee in Grade 4. The examiner started with Item 72 (see 1) on the Word Card. The examinee scored 0 points on Item 74 and did not establish the basal level. Therefore, the examiner applied the reverse rule and administered Item 71 in reverse order (see 2). The item was answered correctly and the basal level was established. The examiner then resumed the forward sequence starting with Item 75 (see 3) and discontinued after 7 consecutive errors (Items 79–85; see 4). The examinee was given credit for Items 1–70 because the basal level was established at Item 71. The Word Reading total raw score for this examinee is 77 (see 5). The examinee self-corrected within the 3" time limit on Items 73 and 79, and a 2 is recorded for Total SC Check Marks (see 6). On Items 72, 75, and 78, the examinee correctly read the words but took more than 3 seconds to respond. Therefore, the total count for >3" Check Marks is 3 (see 6).

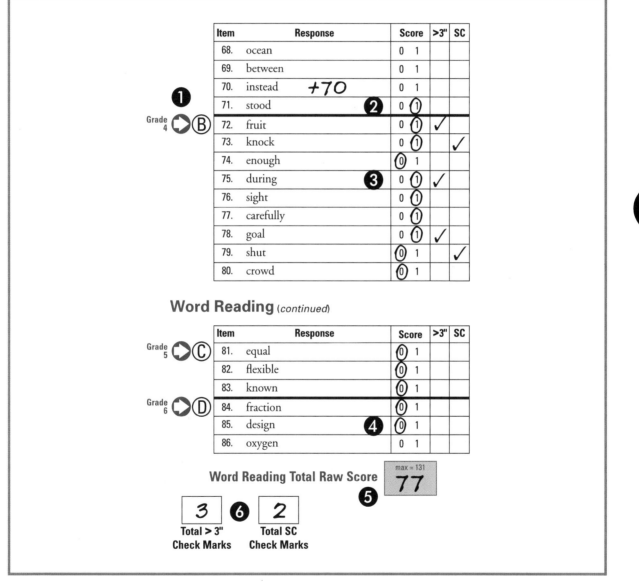

Figure 4.1.
Example of Word Reading Scoring

Maximum Total Raw Score: 131 points

Qualitative Observations

After administration of the subtest, you may complete the Qualitative Observations on the record form. Note how frequently a behavior occurred by checking the appropriate box. Recording of these observations is optional, but strongly recommended because of their value in interpreting subtest results.

Numerical Operations

Materials

- Stimulus Booklet 1
- Record Form
- Response Booklet
- Blank paper
- Pencil without eraser
- 8 pennies
  (Grades K–1 only)

Start Points

Grade PreK:
Do not administer

Grades K–1:
Item 1 Letter A

Grades 2–4:
Item 8 Letter B

Grades 5–8:
Item 13 Letter C

Grades 9–16:
Item 15 Letter D

Adults:
Start at the level of
the last grade completed

Reverse Rule

Score of 0 on **any** of the first 3 items given, administer the preceding items in reverse order until 3 consecutive scores of 1

Discontinue Rule

Discontinue after 6 consecutive scores of 0

Description

Numerical Operations assesses the ability to identify and write numbers, count using 1:1 correspondence, and solve written calculation problems and simple equations involving the basic operations of addition, subtraction, multiplication, and division.

General Directions

To begin, turn to the Administration section for Numerical Operations in Stimulus Booklet 1. For Grades K–1 only, you will need to provide 8 pennies. Follow the administration directions and begin the subtest at the grade-appropriate start point. If you have reason to believe that the examinee's calculation skills are below grade level, you may begin the subtest at the start point for the previous grade level. If an examinee is spending an inordinate amount of time on a single item, encourage him or her to move on to the next problem.

Note that the response booklet contains the consecutively numbered items and the letters A–D. The letters identify the various start points. Monitor the examinee's responses by following along on the record form so that you can apply the reverse and discontinue rules. You will need to observe the examinee's performance until the basal level is established. Make sure the examinee writes in the appropriate spaces in the response booklet. If a numeral is illegible because it is poorly formed, inverted, reversed, or rotated, ask the examinee to read the answer aloud. Then write the verbal response next to the item on the record form and circle it. This will serve as a reminder to you that the examinee's oral response was provided.

Recording and Scoring

Use the record form to score the responses written by the examinee in the response booklet. Score 0 points for an incorrect response and 1 point for a correct response. Note that for the items containing fractions, the directions tell the examinee to express the answer in the simplest or lowest terms. Do not penalize the examinee for failing to reduce the fractions, and score 1 point if the response is otherwise correct. You may wish to make a note that the examinee did not reduce fractions. Fractions that are expressed in correct decimal form also score 1 point.

If the examinee responds correctly to three consecutive items, award 1 point for each of the preceding, unadministered items. The Numerical Operations total raw score is the total number of 1-point responses.

After test administration, review the examinee's response booklet and notes on the scratch paper. Review of the examinee's problem-solving methods can provide valuable error analysis (see Chapter 7).

Maximum Total Raw Score: 54 points

Qualitative Observations

After administration of the subtest, you may complete the Qualitative Observations on the record form. Note how frequently a behavior occurred by checking the appropriate box. Recording of these observations is optional, but strongly recommended because of their value in interpreting subtest results.

Reading Comprehension

Materials

- Stimulus Booklet 1
- Record Form
- Stopwatch

Start Points

Grades PreK–K: Do not administer		**Grade 5:**	Item 55
		Grade 6:	Item 59
Grade 1:	Item 1	**Grades 7–8:**	Item 75
Grade 2:	Item 10	**Grades 9–12:**	Item 94
Grade 3:	Item 20	**Grades 13–16:**	Item 108
Grade 4:	Item 34	**Adults:** Start at the level of the last grade completed	

Reverse Rules

Grades 1–8: Score of 0 on **all** of the grade-specific reversal items given, go back three start points and continue by following the administration rules of the new grade level

Grades 9–12: Score of 0 on **all** of the grade-specific reversal items given, administer Items 75–114

Grades 13–16: Score of 0 on **all** of the grade-specific reversal items given, administer Items 94–127

Stop Points

Grade 1:	After Item 27	**Grade 6:**	After Item 93
Grade 2:	After Item 44	**Grade 7:**	After Item 107
Grade 3:	After Item 54	**Grade 8:**	After Item 114
Grade 4:	After Item 69	**Grades 9–12:**	After Item 127
Grade 5:	After Item 85	**Grades 13–16:**	After Item 140

Description

Reading Comprehension assesses the types of reading comprehension skills taught in the classroom or used in everyday life. On initial items, the examinee matches a written word with its representative picture. On later items, the examinee reads different types of passages and answers questions involving the comprehension of content, such as identifying the main idea and specific details, making inferences, and defining vocabulary by using context cues. The examinee also reads short sentences aloud and responds to comprehension questions. An optional score for Reading Speed can be calculated based on the total of the elapsed times of reading passages. Then the relationship between Reading Speed and Reading Comprehension scores can be used to describe Reading Rate using the Reading Rate graph on the record form.

General Directions

For each grade level, specific basal items have been identified and marked on the record form with grade-specific reversal icons. There is considerable overlap between grades, and the Reading Comprehension reverse rules make it possible for you to measure the reading comprehension of an individual who is reading significantly below grade placement. Once the basal level has been established for an examinee, administer items until you reach the stop point for that grade. All of the items for a grade are administered regardless of examinee performance.

To begin, turn to the Administration section for Reading Comprehension in Stimulus Booklet 1. Follow the administration directions and begin the subtest at the grade-appropriate start point. There are three types of items in the Reading Comprehension subtest: words, sentences, and passages. Examinees must read the sentences aloud, but may read words and passages either aloud or silently, as the examinee chooses. Allow the examinee to continue looking at the reading passage as he or she answers the questions.

Responses that are followed by a **(Q)** indicate that a query is necessary. Query responses by saying **Tell me more**.

Beginning with Item 20, passages are timed using a stopwatch. Begin timing when the examinee begins to read, and stop when the examinee indicates that he or she has finished reading the passage.

Passages are ordered according to reading level, but items related to a passage are not ordered according to the level of difficulty. Do not discontinue prior to the stop point listed for a grade. Start and stop points were determined by identifying a set of items that measured a full range of abilities (based on the performance of the standardization sample) for any given grade group.

Recording and Scoring

For Items 1–5, score 0 points for each incorrect response and 2 points for each correct response.

For the *sentences*, score 1 point for each target word read correctly. The target words are indicated on the record form in **bold type**. The sentences are reproduced on the record form so that you can record errors. Cross out any words the examinee pronounces incorrectly or omits. If the examinee inserts or transposes any words, make a note above the sentence. Figure 4.2 illustrates how to score a sentence item.

Possible 1- and 2-point responses for *passages* are provided in the stimulus booklet. Additional scoring examples are in Appendix A.1 of the supplements. Until you become familiar with the scoring rules, record all responses verbatim. Record the examinee's reading time in seconds for each passage in the space provided.

Figure 4.2.
Example of a Scored Reading Comprehension Sentence Response

To calculate the Reading Comprehension total raw score, add the scores of all the comprehension items, and record the sum in the space provided for the examinee's grade on the record form. For Grades 2–16, give credit for all of the preceding, unadministered items. The credit for preceding items for each grade has been calculated and is noted on the record form. Add the sum of the comprehension items to the total of the preceding, unadministered comprehension items.

To calculate the Target Words total raw score, add the scores from all the Target Words read correctly in the sentences, and record the sum in the space provided for the examinee's grade on the record form. Sentences are shaded on the record form for quick identification. For Grades 2–16, give credit for all of the preceding, unadministered items. The credit for preceding items for each grade has been calculated and is noted on the record form. Add the sum of the Target Words to the total of the preceding, unadministered Target Words items.

To calculate the Reading Speed total raw score, add the elapsed reading times from all passages. Calculate the total, in seconds, and record in the space provided for the examinee's grade on the record form.

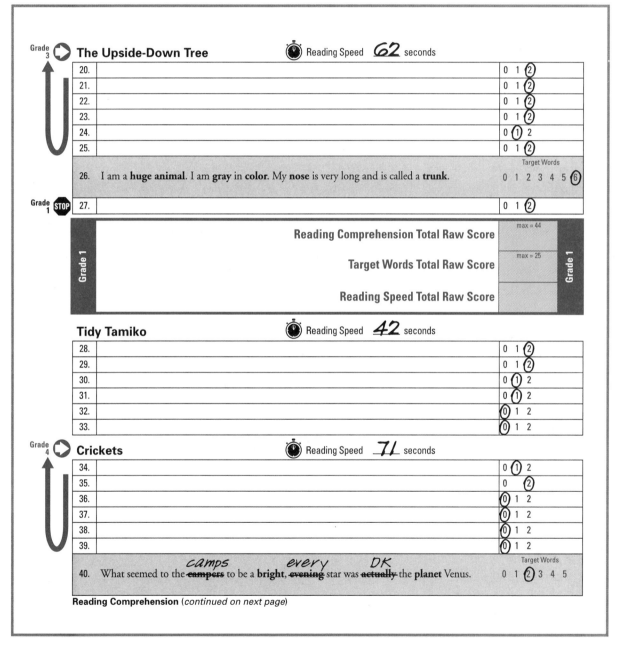

Figure 4.3.
Example of Calculating the Total Raw Scores for Reading Comprehension

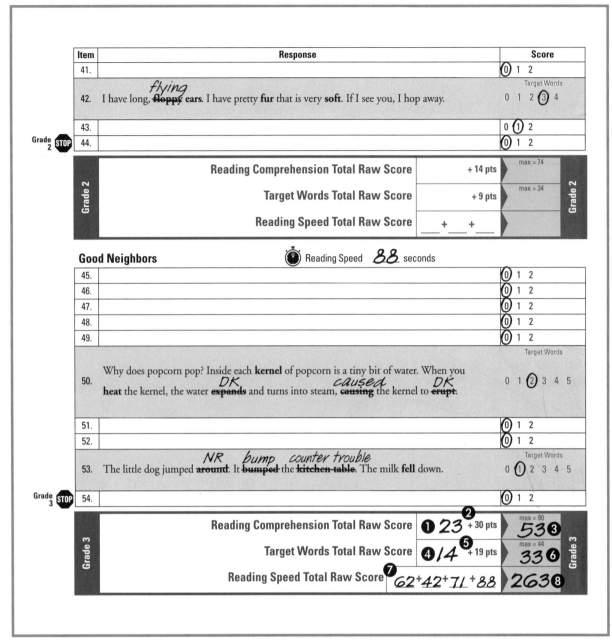

Figure 4.3.
Example of Calculating the Total Raw Scores for Reading Comprehension *(continued)*

Figure 4.3 illustrates how the Reading Comprehension total raw score, the Target Words total raw score, and the Reading Speed total raw score were calculated for a third grade examinee. The examinee scored a raw score of 23 on the comprehension items for Grade 3 (Items 20–25, 27, 28–39, 41, 43–49, 51–52, and 54), and this number is recorded in the Grade 3 space next to Reading Comprehension Total Raw Score (see 1). This score was then added to the credit given for the preceding, unadministered items (see 2), yielding a Reading Comprehension total raw score of 53 (see 3). The sum of the scores for the target words read in sentences (Items 26, 40, 42, 50, and 53) was 14 (see 4). This score was added to the credit given for the preceding items (see 5), for a Target Words total raw score of 33 (see 6). The Reading Speed total raw score was calculated by adding together the elapsed times from The Upside-Down Tree (62 seconds), Tidy Tamiko (42 seconds),

Crickets (71 seconds), and Good Neighbors (88 seconds) for a total of 263 seconds (see 8). The subtest standard score is derived from the Reading Comprehension total raw score. Table 4.1. summarizes the maximum total scores by grade.

Table 4.1.

The Maximum Scores for Reading Comprehension and Target Words by Grade

Grade Level	Reading Comprehension				Target Words		
	Items Administered	Total Points	Credit for Previous Items	Maximum Total Raw Score[a]	Number of Target Words	Credit for Previous Target Words	Maximum Total Raw Score[b]
Grade 1	1–27	44	—	44	25	—	25
Grade 2	10–44	60	14	74	25	9	34
Grade 3	20–54	60	30	90	25	19	44
Grade 4	34–69	60	56	116	25	25	50
Grade 5	55–85	54	90	144	16	44	60
Grade 6	59–93	60	98	158	24	44	68
Grade 7	75–107	56	126	182	26	50	76
Grade 8	75–114	68	126	194	37	50	87
Grades 9–12	94–127	60	158	218	22	68	90
Grades 13–16	108–140	60	182	242	24	76	100

[a] The maximum total raw score for Reading Comprehension is calculated by summing the total Reading Comprehension points for the administered items and the preceding, unadministered items.

[b] The maximum total raw score for Target Words is calculated by summing the total Target Words for the administered items and the preceding, unadministered items.

Qualitative Observations

After administration of the subtest, you may complete the Qualitative Observations on the record form. Note how frequently a behavior occurred by checking the appropriate box. Recording of these observations is optional, but strongly recommended because of their value in interpreting subtest results.

Spelling

Materials	Start Points	Reverse Rule

Materials

- Stimulus Booklet 1
- Record Form
- Response Booklet
- Pencil without an eraser

Start Points

Grade PreK:	Do not administer
Grades K–1:	Item 1
Grade 2:	Item 13
Grades 3–4:	Item 16
Grades 5–7:	Item 19
Grades 8–9:	Item 23
Grades 10–16:	Item 27

Adults: Start at the level of the last grade completed

Reverse Rule

Score of 0 on **any** of the first 3 items given, administer the preceding items in reverse order until 3 consecutive scores of 1

Discontinue Rule

Discontinue after 6 consecutive scores of 0

Description

Spelling assesses the ability to spell dictated letters, letter blends, and words. The inclusion of homonyms requires that the examinee use context clues from the dictated sentences to spell the appropriate word.

General Directions

To begin, turn to the Administration section for Spelling in Stimulus Booklet 1. Follow the administration directions and begin the subtest at the grade-appropriate start point. If you suspect that the examinee's spelling skills are below grade level, you may begin the subtest at the start point that is one grade level lower. You will need to observe the examinee's performance until the basal level is established.

Recording and Scoring

Use the record form to score the examinee's responses. Score 0 points for an incorrect response and 1 point for a correct response.

If the examinee responds correctly to three consecutive items, award 1 point for each of the preceding, unadministered items. The Spelling total raw score is the total number of 1-point responses.

Maximum Total Raw Score: 53 points

Qualitative Observations

After administration of the subtest, you may complete the Qualitative Observations on the record form. Note how frequently a behavior occurred by checking the appropriate box. Recording of these observations is optional, but strongly recommended because of their value in interpreting subtest results.

Pseudoword Decoding

Materials

- Stimulus Booklet 1
- Record Form
- Pseudoword Card
- Pseudoword Audiotape (examiner's use only)

Start Points

Grades PreK–K:
Do not administer

Grades 1–16:
Sample Item 1 (S1)

Adults:
Sample Item 1 (S1)

Discontinue Rule

Discontinue after 7 consecutive scores of 0

Description

Pseudoword Decoding assesses the ability to apply phonetic decoding skills. A list of nonsense words is read aloud from the Pseudoword Card. The words are designed to be representative of the phonetic structure of words in the English language.

General Directions

Before administering this subtest, familiarize yourself with the correct pronunciation of the pseudowords by listening to the Pseudoword Audiotape.

To begin, turn to the Administration section for Pseudoword Decoding in Stimulus Booklet 1. Follow the administration directions and begin the subtest with the first sample item. If the examinee does not respond within 5 seconds or gives an incorrect response on either sample item, provide the correct response. Do not count errors on the sample items when counting errors for the discontinue rule. Do not provide correct responses for items other than for the two sample items.

Be sure the examinee understands that he or she is to read the words going across, not down, the page. If the examinee inadvertently skips a word or row of words, redirect the examinee to the appropriate word or row and make a note on the record form to remind you of this behavior.

Recording and Scoring

Record any incorrect responses verbatim on the record form. Self-corrections count as correct responses. Score 0 points for an incorrect response and 1 point for a correct response. If the examinee responds with only a partial pronunciation of the word, record the abbreviated response and score the item 0 points.

The Pseudoword Decoding total raw score is the total number of 1-point responses. Do not count the sample items when obtaining the total raw score.

Maximum Total Raw Score: 55 points

Math Reasoning

Materials

- Stimulus Booklet 2
- Record Form
- Pencil without an eraser
- Blank paper

Start Points

Grades PreK–K:	Item 1
Grade 1:	Item 4
Grade 2:	Item 16
Grade 3:	Item 21
Grade 4:	Item 23
Grade 5:	Item 28
Grade 6:	Item 30
Grades 7–8:	Item 35
Grades 9–16:	Item 41
Adults:	Start at the level of the last grade completed

Reverse Rule

Score of 0 on **any** of the first 3 items given, administer the preceding items in reverse order until 3 consecutive scores of 1

Discontinue Rule

Discontinue after 6 consecutive scores of 0

Description

Math Reasoning presents a series of problems with both verbal and visual prompts that assess the ability to reason mathematically. The examinee counts, identifies geometric shapes, and solves single- and multi-step word problems, including items related to time, money, and measurement. The examinee solves problems with whole numbers, fractions or decimals, interprets graphs, identifies mathematical patterns, and solves problems related to statistics and probability.

General Directions

To begin, turn to the Administration section for Math Reasoning in Stimulus Booklet 2. Follow the administration directions and begin the subtest at the grade-appropriate start point. If you have reason to believe that the examinee's math skills are below grade level, you may begin the subtest at the start point for the previous grade level.

For those items that allow the examinee to point to a picture in the stimulus booklet, sit so that you can see which picture is selected. Most items require a verbal response. For each item allow the examinee approximately 1 minute to respond. Unless he or she is actively working on the item, go to the next item.

Recording and Scoring

Use the record form to record the examinee's responses verbatim. Score 0 points for an incorrect response and 1 point for a correct response. All of the possible correct responses are provided on the examiner's pages of the stimulus booklet and on the record form. Only one of the correct responses is required to score 1 point.

If the examinee responds correctly to three consecutive items, award 1 point for each of the preceding, unadministered items. The Math Reasoning total raw score is the total number of 1-point responses. After test administration, review the examinee's response booklet and notes on the scratch paper. Review of the examinee's problem-solving methods can provide valuable error analysis (see Chapter 7).

Maximum Total Raw Score: 67 points

Qualitative Observations

After administration of the subtest, you may complete the Qualitative Observations on the record form. Note how frequently a behavior occurred by checking the appropriate box. Recording of these observations is optional, but strongly recommended because of their value in interpreting subtest results.

After you have completed administration of the WIAT–II, gather additional information for error analysis and instructional planning by asking the examinee to talk through the problem solution of incorrect Math Reasoning items.

Written Expression

Materials

- Stimulus Booklet 2
- Record Form
- Response Booklet
- Pencil without an eraser
- Blank paper
- Stopwatch

⮕ Start Points

Grades PreK–2:
Item 1

Grades 3–6:
Item 2

Grades 7–16:
Item 10

Adults:
Start at the level of the last grade completed

🛑 Stop Points

Grades PreK–K:	After Item 1
Grade 1:	After Item 5
Grade 2:	After Item 7
Grades 3–6:	After Item 9
Grades 7–12:	After Item 16
Grades 13–16:	After Item 17

Description

Written Expression assesses the writing process. The subtest has five sections: **Alphabet Writing, Word Fluency, Sentences, Paragraph,** and **Essay**. Alphabet Writing, which is timed, measures automaticity in writing the lowercase letters of the alphabet in order from memory. Word Fluency assesses the ability to generate and write a list of words that match a prescribed category. Sentences evaluate the ability to combine multiple sentences into one, meaningful sentence, or the ability to generate a sentence from visual or verbal cues. Paragraph assesses mechanics, organization, and vocabulary. Essay assesses mechanics, organization, theme development, and vocabulary.

General Directions

The Written Expression subtest is organized so that the most appropriate items are administered to an examinee according to grade. Examinees in Grades PreK–K are administered only Alphabet Writing. Examinees in Grades 1–2 are administered Alphabet Writing, Word Fluency, and Sentences. Examinees in Grades 3–6 are administered Word Fluency, Sentences, and Paragraph. Examinees in Grades 7–16 are administered Word Fluency, Sentences, and Essay.

To begin, turn to the Administration section of Written Expression in Stimulus Booklet 2. Follow the administration directions and begin the subtest at the grade-appropriate start point. If you have reason to believe that the examinee's writing skills are below grade level, you may begin the subtest at the start point for the previous grade level.

Alphabet Writing

Prior to test administration, decide if you will "test the limits" on this item by allowing the examinee to continue writing past the 15-second time limit until the alphabet is completed. Although there are no norms by which to measure testing the limits, the qualitative information can be helpful when talking with parents and planning intervention.

Word Fluency

Administration requires the use of a stopwatch. Stop at 60 seconds. Item 2 is administered to examinees in Grades 3–6 and Item 10 is administered to Grades 7–16. Make sure the response booklet is open to page 8 for Grades 3–6 or page 11 for Grades 7–16.

Sentences

To administer the Sentences, go to the grade-appropriate item in the stimulus booklet. Direct the examinee to the appropriate sample item in the response booklet. Follow the instructions for the sample item in the stimulus booklet. The sample item is provided as a model or teaching item, therefore it is not scored. At the examinee's request you may read unknown words in the stimulus booklet. Examinees may not use a dictionary or spelling tool.

Paragraph

Only one of the prompts (Prompt A or Prompt B) should be administered. Use Prompt B if Prompt A is spoiled or for purposes of reevaluation. Direct the examinee to turn to the page in the response booklet for the selected prompt. Allow the examinee up to 10 minutes to write a paragraph. Examinees may not use a dictionary or spelling tool.

Essay

Grades 7–12 are administered Item 16 and Grades 13–16 are administered Item 17. Item 16 and Item 17 each have 2 prompts (Prompt A and Prompt B). Only one of the prompts should be administered. Use Prompt B if Prompt A is spoiled or for purposes of reevaluation. Give the examinee some blank paper and direct him or her to the selected prompt for the grade-appropriate item in the response booklet. Allow the examinee up to 15 minutes to write the essay. Examinees may not use a dictionary or spelling tool.

Recording and Scoring

Refer to Appendix A.2 of the supplements for comprehensive scoring guidelines and examples for Alphabet Writing (*WIAT–II Scoring and Normative Supplement for Grades PreK–12* only), Word Fluency, Sentences, Paragraph, and Essay.

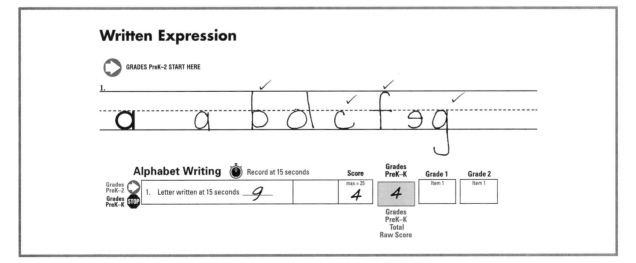

Figure 4.4.
Example of a Scored Alphabet Writing Response

Alphabet Writing

After 15 seconds have elapsed, record the last letter written by the examinee in the space provided for Alphabet Writing on the record form. Score only the letters written during this 15-second time period. Figure 4.4 is an example of a scored Alphabet Writing response. The figure includes the appropriate sections from the response booklet and the record form.

For Grades PreK–K, transfer the Alphabet Writing score to the Supplemental Score Conversion Worksheet where it will be converted to a decile. For Grades 1–2, copy the Alphabet Writing score in the box provided for the appropriate grade on the record form next to Item 1. Figure 4.7 illustrates how to record the Alphabet Writing score for an examinee in Grade 2.

Word Fluency

To score the Word Fluency items, record the score in the space provided on the record form. Use Table B.5 (grade-based) or Table E.5 (age-based) to convert the score to a quartile score. The quartile score is added to the scores from the other sections in Written Expression to calculate the subtest total raw score.

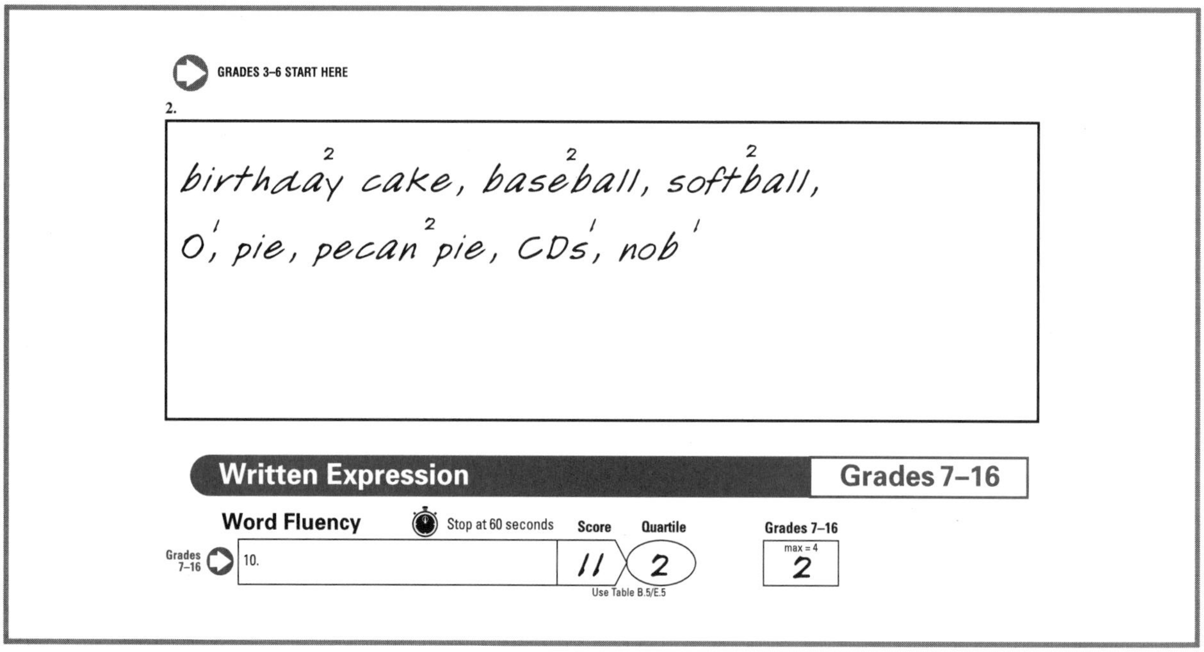

Figure 4.5.
Example of Written Expression Word Fluency Scoring

Figure 4.5 provides an example of Word Fluency scoring. The figure includes the appropriate sections from the response booklet and the record form. This example would receive a score of 11. Four items receive 2 points each: *birthday cake, baseball, softball,* and *pecan pie* because they are acceptable, multi-syllable words. Three items receive 1 point each: *0 (zero) CDs,* and *nob* because they are acceptable as single syllable or abbreviated words. Credit is given to *0* even though it is not spelled out, and to *nob* even though it is spelled incorrectly. *Pie* does not receive credit because it is a different description of *pecan pie.* The examinee is awarded the 2 points for the multi-syllable response *pecan pie* rather than the single point for *pie* even though *pie* was written first. Figure 4.5 also illustrates how the Written Expression Word Fluency score is recorded on the record form.

Sentences

Score each item 2, 1, or 0 points depending on the quality of the response. Appendix A. 2 includes examples and explanations of scored responses for each item. After the sentence items are scored, the points earned are totaled and recorded by grade in the space provided on the record form.

Paragraph

The paragraph can be scored analytically using the scoring rubric on the record form or by following the guidelines for holistic scoring. Appendix A.2 includes sample responses that have been scored using the scoring rubric and holistic scoring. For analytic scoring, the scoring rubric has three evaluation categories: Mechanics, Organization, and Vocabulary. Figure 4.6 illustrates the paragraph scoring rubric on the record form.

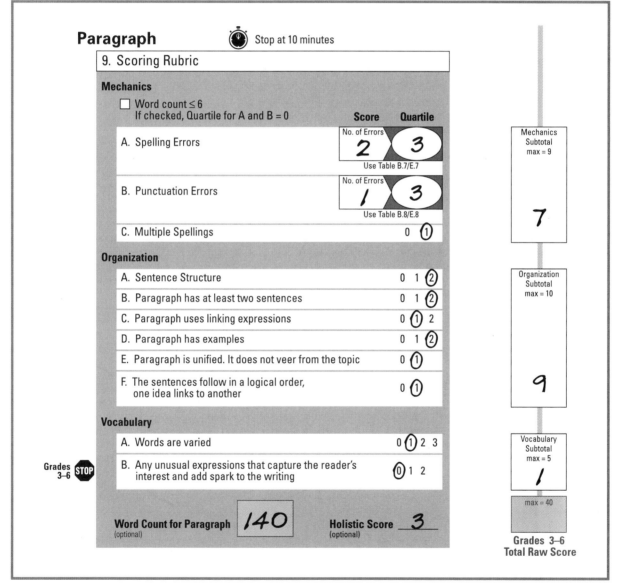

Figure 4.6.
Example of the Written Expression Scoring Rubric for Paragraph

Mechanics Subtotal

To determine the Mechanics subtotal, evaluate if the paragraph includes at least *seven words*. If there are six or fewer words, do *not* count spelling and punctuation errors and record 0 points in the spaces provided for the Spelling Errors Quartile and the Punctuation Errors Quartile. If the paragraph contains at least seven words, use Tables B.7 and B.8 or E.7 and E.8 to convert the spelling error and punctuation error scores to quartile scores. The third score for Mechanics is dependent on whether the examinee has multiple spellings for the same word. A score of 0 points is recorded if there are multiple spellings; a score of 1 point is recorded if there are not.

The Mechanics subtotal score is the sum of the spelling and punctuation quartiles and the multiple spellings score. The maximum score is 9.

Organization Subtotal

To determine the Organization subtotal, assess the sentence structure, number of sentences, use of linking expressions, use of examples to illustrate or expand ideas, and the unity and logical order of the paragraph.

The Organization subtotal score is the sum of the number of points earned in the six elements. The maximum score is 10.

Vocabulary Score

To determine the Vocabulary subtotal, evaluate the word variety and style of the paragraph.

The Vocabulary subtotal score is the sum of points earned in the two elements. The maximum score is 5.

Word Count

Word Count is an optional supplemental score that can be calculated for the paragraph. To calculate the Word Count total raw score, count the number of words written by the examinee. Do not include the words of the prompt in the score. Abbreviations (e.g., PE) count as a single word. Transfer the Word Count total raw score to the Supplemental Score Conversion Worksheet and convert it to a quartile by using Table B.6 (grade-based) or Table E.6 (age-based).

Using Holistic Scoring

The paragraph can also be scored using a holistic scoring system that is similar to the holistic scoring on the WIAT. Due to the wide variation in responses, the holistic scoring criteria were designed to be very general. To understand holistic scoring, refer to the holistic scoring criteria. Paragraphs can be scored 0, 1, 2, 3, 4, 5, or 6 points. A paragraph that demonstrates a basic response to the prompt is probably enough to earn a low score; however, to achieve a higher score, the paragraph must include appropriate details that provide the reader with a fuller, richer knowledge of the examinee's opinions or ideas. Do not penalize if the paragraph contains incorrect spelling, punctuation, or mechanics. Refer to Table 4.2 for the holistic scoring criteria for specific score information.

To calculate the Written Expression total raw score for Grades PreK–6, identify the column that represents the grade level of the examinee, then record the various scores for Alphabet Writing (Grades PreK–2), Word Fluency (Grades 1–6), Sentences (Grades 1–6), and Paragraph (Grades 3–6) including the subtotal scores for Mechanics, Organization, and Vocabulary. Sum the scores in the grade-specific space provided above Total Raw Score. Figure 4.7 illustrates how to calculate the total raw score for an examinee in Grade 2.

Table 4.2.
Holistic Scoring Criteria for Paragraphs

Score	Response
6 points	Well written and presents **clear, organized, and developed descriptions** of the topic. The ideas and details are **clarified and related through the use of effective transitions,** resulting in an overall sense of the subject.
	Effectiveness is enhanced through the use of vivid imagery.
5 points	Presents a **substantial amount of descriptive and varied detail** of the topic. The ideas and details are **clarified with several descriptions or through elaboration.**
	Features are related to each other or to the whole.
	Organization is weak but several ideas are clarified with added details, or organization is clear but the ideas are less well developed.
4 points	Generally well written and contains a **moderate amount of description** of the topic. The ideas or activities are related to each other or to the main idea.
	Mentions a few activities that the examinee enjoys and **adds clarifying descriptive details to each** activity.
	Mentions several activities but **clarifies only a few** of the activities **with several added details.**
	Organized around a **single activity** that the examinee enjoys **with a moderate amount of description** about the activity.
3 points	Contains a **limited amount of description** of the topic. The ideas or activities are related to each other or to the main idea.
	Mentions a few activities that the examinee enjoys and **clarifies many** of the activities **through additional descriptive details.**
	Mentions several activities that are related to each other or to the whole, some of which are **clarified through an additional detail.**
2 points	Contains a **minimal amount of description** of the topic with a **few activities** that the examinee enjoys and **clarifies through additional descriptive details of at least one of the activities.**
	Mentions a single activity and provides **a few descriptive details** about the activity.
1 point	Indicates that the examinee attempted to respond to the prompt with a coherent **listing of one or more general activities** (e.g., *play games, play outside*). There is **no attempt to further clarify with additional descriptive details.**
0 points	Demonstrates no relationship to the prompt.

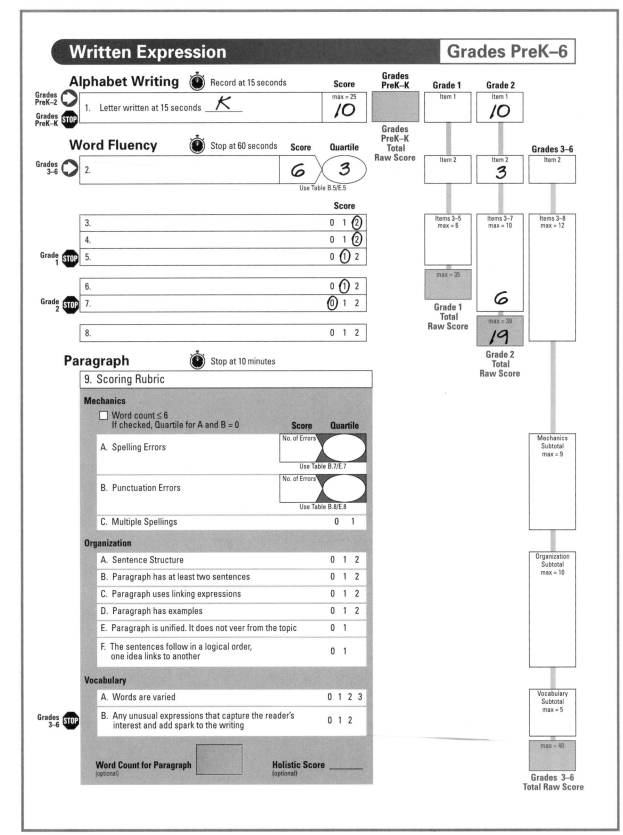

Figure 4.7.

Example of Written Expression Scoring for Grade 2

Essay

The essay can be scored using the scoring rubric on the record form or by following the guidelines for holistic scoring. Appendix A.2 includes sample responses that have been scored using the scoring rubric and holistic scoring. For analytic scoring, the scoring rubric has four evaluation categories: Mechanics, Organization, Theme Development, and Vocabulary. Figure 4.8 illustrates the essay scoring rubric on the record form.

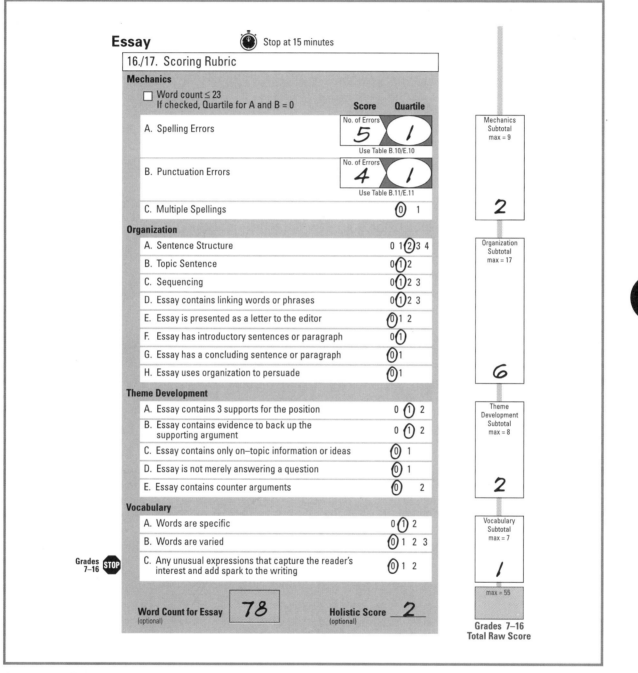

Figure 4.8.
Example of the Written Expression Scoring Rubric for Essay

Mechanics Subtotal

To determine the Mechanics subtotal, first count the words in the essay. The essay should contain at least *24 words*. If there are 23 or fewer words, do *not* count spelling and punctuation errors and record 0 points in the spaces provided for the Spelling Errors Quartile and the Punctuation Errors Quartile. If the essay contains at least 24 words, count the spelling errors and convert the number to a quartile using Table B.10 (grade-based) or E.10 (age-based) in the supplements. Similarly, count the punctuation errors and convert the number to a quartile using Table B.11 (grade-based) or E.11 (age-based) in the supplements. The third score for Mechanics is dependent on whether the examinee has multiple spellings for the same word. A score of 0 points is recorded if there are multiple spellings; a score of 1 point is recorded if there are not.

The Mechanics subtotal score is the sum of the spelling and punctuation quartiles and the multiple spellings score. The maximum score is 9.

Organization Subtotal

To determine the Organization subtotal, assess the sentence structure, use of topic sentences, correct sequencing of ideas, use of linking expressions, adherence to the requirement of a letter to the editor, inclusion of introductory and concluding sentences, and the examinee's ability to use organization to persuade.

The Organization subtotal score is the sum of the number of points earned in the eight elements. The maximum score is 17.

Theme Development Subtotal

Theme Development is evaluated by determining if the essay includes the required three supports, evidence to back up any supporting argument, on-topic information, and any counter arguments. The essay cannot be limited to merely answering a question.

The Theme Development subtotal score is the sum of points earned in the five elements. The maximum score is 8.

Vocabulary Subtotal

Vocabulary is evaluated by determining if the examinee's words are specific and varied, and if any unusual expressions were employed to capture the reader's interest and add spark to the writing.

The Vocabulary subtotal score is the sum of the points earned in the three elements. The maximum score is 7.

Word Count

Word Count is an optional supplemental score that can be calculated for the essay. To calculate the Word Count total raw score, count the number of words written by the examinee. Abbreviations count as a single word. Transfer the Word Count total raw score to the Supplemental Score Conversion Worksheet and convert it to a quartile using Table B.9 (grade-based) or Table E.9 (age-based).

Using Holistic Scoring

The essay can also be scored using a holistic scoring system that is similar to the holistic scoring on the WIAT. Due to the wide variation in responses, the holistic scoring criteria were designed to be very general. To understand holistic scoring, refer to the holistic scoring criteria. Essays can be scored 0, 1, 2, 3, 4, 5, or 6 points. An essay that demonstrates a basic response to the prompt is probably enough to earn a low score; however, to achieve a higher score, the essay must include appropriate details that provide the reader with a fuller, richer knowledge of the examinee's opinions or ideas. Do not penalize if the essay contains incorrect spelling, punctuation, or mechanics. Refer to the following holistic scoring criteria for specific score information.

Table 4.3.
Holistic Scoring Criteria for Essays

Score	Response
6 points	**Clearly states or implies a position** and supports it with a **substantial amount of evidence,** so that the essay presents a **cogent, persuasive argument** in favor of the position. **Well-organized, fluent, vivid, and interesting.** The essay shows a strong sense of audience and purpose and uses language effectively and efficiently to influence the reader. Does not contain illogical or irrelevant arguments, redundancy, or a verbal assault.
5 points	**States or implies a position** and supports it with a **substantial amount of evidence.** Although only **three supports are required,** the essay **may provide additional reasons.** Expands on each support or reason with **many clarifying details. The details are well developed and support the position.** Usually a paragraph will be dedicated to each reason and the surrounding details. Message is on topic, logical, well stated, and organized.
4 points	**States or implies a position** and supports it with **no fewer than three reasons,** and provides **clarifying detail for at least three of the reasons.** The detail is developed, with generally two or three sentences written for each reason. On topic and logical, and has few language problems but may have minor problems with unity or organization.
3 points	**States or implies a position** and supports it with **at least two reasons,** and provides **some clarifying detail** for at least two of the reasons. Provides **three or more specific reasons, but clarifies only one** of the reasons. Clarifying **details are generally one or two sentences** in length. On topic and logical, but may include language problems or poor organization.
2 points	**States or implies a position** and supports it with **at least one reason that is somewhat clarified by details.** Provides **several nonspecific or undeveloped reasons.** Provides a **few reasons, but only one reason is clarified** with additional detail. Provides a **number of reasons, some of which may be illogical, vague, redundant, or have language problems.**
1 point	**States or implies a position** and supports it with **enough details to determine that the response is on topic.** Contains **a persuasive tone, but no reasons** for a position **or only a vague, or illogical reason.** Contains **extraneous information** or **considerable repetition.** Organization, logic, or language control problems interfere with meaning and may confuse the reader.
0 points	Contains no relationship to the prompt. Attempt to persuade the reader is not noticeable.

To calculate the Written Expression total raw score for Grades 7–16, record the various scores for Word Fluency, Sentences, and Essay (including subtotal scores for Mechanics, Organization, Theme Development, and Vocabulary). Sum the scores in the space provided above total raw score. Figure 4.9 illustrates how to calculate the total raw score for an examinee in Grades 7–16.

Written Expression — Grades 7–16

Word Fluency

Stop at 60 seconds

Grades 7–16	Item	Score	Quartile	Grades 7–16 (max = 4)
	10.	13	2	2

Use Table B.5/E.5

Sentences

Item	Score	Items 11–15 (max = 10)
11.	0 1 (2)	
12.	0 1 (2)	
13.	0 (1) 2	
14.	0 (1) 2	
15.	(0) 1 2	6

Essay

Stop at 15 minutes

16./17. Scoring Rubric

Mechanics

☐ Word count ≤ 23
If checked, Quartile for A and B = 0

	Score	Quartile
A. Spelling Errors	No. of Errors 5	1
	Use Table B.10/E.10	
B. Punctuation Errors	No. of Errors 3	2
	Use Table B.11/E.11	
C. Multiple Spellings	0 (1)	

Mechanics Subtotal (max = 9): 4

Organization

	Score
A. Sentence Structure	0 1 (2) 3 4
B. Topic Sentence	0 (1) 2
C. Sequencing	0 (1) 2 3
D. Essay contains linking words or phrases	0 (1) 2 3
E. Essay is presented as a letter to the editor	0 1 (2)
F. Essay has introductory sentences or paragraph	0 (1)
G. Essay has a concluding sentence or paragraph	(0) 1
H. Essay uses organization to persuade	(0) 1

Organization Subtotal (max = 17): 8

Theme Development

	Score
A. Essay contains 3 supports for the position	0 (1) 2
B. Essay contains evidence to back up the supporting argument	(0) 1 2
C. Essay contains only on–topic information or ideas	0 (1)
D. Essay is not merely answering a question	0 (1)
E. Essay contains counter arguments	(0) 2

Theme Development Subtotal (max = 8): 3

Vocabulary

	Score
A. Words are specific	0 (1) 2
B. Words are varied	0 (1) 2 3
C. Any unusual expressions that capture the reader's interest and add spark to the writing	(0) 1 2

Grades 7–16 STOP

Vocabulary Subtotal (max = 7): 2

Word Count for Essay (optional): 84

Holistic Score (optional): 2

max = 55: 25
Grades 7–16 Total Raw Score

Figure 4.9.
Example of Written Expression Scoring for Grades 7–16

Mastering the Scoring Procedures

After you have carefully reviewed the scoring guidelines, use the sample responses in Appendix A.2 of the supplements to practice scoring paragraphs or essays before scoring an examinee's protocol. The sample responses in Appendix A.2 were selected from the standardization sample to represent a variety of scores and score combinations. Each response includes an excerpt from the record form that displays the scores and a description of the reasoning that guided scoring. The sample responses are scored using the scoring rubric and holistic scoring.

Although the decision of which scoring method to use depends on the purpose of assessment, both the holistic and analytic methods can be used to score a response. For example, if you administer the paragraph item to obtain a general idea of an examinee's writing ability, you can score the response holistically. If the score is lower than you expect, you can then use the analytic scoring rubric to evaluate specific problems. Holistic scoring, which is more subjective, allows you to assign a single score (0–6 points) to a paragraph based on the *overall* quality of the writing. **A holistic score cannot be used to calculate the Written Expression total raw score.** Therefore, to obtain a standard score, you must use the analytic scoring rubric. Effective and reliable scoring of the writing sample, whether analytic or holistic, requires more effort than does the scoring of other WIAT–II subtests. Therefore, practice scoring responses. First, score the sample responses provided in Appendix A.2 of the supplements, compare your results with the actual scores supplied, and review the accompanying annotations. Then practice scoring "practice" responses from friends or colleagues. If possible, have another examiner also review the scoring criteria and score the practice response. Compare the two scores and explore any discrepancies by referring to the scoring criteria and the scored samples in Appendix A.2. If, after completing the preceding steps, you are still unsure of certain aspects of scoring, consult further with a language-arts specialist or composition specialist or both. Remember that scoring criteria were developed based on widely accepted expectations for examinees in the assigned grades. If the writing requirements for a grade are significantly different in your school, you should score the response according to the rules included in this manual, but note the discrepancy in expectations in your report.

Listening Comprehension

Receptive Vocabulary

Materials
- Stimulus Booklet 2
- Record Form

Start Points

Grades PreK–5: Item 1

Grades 6–16: Item 7

Adults: Start at the level of the last grade completed

Reverse Rule

Score of 0 on **any** of the first 3 items given, administer the preceding items in reverse order until 3 consecutive scores of 1

Discontinue Rule

Discontinue after 6 consecutive scores of 0

Sentence Comprehension

Start Points

Grades PreK–5: Item 17

Grades 6–16: Item 21

Adults: Start at the level of the last grade completed

Reverse Rule

Score of 0 on **any** of the first 3 items given, administer the preceding items in reverse order until 3 consecutive scores of 1

Discontinue Rule

Discontinue after 6 consecutive scores of 0

Expressive Vocabulary

Start Points

Grades PreK–5: Item 27

Grades 6–16: Item 31

Adults: Start at the level of the last grade completed

Reverse Rule

Score of 0 on **any** of the first 3 items given, administer the preceding items in reverse order until 3 consecutive scores of 1

Discontinue Rule

Discontinue after 6 consecutive scores of 0

Description

Listening Comprehension assesses the ability to listen for detail by selecting the picture that matches a word or sentence and by generating a word that matches a picture and an oral description. There are three sections: **Receptive Vocabulary, Sentence Comprehension,** and **Expressive Vocabulary.**

General Directions

To begin, turn to the Administration section of Listening Comprehension in Stimulus Booklet 2. Follow the administration directions and begin the subtest at the grade-appropriate start point. Position yourself so that you can see where the examinee points if he or she does not provide a verbal response for Items 1–26. If you have reason to believe that the examinee's vocabulary is below grade level, you may begin with the first item in each section. Allow the examinee approximately 10 seconds to begin responding before going on to the next item. Any prompt may be repeated once at the examinee's request. Make a notation of the request on the record form by writing a circled **R**.

If the examinee's response to an item in the Expressive Vocabulary section is more than a single word, remind the examinee of the one-word requirement.

Recording and Scoring

Score 0 points for an incorrect response and 1 point for a correct response. For each section, if the examinee responds correctly to three consecutive items, award 1 point for each of the preceding, unadministered items. To obtain the subtotal raw scores, add the correct responses in each section and record the number in the space provided on the record form.

For the Expressive Vocabulary section, record responses verbatim. The correct responses for Expressive Vocabulary are in the stimulus booklet.

To obtain the Listening Comprehension total raw score, add the subtotal raw scores for Receptive Vocabulary, Sentence Comprehension, and Expressive Vocabulary, and record the number in the space provided on the record form. Figure 4.10 illustrates how to calculate the Listening Comprehension total raw score.

Maximum Total Raw Score: 41 points

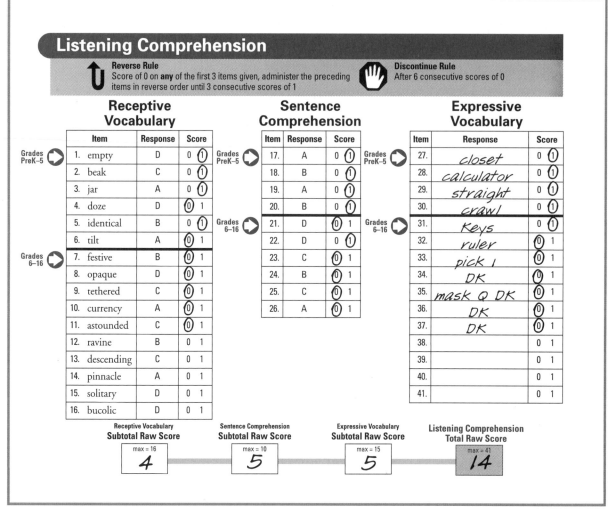

Figure 4.10.
Example of Listening Comprehension Scoring

Oral Expression

Sentence Repetition

Materials

- Stimulus Booklet 2
- Record Form
- Stopwatch
- Tape recorder (optional)

Start Points

Grades PreK–K: Item 1

Grades 1–3: Item 5

Grades 4–16: Do not administer

Adults: Do not administer

Reverse Rule

Score of 0 on **any** of the first 3 items given, administer the preceding items in reverse order until 3 consecutive scores of 1

Discontinue Rule

Discontinue after 6 consecutive scores of 0

Word Fluency, Visual Passage Retell, and Giving Directions

Start Points

All Grades: Start with Item 10 and administer *each* Item 10–15

Description

Oral Expression assesses the examinee's general ability to use oral language effectively to communicate with others. There are four sections: **Sentence Repetition** (administered only to Grades PreK–3), **Word Fluency**, **Visual Passage Retell**, and **Giving Directions**.

General Directions

Sentence Repetition has its own Start Points, Reverse Rule, and Discontinue Rule. For the other sections, all examinees begin at the same start point and attempt all of the items.

The examinee's responses for every section must be recorded verbatim. If necessary, you may use a tape recorder. After completing one section, proceed to the next section. Allow approximately 10 seconds for the examinee to begin responding, then go on to the next item.

Sentence Repetition

Sentence Repetition is administered to examinees in Grades PreK–3 only. To begin, turn to the Administration section of Oral Expression in Stimulus Booklet 2. Follow the administration directions and begin the subtest at the grade-appropriate start point. Present each sentence *only once*. Use your normal speaking voice and rate.

Word Fluency

There are two Word Fluency tasks, Word Fluency A and Word Fluency B. After administering Word Fluency A (Item 10), you should administer the Visual Passage Retell Section (Items 11 and 12), then Word Fluency B (Item 13). To begin, turn to the Administration section of Word Fluency A and follow the administration directions.

Visual Passage Retell

Proceed by reading the short story from the stimulus booklet. Your purpose is to model story telling. Use your voice to make the story animated and interesting.

Giving Directions

Allow the examinee approximately 10 seconds to begin responding. Continue to follow the administration directions in the stimulus booklet.

If the examinee is unable to continue through the task to a conclusion, you can cue him or her *only once* by saying **Tell me more**.

Recording and Scoring

Refer to Appendix A.3 of the supplements for comprehensive scoring guidelines and examples for Sentence Repetition, Word Fluency, Visual Passage Retell, and Giving Directions.

Sentence Repetition

Record response errors on the record form by drawing a line through any omitted words and recording any instances in which the student omits, changes, adds a word, or changes word order. Note with a circled **R** each time the student asks for a repetition. Score 0 points for an incorrect response and 1 point for a correct response. If the examinee responds correctly to three consecutive items, award 1 point for each of the preceding, unadministered Sentence Repetition items. **Do not give credit to examinees in Grades 4–16 for the Sentence Repetition items.** To obtain the Sentence Repetition subtotal raw score, add the correct responses and record the number in the space provided.

Word Fluency

To facilitate scoring, you must record all responses verbatim as quickly as possible without interrupting the examinee.

Add the total number of points earned for Word Fluency A (Item 10) and Word Fluency B (Item 13). Record the number in the space provided on the record form. Use Table B.12 (grade-based) or Table E.12 (age-based) to convert the Word Fluency score. The converted score is doubled in the table for purposes of assigning the appropriate weight to Word Fluency when calculating the Oral Expression total raw score. An example of Word Fluency scoring for an examinee in Grade 4 is presented in Figure 4.11.

The circled responses in Figure 4.11 did not score points. For Item 10, *bear* did not score a point because it was part of the prompt, and *lion* was only scored 1 point because it appears twice on the list. For Item 13, *drive a train* and *drive a bus* did not score points because 1 point had already been given for the verb *drive*. The response *go in a helicopter* did not score a point because it is a variation of the verb *go*. The score for Item 10 (Word Fluency A) and the score for Item 13 (Word Fluency B) were added and recorded in the space provided for the Word Fluency Score. Table B.12 was employed to determine the Word Fluency Converted Score.

Word Fluency A

All Grades ⏱ Stop at 60 seconds

10. Different Animals

bird, eagle, tiger, lion, (bear,) monkey, zebra, (lion,) cat, deer, snake, bug, butterfly, hippo

Score

12

Word Fluency B

All Grades ⏱ Stop at 60 seconds

13. Ways to move

drive, jump, roll, march, slide, (drive a train,) (drive a bus,) skip, swim, (go in a helicopter,) ride a horse

Score

8

Word Fluency Converted Score

| 12 | 8 | 20 | 2 |

Word Fluency A   Word Fluency B   Word Fluency Score
Use Table B.12/E.12

Figure 4.11.
Example of Oral Expression Word Fluency Scoring

11. Scoring Rubric	No Evidence	Evidence	Skilled	
A. Explains what the story is about (**main idea**)	0	1	2	
B. States **details** about the pictures	0	1	2	
C. Labels characters (**names**)	0	1	2	
D. Describes or tells where story occurs (**setting**)	0	1	2	
E. Tells what happens or what is happening (**plot**)	0	1	2	
F. Relates a logical order of events (**sequencing**)	0	1	2	
G. Summarizes and/or states a final outcome (**conclusion**)	0	1	2	**Item 11 Score**
H. **Predicts** what might happen next	0	1	2	max = 18
I. **Compares** story to own experiences or to another story	0	1	2	

Figure 4.12.
Example of the Visual Passage Retell Scoring Rubric

Visual Passage Retell

To facilitate accurate scoring, responses must be recorded verbatim. You may wish to use a tape recorder. Each of the two passages is scored independently using the scoring rubric that appears on the record form. Figure 4.12 is an example of Visual Passage Retell scoring rubric. Each of the scoring criteria requires you to determine whether the examinee demonstrated a specific skill, and if he or she elaborated in the skill area. Some more creative examinees may elaborate differently. As long as the elaboration makes sense with the pictures, do not penalize for creativity.

To calculate the Visual Passage Retell subtotal raw score, add the points earned for Items 11 and 12. Record the number in the space provided on the record form. The maximum score is 36.

Giving Directions

To facilitate accurate scoring, responses must be recorded verbatim. You may wish to use a tape recorder. Each of the two items is scored independently using the scoring rubric that appears on the record form. Figure 4.13 illustrates the scoring rubric for Item 14, and Figure 4.14 illustrates the scoring rubric for Item 15. The scoring criteria require you to determine whether the examinee included the required information, and to what extent he or she elaborated on the information. The examinee should not be penalized for using a different term for the same object or action (e.g., if the word *money* is used instead of *coin*). As long as the elaboration follows instructions, do not penalize for creativity.

14. Scoring Rubric	No Evidence	Evidence	Skilled	
A. Response includes the words *vending machine* or *snack machine*	0	1	2	
B. Reference made to putting money in machine	0	1	2	
C. Reference made to selecting a snack	0	1	2	**Item 14 Score**
D. Reference made to opening bottom door of machine	0	1	2	
E. Reference made to getting snack	0	1	2	max = 12
F. Reference made to eating snack	0	1	2	

Figure 4.13.
Example of the Giving Directions Scoring Rubric for Item 14

15. Scoring Rubric	No Evidence	Evidence	Skilled	
A. Reference made to getting bread	0	1	2	
B. Reference made to getting peanut butter	0	1	2	
C. Reference made to spreading or putting peanut butter on bread	0	1	2	**Item 15 Subtotal Raw Score**
D. Reference made to getting jelly	0	1	2	
E. Reference made to spreading or putting jelly on bread	0	1	2	max = 12
F. Reference made to a completed peanut butter and jelly sandwich	0	1	2	

Figure 4.14.
Example of the Giving Directions Scoring Rubric for Item 15

To calculate the Giving Directions subtotal score, add the points earned for Items 14 and 15. Record the number in the space provided on the record form. The maximum score is 24.

To obtain the Oral Expression total raw score, add the subtotal raw scores for Sentence Repetition (only for Grades PreK–3), Visual Passage Retell, Giving Directions, and the converted score for Word Fluency. Record the number in the space provided on the record form.

Maximum Total Raw Score for Grades PreK–3: 77 points

Maximum Total Raw Score for Grades 4–16: 68 points

5 Development and Standardization

Development

The primary goal of the WIAT revision was to preserve the test's strengths yet still address any concerns regarding the content, utility, or psychometric properties. The initial step was an in-depth critique of all aspects of the WIAT, including the factor structure, normative and linking information, subtest content, administration and scoring procedures, and interpretation and intervention issues. In 1996, item revision began with focus groups conducted in the four geographic regions of the United States. School and clinical psychologists, neuropsychologists, educational diagnosticians, speech-language pathologists, elementary and secondary level general and special educators, directors of special education, directors of university training programs, and parents were invited to discuss pertinent WIAT issues. More than 500 achievement test users in public and private schools, clinical settings, and post-secondary programs completed a comprehensive survey about achievement tests. Concurrently, discussions with curriculum specialists and the leading researchers in reading, writing, spelling, language, and math led to the formation of an expert advisory panel that assisted the development team.

The development process of the WIAT–II was rigorous. A blueprint of the constructs for each subtest was developed based on information from the focus group discussions, recommendations from the expert advisory panel, review of available state standards and curricula, and an extensive literature search. The WIAT–II continues to be linked with the Wechsler intelligence scales and was developed in conjunction with the PAL–RW (Berninger, 2001). The WIAT–II is designed to identify an individual's skill set in basic reading, reading comprehension, mathematics calculation, mathematics reasoning, oral expression, listening comprehension, spelling, and written expression and compare an individual's performance either to age or grade peers. The PAL–RW is designed to identify the underlying reading or writing process skills that contribute to reading or writing deficits. Using the PAL–RW in conjunction with the WIAT–II enables the examiner to comprehensively test an individual in the area of need.

Subtest and Item Specifications

Several sources defined the scope and sequence of the curriculum areas represented in the WIAT–II. The subtests represent a composite of typical curriculum specifications across the United States. The curriculum specifications were strongly influenced by (a) the current research findings as outlined in the report by the National Reading Panel, *Teaching Children To Read: An Evidence-Based Assessment of the Scientific Research Literature on Reading and its Implications for Reading Instruction* (2000); (b) state standards; (c) *Principles and Standards for School Mathematics* (National Council of Teachers of Mathematics, 2000); and (d) recommendations of the advisory groups. To ensure content coverage, the subtest items were reviewed by experts before the national tryout studies.

Field Testing

Pilot testing was conducted during the spring semester of 1997 with approximately 400 individuals in Grades PreK through 16. During the following school year, a large-scale tryout was conducted with approximately 1,900 students from Grades PreK through 16. The four geographic regions of the United States were represented with an equal distribution of diverse communities (rural, suburban, and urban), socioeconomic levels, and ethnic compositions. The total tryout sample for Grades PreK–16 was 54% female and 46% male. Approximately 51% were White and 49% were of African American, Hispanic, Asian, or other racial/ethnic origin. In addition, a sample of sixty 4- and 5-year-old PreK students, identified by their schools as being "at risk," were included in the tryout studies to ensure adequate item coverage. Items were also administered to a sample of 350 individuals identified with specific reading, math, or reading and math disabilities.

Item Analysis

The data obtained during the pilot and tryout testing was used to evaluate each item to determine the best items to retain for the WIAT revision. Item analysis used conventional percent-correct statistics, item-total correlations, grade-to-grade progressions in mean scores, and internal-consistency reliability of scales. Estimates were used to establish the order of item presentation. Items were further examined for possible bias by a panel of experienced reviewers and analyzed using item response theory (IRT) bias analysis, which considers statistical significance and effect size.

Standardization

Description of the Grades PreK–12 Standardization Sample

The WIAT–II age-based and grade-based normative information presented in this manual and in the *WIAT-II Scoring and Normative Supplement for Grades PreK–12* are derived from a standardization sample of individuals in Grades PreK–12, aged 4–19 years. The normative information for the college and adult standardization sample are reported in the *WIAT–II Supplement for College Students and Adults*. The standardization sample was collected during the 1999–2000 and 2000–2001 school years and is based on national standardization samples representative of the U.S. population. A stratified random sampling plan ensured that the standardization samples included representative proportions of individuals according to each demographic variable. An analysis of data gathered in October 1998 by the U.S. Bureau of the Census provided the basis for stratification along the following variables: grade, age, sex, race/ethnicity, geographic region, and parent education level (PEL; parent refers to parent or guardian). The following sections present the characteristics of the WIAT–II standardization sample.

▪ **Grade.** The grade-based standardization sample included individuals ranging from Grade PreK to Grade 12. The sample was divided into two grade groups: Grades PreK–8 and Grades 9–12. The Grades PreK–8 group consisted of 2,900 participants including 200 children in Grade PreK and aged 5 years (PreK [age 5]) and 300 participants in each of the other grades. The Grades PreK–8 group was further divided into two collection groups, with half of the sample gathered during the fall semester and half of the sample gathered during the spring semester (see Table 5.1). The Grades 9–12 group consisted of 700 participants including 200 students each in Grades 9 and 10, and 150 participants each in Grades 11 and 12 (see Table 5.2). Of the 3,600 participants in the total grade-based sample, 2,171 individuals were also included in the age-based sample.

- **Age.** The age-based standardization sample included 2,950 participants ranging in age from 4 years, 0 months to 19 years, 11 months. The sample was divided into two groups: ages 4:0–14:11 and ages 15:0–19:11. The 4:0–14:11 group consisted of 2,400 participants (see Table 5.1) and the 15:0–19:11 group included 550 participants (see Table 5.2). Individuals attending college were excluded from the 15:0–19:11 group.

- **Sex.** The grade-based standardization sample included 1,806 females and 1,794 males, with an approximately equal number in each grade. The age-based standardization sample included 1,473 females and 1,477 males, with an approximately equal number for each age.

- **Race/Ethnicity.** The proportions of Whites, African Americans, Hispanics, Asians, and other racial/ethnic groups for each age-based and grade-based standardization sample were based on the racial/ethnic group proportions of U.S. students in Grades PreK–12 or ages 4–19 years. The racial/ethnic designation of each participant in the sample was provided by his or her parent. The parent also indicated whether or not the student was of Hispanic origin. To be consistent with the U.S. Census procedures, if the parent indicated that the participant was of Hispanic origin, regardless of the parent's response to the other racial/ethnic group categories, the participant was assigned to the Hispanic category. For purposes of sampling, Native American and Eskimo participants were placed in the other racial/ethnic category. Pacific Islanders were included in the Asian category. The racial/ethnic proportions were balanced within each grade or age, sex, geographic region, and parent education level.

- **Geographic Region.** The United States was divided into four major geographic regions specified by the U.S. Census reports (see Figure 5.1): Northeast, North Central, South, and West. The number of participants from each region was proportionate to the population in each region.

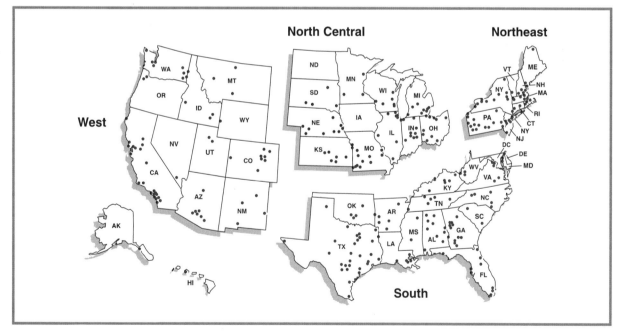

Figure 5.1.
Standardization Testing Sites

- **Parent Education Level.** The grade-based and age-based standardization samples were stratified according to the following four parent education levels: less than 12th grade (<12), high-school graduate or equivalent (12), 1 through 3 years of college or technical school (13–15), or 4 or more years of college (≥16). The parent was asked to specify the highest grade completed by each parent living in the home. If both parents lived with the child, the average (rounding up) of the two education levels was used. If only one parent lived with the child, the education level of that parent was used. A matrix of four parent education levels by the participant's race/ethnicity for each combination of grade, age, sex, and geographic region formed the basis of the sampling plan.

Locating and Testing the Sample

The collection of standardization data was achieved primarily through the use of qualified examiners including school and clinical psychologists, neuropsychologists, speech-language pathologists, special education teachers, university counselors, and university school psychology trainers, as well as public and private school districts in the United States. Examiners were selected based on their professional qualifications and their access to participants who met the WIAT–II standardization requirements. Examiners received parent consent forms and instructions for obtaining informed consent. The consent form requested the participant's age, grade, sex, race/ethnicity, region of residence, and PEL. Consent forms were also available in Spanish. A database was compiled containing demographic information on all available sample participants. A stratified random sampling approach was used to select participants representative of the population.

Student participants were enrolled in public or private school settings. Students who received special education services in school settings were not excluded from participation. According to the *Digest of Education Statistics, 2000* (Snyder & Hoffman, 2001), approximately 6% of students enrolled in public schools are identified as having a specific learning disability. In addition, 2.3% of students are diagnosed with speech or language impairments, 1.3% are diagnosed with mental retardation, 1% are diagnosed with serious emotional disturbance, and less than 1% are diagnosed with hearing impairments. As a result, 8% to 10% of the standardization sample at each grade level consisted of students classified by their schools as having a learning disability, a speech or language impairment, an emotional disturbance, mild mental impairment, an attention-deficit hyperactivity disorder (ADHD), or a mild hearing impairment. In addition, approximately 3% of the sample at each grade level consisted of students in gifted and talented programs. Specific exclusion criteria for the standardization sample included the following:

- Individuals who did not speak and understand English and children ages 4 and 5 from non-English speaking homes.

- Individuals who were previously diagnosed with a neurological disorder such as epilepsy, stroke, brain tumor, or significant head injury.

- Individuals who were taking medications that might depress performance (e.g., anti-convulsants).

Representativeness of the Sample

The percentages of the U.S. population and the grade-based standardization sample according to PEL, race/ethnicity, and geographic region are presented in Figure 5.2. Percentages according to the U.S. population and the age-based standardization sample according to PEL, race/ethnicity, and geographic region are presented in Figure 5.3. Tables 5.1–5.10 present detailed demographic information for the U.S. population and the grade-based and age-based standardization samples.

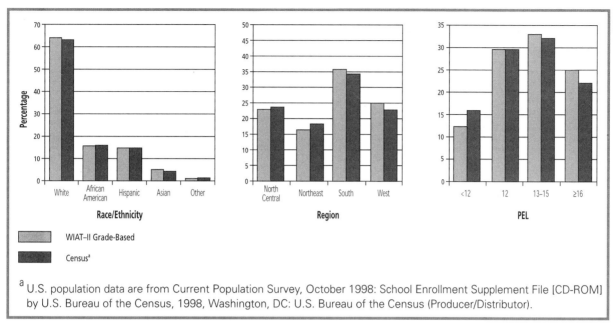

Figure 5.2.
Demographic Characteristics of the Grade-Based Standardization Sample and the U.S. Population

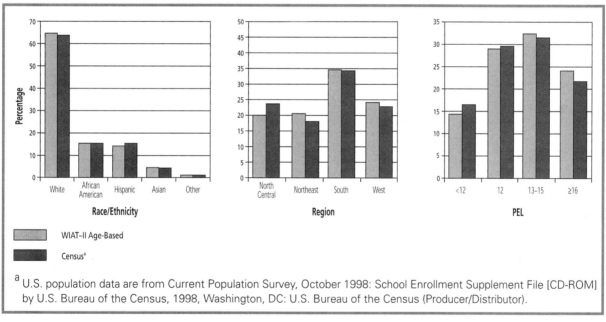

Figure 5.3
Demographic Characteristics of the Age-Based Standardization Sample and the U.S. Population

Table 5.1.

Demographic Characteristics of the Standardization Samples: Number by Grades PreK–8 and Sex (Fall and Spring) and by Ages 4–14 and Sex

Number by Grade and Sex (Fall)				Number by Grade and Sex (Spring)				Number by Age and Sex			
Grade	Female	Male	Total	Grade	Female	Male	Total	Age	Female	Male	Total
PreK[1]	54	46	100	PreK[1]	50	50	100	4	150	150	300
K	75	75	150	K	73	77	150	5	150	150	300
1	75	75	150	1	74	76	150	6	100	100	200
2	75	75	150	2	76	74	150	7	100	100	200
3	75	75	150	3	75	75	150	8	101	99	200
4	75	75	150	4	77	73	150	9	98	102	200
5	75	75	150	5	74	76	150	10	101	99	200
6	76	74	150	6	76	74	150	11	100	100	200
7	75	75	150	7	76	74	150	12	100	100	200
8	75	75	150	8	76	74	150	13	99	101	200
								14	100	100	200
Total	730	720	1450	**Total**	727	723	1450	**Total**	1199	1201	2400

[1] (Age 5)

Table 5.2.

Demographic Characteristics of the Standardization Samples: Number by Grades 9–12 and Sex and by Ages 15–19 and Sex

Number by Grade and Sex				Number by Age and Sex			
Grade	Female	Male	Total	Age	Female	Male	Total
9	100	100	200	15	102	98	200
10	99	101	200	16	99	101	200
11	75	75	150	17–19	73	77	150
12	75	75	150				
Total	349	351	700	**Total**	274	276	550

Table 5.3.

Demographic Characteristics of the Standardization Samples: Percentages by Grades PreK–8 and Race/Ethnicity (Fall and Spring) and by Ages 4–14 and Race/Ethnicity

Percentage by Grade and Race/Ethnicity (Fall)						
Grade	*n*	White	African American	Hispanic	Asian	Other
PreK (Age 5)	100	63.00	9.00	23.00	4.00	1.00
K	150	63.33	16.67	15.33	4.00	0.67
1	150	63.33	16.67	15.33	4.00	0.67
2	150	63.33	16.67	15.33	4.00	0.67
3	150	63.33	16.67	15.33	4.00	0.67
4	150	63.33	16.67	15.33	4.00	0.67
5	150	63.33	16.67	15.33	4.00	0.67
6	150	64.00	15.33	15.33	4.67	0.67
7	150	64.00	16.00	14.67	4.67	0.67
8	150	65.33	16.00	13.33	4.67	0.67
Total	1450	63.63	15.64	15.83	4.20	0.70
U.S. Population[a]		63.83	15.83	15.15	4.22	0.96

Percentage by Grade and Race/Ethnicity (Spring)						
Grade	*n*	White	African American	Hispanic	Asian	Other
PreK (Age 5)	100	64.00	17.00	15.00	3.00	1.00
K	150	62.67	16.67	16.00	4.00	0.67
1	150	62.67	16.67	16.67	3.33	0.67
2	150	62.67	16.67	16.00	4.00	0.67
3	150	62.67	16.67	16.00	4.00	0.67
4	150	63.33	16.00	16.00	4.00	0.67
5	150	62.67	16.67	16.00	4.00	0.67
6	150	64.67	15.33	14.67	4.67	0.67
7	150	64.00	15.33	15.33	4.67	0.67
8	150	67.33	10.67	15.33	5.33	1.33
Total	1450	63.66	15.77	15.70	4.10	0.77
U.S. Population[a]		63.83	15.83	15.15	4.22	0.96

Percentage by Age and Race/Ethnicity						
Age	*n*	White	African American	Hispanic	Asian	Other
4	300	63.33	15.00	15.33	5.00	1.33
5	300	63.00	16.33	15.67	4.00	1.00
6	200	63.00	16.50	15.50	4.00	1.00
7	200	63.00	16.50	15.50	4.00	1.00
8	200	63.00	16.50	15.50	4.00	1.00
9	200	63.00	16.50	15.50	4.00	1.00
10	200	63.00	16.50	15.50	4.00	1.00
11	200	66.00	15.00	14.00	4.50	0.50
12	200	66.00	15.00	15.00	3.50	0.50
13	200	64.50	16.50	14.00	4.50	0.50
14	200	66.50	15.50	13.00	4.00	1.00
Total	2400	64.03	15.98	14.95	4.14	0.89
U.S. Population[a]		63.83	15.83	15.15	4.22	0.96

[a] U.S. Bureau of the U.S. Population. (1998). Current population survey. October 1998: School Enrollment Supplement File [CD-ROM]. Washington, DC: Bureau of the U.S. Population (Producer/Distributor).

Table 5.4.

Demographic Characteristics of the Standardization Samples: Percentages by Grades 9–12 and Race/Ethnicity and by Ages 15–19 and Race/Ethnicity

Percentage by Grade and Race/Ethnicity						
Grade	n	White	African American	Hispanic	Asian	Other
9	200	65.50	16.00	13.50	4.50	0.50
10	200	65.50	16.50	13.00	4.00	1.00
11	150	66.00	16.67	13.33	3.33	0.67
12	150	65.33	14.67	13.33	5.33	1.33
Total	700	65.58	15.96	13.29	4.29	0.88
U.S. Population[a]		63.77	16.36	15.24	3.63	1.01

Percentage by Age and Race/Ethnicity						
Age	n	White	African American	Hispanic	Asian	Other
15	200	65.50	16.50	13.00	4.00	1.00
16	200	65.50	17.00	12.50	4.00	1.00
17–19	150	67.87	15.08	13.34	2.97	0.75
Total	550	66.29	16.19	12.95	3.66	0.91
U.S. Population[a]		63.77	16.36	15.24	3.63	1.01

[a] U.S. Bureau of the U.S. Population. (1998). Current population survey. October 1998: School Enrollment Supplement File [CD-ROM]. Washington, DC: Bureau of the U.S. Population (Producer/Distributor).

Table 5.5.

Demographic Characteristics of the Standardization Samples: Percentages by Grades PreK–8 and Geographic Region (Fall and Spring) and by Ages 4–14 and Geographic Region

Percentage by Grade and Geographic Region (Fall)					
Grade	*n*	North Central	Northeast	South	West
PreK (Age 5)	100	23.00	5.00	29.00	43.00
K	150	22.67	19.33	34.67	23.33
1	150	22.67	20.00	34.67	22.67
2	150	19.33	20.00	34.67	26.00
3	150	22.67	19.33	34.67	23.33
4	150	22.67	19.33	34.67	23.33
5	150	22.67	19.33	34.67	23.33
6	150	24.67	13.33	34.67	27.33
7	150	18.67	17.33	38.67	25.33
8	150	25.33	11.33	37.33	26.00
Total	1450	22.43	16.43	34.77	26.37
U.S. Population[a]		23.26	18.92	34.17	23.65

Percentage by Grade and Geographic Region (Spring)					
Grade	*n*	North Central	Northeast	South	West
PreK (Age 5)	100	24.00	14.00	43.00	19.00
K	150	20.00	18.00	38.00	24.00
1	150	22.67	16.67	37.33	23.33
2	150	22.67	17.33	34.00	26.00
3	150	21.33	17.33	37.33	24.00
4	150	23.33	15.33	36.00	25.33
5	150	24.67	15.33	34.00	26.00
6	150	22.00	16.00	39.33	22.67
7	150	22.00	12.00	39.33	26.67
8	150	25.33	10.00	34.67	30.00
Total	1450	22.80	15.20	37.30	24.70
U.S. Population[a]		23.26	18.92	34.17	23.65

Percentage by Age and Geographic Region					
Age	*n*	North Central	Northeast	South	West
4	300	25.33	16.67	35.00	23.00
5	300	18.67	23.33	34.00	24.00
6	200	19.00	23.00	33.50	24.50
7	200	18.50	23.50	34.00	24.00
8	200	18.50	23.50	34.50	23.50
9	200	18.50	23.50	34.00	24.00
10	200	18.50	23.50	34.00	24.00
11	200	18.00	24.00	35.50	22.50
12	200	18.50	20.50	37.00	24.00
13	200	18.50	19.50	36.50	25.50
14	200	19.00	20.00	37.50	23.50
Total	2400	19.18	21.91	35.05	23.86
U.S. Population[a]		23.26	18.92	34.17	23.65

[a] U.S. Bureau of the U.S. Population. (1998). Current population survey. October 1998: School Enrollment Supplement File [CD-ROM]. Washington, DC: Bureau of the U.S. Population (Producer/Distributor).

Table 5.6.

Demographic Characteristics of the Standardization Samples: Percentages by Grades 9–12 and Geographic Region and by Ages 15–19 and Geographic Region

Grade	n	North Central	Northeast	South	West
		Percentage by Grade and Geographic Region			
9	200	23.50	19.50	34.00	23.00
10	200	23.50	17.50	36.00	23.00
11	150	24.00	16.00	36.00	24.00
12	150	23.33	19.33	34.00	23.33
Total	700	23.58	18.08	35.00	23.34
U.S. Population[a]		24.47	18.50	34.60	22.44

Age	n	North Central	Northeast	South	West
		Percentage by Age and Geographic Region			
15	200	24.00	19.00	32.00	25.00
16	200	23.00	18.00	36.00	23.00
17–19	150	25.66	13.53	30.90	29.91
Total	550	24.22	16.84	32.97	25.97
U.S. Population[a]		24.47	18.50	34.60	22.44

[a] U.S. Bureau of the U.S. Population. (1998). Current population survey. October 1998: School Enrollment Supplement File [CD-ROM]. Washington, DC: Bureau of the U.S. Population (Producer/Distributor).

Table 5.7.

Demographic Characteristics of the Standardization Samples: Percentages by Grades PreK–8 and Parent Education Level (Fall and Spring) and by Ages 4–14 and Parent Education Level

Percentage by Grade and Parent Education Level (Fall)					
Grade	*n*	< 12	12	13-15	≥ 16
PreK (Age 5)	100	10.00	24.00	33.00	33.00
K	150	14.67	28.67	32.00	24.67
1	150	14.67	28.67	32.00	24.67
2	150	11.33	29.33	33.33	26.00
3	150	11.33	30.00	33.33	25.33
4	150	14.67	29.33	31.33	24.67
5	150	14.67	28.00	32.67	24.67
6	150	8.67	30.67	34.00	26.67
7	150	14.00	28.00	32.00	26.00
8	150	13.33	28.67	34.00	24.00
Total	1450	12.73	28.53	32.77	25.97
U.S. Population[a]		14.68	28.57	32.31	24.45

Percentage by Grade and Parent Education Level (Spring)					
Grade	*n*	< 12	12	13-15	≥ 16
PreK (Age 5)	100	14.00	29.00	32.00	25.00
K	150	13.33	29.33	33.33	24.00
1	150	13.33	28.67	34.00	24.00
2	150	13.33	29.33	33.33	24.00
3	150	14.00	28.67	32.67	24.67
4	150	12.67	30.00	32.67	24.67
5	150	13.33	29.33	33.33	24.00
6	150	12.00	30.00	33.33	24.67
7	150	12.00	30.00	33.33	24.67
8	150	12.00	30.00	33.33	24.67
Total	1450	13.00	29.43	33.13	24.44
U.S. Population[a]		14.68	28.57	32.31	24.45

Percentage by Age and Parent Education Level					
Age	*n*	< 12	12	13-15	≥ 16
4	300	12.33	25.67	31.67	30.33
5	300	15.00	29.00	31.67	24.33
6	200	15.00	29.00	32.00	24.00
7	200	15.00	29.00	32.00	24.00
8	200	15.00	29.00	32.00	24.00
9	200	15.00	29.00	32.00	24.00
10	200	15.00	29.00	32.00	24.00
11	200	14.00	28.50	34.00	23.50
12	200	14.50	27.50	34.50	23.50
13	200	14.00	28.00	34.00	24.00
14	200	10.50	30.00	34.00	25.50
Total	2400	14.12	28.52	32.71	24.65
U.S. Population[a]		14.68	28.57	32.31	24.45

[a] U.S. Bureau of the U.S. Population. (1998). Current population survey. October 1998: School Enrollment Supplement File [CD-ROM]. Washington, DC: Bureau of the U.S. Population (Producer/Distributor).

Table 5.8.

Demographic Characteristics of the Standardization Samples: Percentages by Grades 9–12 and Parent Education Level and by Ages 15–19 and Parent Education Level

		Percentage by Grade and Parent Education Level			
Grade	*n*	< 12	12	13-15	≥ 16
9	200	13.00	29.50	32.50	25.00
10	200	15.00	29.50	32.50	23.00
11	150	11.33	29.33	32.00	27.33
12	150	8.67	34.00	34.00	23.33
Total	700	12.00	30.58	32.75	24.67
U.S. Population[a]		14.75	28.76	33.10	23.38

		Percentage by Age and Parent Education Level			
Age	*n*	< 12	12	13-15	≥ 16
15	200	13.50	30.00	32.50	24.00
16	200	15.00	29.00	33.00	23.00
17–19	150	18.47	32.67	27.60	21.27
Total	550	15.66	30.55	31.03	22.76
U.S. Population[a]		14.75	28.76	33.10	23.38

[a] U.S. Bureau of the U.S. Population. (1998). Current population survey. October 1998: School Enrollment Supplement File [CD-ROM]. Washington, DC: Bureau of the U.S. Population (Producer/Distributor).

Table 5.9.

Demographic Characteristics of the Grade-Based Standardization Samples: Percentages by Parent Education Level and Race/Ethnicity

Parent Education Level[a]	White	African American	Hispanic	Asian	Other
<12	25.87	23.91	43.70	3.48	3.04
	25.44	21.48	46.92	5.25	0.90
12	61.17	19.13	17.23	2.18	0.28
	62.33	20.68	13.26	2.61	1.12
13–15	71.90	14.68	10.04	2.87	0.51
	71.50	15.95	8.38	2.96	1.22
≥16	76.53	9.34	5.01	8.68	0.44
	80.73	7.89	3.97	6.97	0.45

Note. The first number appearing in a pair is the percentage obtained for the standardization sample; the second number is the percentage of the U.S. population. U.S. Bureau of Census. (1998). Current population survey. October 1998: School Enrollment Supplement File [CD-ROM]. Washington, DC: Bureau of the Census (Producer/Distributor).

[a] Number of years of parent education, which is the average number of grades completed by the parent living with the child.

Table 5.10.

Demographic Characteristics of the Age-Based Standardization Samples: Percentages by Parent Education Level and Race/Ethnicity

Parent Education Level[a]	White	African American	Hispanic	Asian	Other
<12	27.82	22.30	43.41	3.84	2.64
	25.44	21.48	46.92	5.25	0.90
12	63.23	19.34	14.00	2.61	0.83
	62.33	20.68	13.26	2.61	1.12
13–15	72.07	15.06	9.55	2.49	0.83
	71.50	15.95	8.38	2.96	1.22
≥16	75.93	10.04	5.50	8.25	0.28
	80.73	7.89	3.97	6.97	0.45

Note. The first number appearing in a pair is the percentage obtained for the standardization sample; the second number is the percentage of the U.S. population. U.S. Bureau of Census. (1998). Current population survey. October 1998: School Enrollment Supplement File [CD-ROM]. Washington, DC: Bureau of the Census (Producer/Distributor).

[a] Number of years of parent education, which is the average number of grades completed by the parent living with the child.

WIAT–II Linking Sample

The WIAT–II linking samples were developed from a subset of standardization participants who were administered one of three Wechsler intelligence scales: the WPPSI–R, the WISC–III, or the WAIS–III. The linking samples consisted of 1,069 participants (51% female and 49% male). The WPPSI–R was administered to 199 participants aged 4:0–6:11 years, the WISC–III was administered to 775 participants aged 6:0–16:11 years, and the WAIS–III was administered to 95 participants aged 16–19 years. Figures 5.4, 5.5, and 5.6 present the demographic characteristics of the WIAT–II linking samples according to race/ethnicity, parent/self education level, and geographic region.

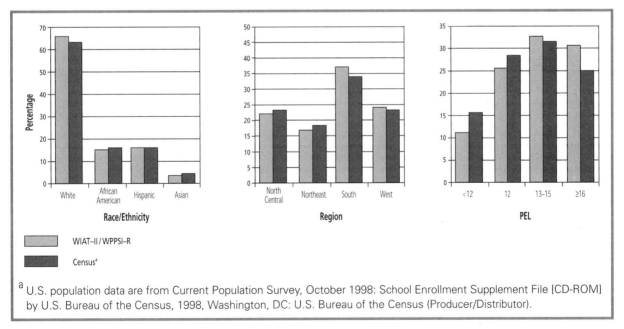

[a] U.S. population data are from Current Population Survey, October 1998: School Enrollment Supplement File [CD-ROM] by U.S. Bureau of the Census, 1998, Washington, DC: U.S. Bureau of the Census (Producer/Distributor).

Figure 5.4.

Demographic Characteristics of the WIAT–II and WPPSI–R Linking Sample and the U.S. Population

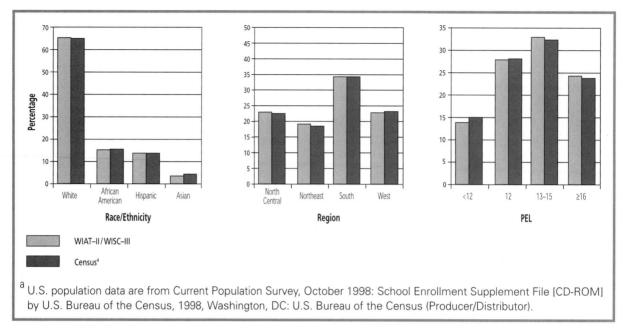

Figure 5.5.
Demographic Characteristics of the WIAT–II and WISC–III Linking Sample and the U.S. Population

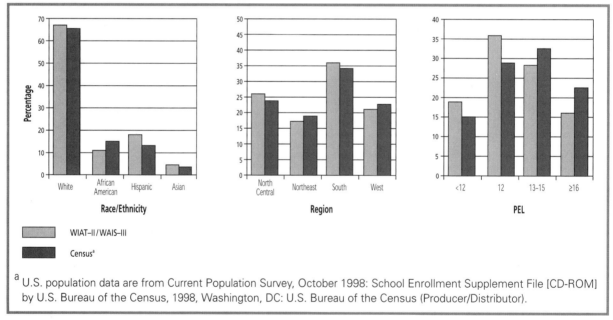

Figure 5.6.
Demographic Characteristics of the WIAT–II and WAIS–III Linking Sample and the U.S. Population

The WPPSI–R linking sample was balanced by sex (49.2% female, 50.8% male) and had representative proportions of race/ethnicity with 64.8% White, 15.6% Hispanic, 15.1% African American, and 3.5% Asian. The sample had various levels of PEL (11.1% less than high school, 25.6% high school or equivalent, 32.7% some college, and 30.7% college) and was representative of the census regions of the U.S. (37.2% South, 24.6% West, 21.6% North Central, and 16.6% Northeast). The WISC–III linking sample was balanced by sex (50.6% female; 49.4% male), race/ethnicity

(64.7% White, 15.7% African American, 14.6% Hispanic, and 3.8% Asian), PEL (14.1% less than high school, 28.5% high school or equivalent, 33.1% some college, and 24.3% college), and representative of the census regions (34.5%, 23.4%, 23%, and 19%, for South, North Central, West, and Northeast, respectively). The WAIS–III linking sample was balanced by sex (52.9% female, 47.1% male), race/ethnicity (66.3% White, 18.3% Hispanic, 10.6% African American, and 4.8% Asian), PEL (19.2% less than high school, 35.6% high school or equivalent, 28.3% some college, and 16.3% college), and representative of the census regions (35.6%, 26%, 21.2%, and 17.3% for South, North Central, West, and Northeast, respectively).

The mean WPPSI–R, the WISC–III, and the WAIS–III FSIQ scores for the linking samples were 102.94 (SD = 15.26), 102.86 (SD = 15.09), and 101.70 (SD = 13.41), respectively. (Note: A small degree of case weighting (five cases) was applied to the WPPSI–R linking sample to adjust the standard deviation to near 15. Similarly, case weighting (9 cases) was applied to the WAIS–III linking sample.) The slightly higher means observed for the WPPSI–R and the WISC–III were expected due to the known inflation of norms over time (Flynn, 1984, 1987; Matarazzo, 1972). It was important that the ability–achievement discrepancy tables be based on scores that were normed during the same time period to ensure comparable norms (Berk, 1984; Reynolds, 1990). Therefore, the WPPSI–R and the WISC–III linking samples were used to re-anchor the WISC–III and WPPSI–R IQ and Index scores to a mean of 100 and a standard deviation of 15. (This was not necessary in the case of the WAIS–III which was normed close to the same period as the WIAT–II.) These re-anchored IQ and Index scores were used to create the ability–achievement discrepancy tables in Appendix H of the *Scoring and Normative Supplement for Grades PreK–12*. This adjustment of the WISC–III and the WPPSI–R IQ and Index scores is incorporated into the tables that are based on the regression or predicted-achievement method and increases the technical accuracy of the prediction. The tables in Appendix H report the predicted-achievement score based on the re-anchored IQ and Index scores that correspond to the examinee's obtained ability score.

Quality Control Procedures

The quality-control procedures used in collecting the WIAT–II standardization data were designed to facilitate proper test administration and scoring. One of the first steps to ensure the quality of the administration was to recruit examiners who had extensive testing experience. Before being selected to participate in the standardization, examiners provided information about their education and professional experience, assessment experience, and certification or licensing status. The majority of examiners selected were certified or licensed professionals working in school or university systems, and the remainder were clinicians working in clinical settings.

Each examiner received a standardization manual detailing the test administration, recording, and scoring information. Each examiner submitted a WIAT–II practice protocol. The practice protocols were evaluated according to guidelines that focused on the examiner's adherence to test administration and scoring procedures. Examiners received detailed written and oral critiques of their practice protocols and were contacted if any irregularity or missing information appeared with a submitted case. Newsletters and information sheets, which addressed administration and scoring concerns and potential problem areas, were sent to all examiners throughout the standardization process.

The second step to ensure the quality-control procedure was the rescoring of each protocol. Each protocol was initially scored by the examiner and then rescored by two well-trained scorers working independently. The scores were then compared for consistency. A member of the development team resolved discrepancies between any two sets of scores for a protocol. Following this stage, the data set was carefully examined to ensure that all scores were within the range of possible scores; extreme scores (e.g., outliers) were re-examined to ensure that the test was administered and scored correctly and any missing data were verified. After all protocols were double-scored, the scores double-entered, and discrepancies resolved, reliability, validity, and norming studies were conducted. Finally, the development team worked independently to verify data by comparing all manual tables to the original computer printouts.

Derivation of Scores

Determination of Start Points, Discontinue Rules, and Stop Points

Because the WIAT–II is designed for ages 4 through adulthood, some items are too difficult for younger children, and other items are too easy for older individuals. To avoid frustrating the examinee by administering overly easy or overly difficult items, start points, discontinue rules, and stop points are used as much as possible. In the standardization version of the WIAT–II subtests, items were ordered according to increasing difficulty as indicated by the pilot and tryout data. Start points and discontinue rules for the subtests were set generously in order to allow the examinee to attempt all of the items that he or she might be expected to pass, yet limit the number of items presented. Final adjustments in the rules for starting, discontinuing, and stopping each subtest were made on the basis of empirical studies of the standardization data. The start point for each age group was set so that if more than 95% of the examinees in a particular grade responded correctly to all preceding items administered, the start point for that grade was moved to a more difficult item for which 90% or fewer of the examinees responded correctly. To set the final adjustments in the discontinue rules, the probability of an examinee obtaining additional points after each of several possible discontinue points was examined.

The Reading Comprehension subtest items were administered according to a pre-established item set. In the WIAT–II tryout, these items represented a wide range of abilities for the assigned grade group. Unlike the majority of subtests, the Reading Comprehension subtest items are not presented in order of increasing difficulty; instead, each reading passage includes items of various degrees of difficulty. This format enables the examiner to administer various types of comprehension items specific to a reading passage and encourages the examinee to stay engaged in the task.

Derivation of the Subtest Standard Scores

For each of the WIAT–II subtests, the distribution of total raw scores for each age and grade group were converted to a scale with a mean of 100 and a standard deviation of 15. This conversion was accomplished by preparing a cumulative frequency distribution of total raw scores for each age and grade group, normalizing these distributions, and calculating the appropriate standard score for each total raw score. The progression of standard scores within each age and within each grade and from age-to-age and grade-to-grade was then examined and smoothing eliminated minor irregularities. Across-age and across-grade smoothing was accomplished through computerized plotting of the standard score conversions for each age and each grade and smoothing the shapes of each resulting curve. Total raw-to-standard score conversions for those ages divided into 4-month spans (i.e., ages 4:0–13:11) were interpolated from the scores at the midyear points. Interpolation for age spans above age 13:11 was not necessary because the progression of mean scores by age did not differ significantly. Total raw-to-standard score conversions for each grade in the Grades PreK–8 range were interpolated to create winter norms from the scores midway between the fall and spring scores. Fall, winter, and spring norms are available for examinees in Grades PreK–8. Annual norms are available for examinees in Grades 9–12. Table C.1 in Appendix C of the supplement presents grade-based standard scores for subtest total raw scores, and Table C.2 presents composite standard scores based on the sums of the subtest standard scores. Table F.1 in Appendix F of the supplement presents the age-based standard score equivalents of subtest total raw scores, and Table F.2 presents standard scores for each composite. The standard scores for each subtest and composite range from 40 to 160.

Derivation of Total and Composite Standard Scores

The five composite standard scores were formed by summing each individual's actual subtest standard scores on the relevant subtests. An analysis of variance revealed no statistically significant variation by age or grade in the mean sum of standard scores for each composite. Moreover, the results of Bartlett's test for homogeneity of variance applied across the 14 age groups and the 14 grades indicated that the variance of the sums did not differ significantly by age or grade (spring and fall). Consequently, the age groups were combined ($N = 2,950$) and the grade groups were combined ($N = 3,600$) to construct the tables of composite score equivalents of sums of standard scores (Tables C.2 and F.2, respectively).

For each of the composite scales, the distribution of the sum of standard scores was converted to a scale with a mean of 100 and standard deviation of 15. This was accomplished by preparing a cumulative frequency distribution of actual sums of standard scores for each of the five composite scales, normalizing, and smoothing these distributions, and then calculating the appropriate composite score equivalent for each sum of standard scores. The smoothing of the sum-of-standard-score frequency distributions included an initial computerized smoothing and visual inspection of the distributions. Minor irregularities were smoothed by hand. Departures from normality in the resulting distributions were tested and found to be nonsignificant.

Derivation of the Supplemental Scores

Supplemental scores were derived by converting raw scores to quartile- or decile-based scores using Tables B.1–B.12 (grade-based) or E.1–E.12 (age-based) in the *WIAT–II Scoring and Normative Supplement for Grades PreK–12*. The quartile and decile tables were created using the SAS Univariate procedure (SAS Institute, 1990). Tables for the winter scores were interpolated by computing the arithmetic mean of the fall and spring raw score ranges. Decile scores for Alphabet Writing were employed to match the use of decile scores on the PAL–RW, where the identical item appears.

For the Written Expression Word Fluency and the Oral Expression Word Fluency supplemental scores, the lowest quartile was divided into two groups according to frequency distributions. Raw scores that fell within the 5th percentile and occurred with low frequency were assigned a score of 0; the remaining scores within this quartile were assigned a score of 1.

For the Spelling Errors (Paragraph and Essay) and Punctuation Errors (Paragraph and Essay) supplemental scores, the highest quartile was divided into two groups: a raw score of 0 (i.e., no errors) was assigned a score of 4; the remaining scores within this quartile were assigned a score of 3. These scores were created using quartile-based scores to make the process of calculating the subtest total raw score less cumbersome.

6 Reliability and Validity

The fundamental concepts of psychoeducational measurement include the reliability of scores obtained on a test, statistical significance of the differences between scores, and validity of the interpretations derived from the scores. The statistical data presented in this chapter determine the confidence examiners can have in the accuracy of obtained scores. This chapter reports and discusses the statistical data as they relate to the quantitative interpretations of scores on the WIAT–II.

Reliability

The reliability of a test refers to the precision, consistency, and stability of test scores across equivalent sets of items, across time, and among examiners. If a test is reliable, the results will be an accurate measure of the underlying construct the test is intended to measure. The results of a test that is statistically reliable will not have been influenced by irrelevant, chance factors including momentary fatigue, fluctuations in mood or memory, or temporary alterations in testing conditions. Reliability values range from 0 (*no consistency*) to 1 (*perfect consistency*). Several statistics are useful for describing a test's reliability, including estimates of internal consistency and precision, interitem comparison, standard errors of measurement and confidence intervals, test–retest stability, and interscorer agreement.

Internal Consistency and Precision

Internal consistency measures evaluate the homogeneity of item responses within subtests. Dividing the items in a subtest into two equivalent forms and comparing scores between the two (i.e., split-half reliability), assesses interitem consistency. To measure the consistency of how a test is scored, interscorer reliability is assessed by requiring two examiners to independently score the same responses, and then comparing the scores for consistency. Strong interscorer reliability indicates that the test is less prone to discrepancies when examiners score responses. To measure the test–retest reliability, the test is administered more than once to the same examinee and the stability of scores over a specified period is compared. For a test to be reliable, the examinee's scores should remain relatively consistent between the first and second testings.

Interitem Comparisons

One estimate of test-score consistency, obtained internally from data on a single administration of the test, is derived with the split-half method. For the WIAT–II, equivalent halves of each subtest, representing parallel forms with approximately equal variances, were selected. The scores on these half-tests were intercorrelated and corrected for the score on the full-length subtest by the

Spearman-Brown formula $\frac{2r}{r+1}$ in which r refers to the half-test intercorrelations. This procedure provides an assessment of the degree to which both halves of the subtest measure achievement in the same domain. The split-half method was selected for analyzing the internal consistency of the WIAT–II subtests because it is the same method used to estimate reliability for the majority of the WISC–III subtests. Reynolds (1985) has recommended the use of the same type of reliability estimates for both ability and achievement test scores when discrepancies between them are evaluated.

Table 6.1 presents the split-half reliability coefficients for the subtest standard scores for ages 4–19. Split-half coefficients were not computed for the Written Expression and Oral Expression subtests because the nature of the item content (assessing the quality of a single response) prevented separating the items into equivalent halves. Instead, test–retest reliability coefficients were computed for the two subtests. Tables 6.3 and 6.5 present the coefficients calculated at each grade for fall and spring, respectively. The Oral Expression test–retest reliability coefficients for ages 4–5 and Grades Pre-Kindergarten–Kindergarten were estimated based on data from age 6 and Grade 1 data, respectively, due to insufficient sample sizes for the younger ages and grades. For the five composite scores, reliability coefficients were computed according to a formula for the reliability of a composite of several tests (Nunnally, 1978, p. 246).

The reliability scores reflect strong interitem consistency within subtests. As indicated in Tables 6.1, 6.3, and 6.5, the reliability coefficients for the composites are generally greater than those for the individual subtests because the composite scores summarize an examinee's performance on a broader sample of achievement than can be sampled by a single subtest. The higher the reliability coefficient, the greater the confidence one can place in the consistency and precision of scores. As evidenced in the Tables 6.1, 6.3, and 6.5, the WIAT–II possesses moderately high to high interitem reliability, with average reliability coefficients ranging from .80 to .98. The overall total composite reliability is .98.

Standard Errors of Measurement and Confidence Intervals

The standard error of measurement (SE_M) provides an estimate of the amount of error, due to unreliability, in an individual's observed test score. Table 6.2 presents the SE_M for each subtest and composite standard score at each age. Tables 6.4 and 6.6 present the SE_M for each subtest and composite standard score at each grade, for fall and spring, respectively. The SE_M is inversely related to the reliability coefficient (see Tables 6.1, 6.3, and 6.5), the greater the reliability is, the smaller the SE_M is, and the more confidence the examiner can have in the precision of the observed test score.

The SE_M is used to calculate the confidence interval, or the band of scores, around the observed score in which the individual's true score is likely to fall. Confidence intervals provide another means of expressing the precision of test scores. The examiner can use confidence intervals to report an individual's true score. Confidence intervals also serve as a reminder that measurement error is inherent in all test scores and the observed test score is only an estimate of true ability. Three intervals of confidence are typically used: 68%, 90%, and 95%. The magnitude of the interval required for 68% confidence is on either side of the obtained standard score. To construct intervals at the 68% level of confidence, use Table 6.2 for age-based standard scores, and Table 6.4 or Table 6.6 for grade-based standard scores. For example, if a 13-year-old examinee obtained a Word Reading age-based standard score of 100, the examiner can be 68% confident that the individual's true score falls in the range of 97–103 (1 SE_M or 3.00 points, on either side of the obtained score). The magnitudes needed to set confidence intervals at the 90% and 95% levels for grade-based scores are provided in Appendix D (Tables D.1 and D.2) and for age-based scores, in Appendix G (Tables G.1 and G.2). To construct the confidence interval, use the appropriate table to identify the amount that corresponds to the examinee's grade (or age), the subtest (or composite) of interest, and the confidence level (95% or 90%). Subtract the indicated amount from the examinee's score and add the indicated amount to the score. The resulting numbers are the lower and upper limits of the confidence interval within which the true score is likely to fall. For example, if a 13-year-old examinee obtained a Word Reading age-based standard score of 100, the examiner can be 90% confident that the individual's true score is in the range of 95–105 (100 ± 5 SE_M) and 95% confident that the individual's true score is in the range of 94–106 (100 ± 6 SE_M).

Test-Retest Stability

The stability of scores of the WIAT–II was assessed in separate studies of 297 examinees who were tested twice. This age-based sample was drawn from three age bands in the standardization sample: ages 6–9, 10–12, and 13–19 years. The test–retest interval ranged from 7 to 45 days, with a mean retest interval of 10 days. The sample had the following composition: 54% female and 46 % male; and 73% White, 10% African American, 15% Hispanic, 1% Asian, and 1% of other racial/ethnic origin.

For evaluation of the test–retest reliabilities, the means and standard deviations (*SD*) of the scores from the first and second testings and the stability coefficients between the two scores were calculated. The retest coefficients were corrected for the variability of the standardization sample in order to obtain accurate estimates of score stability in the sample. Tables 6.7–6.9 present, for each of the three age bands, the means and standard deviations from the first and second testings and the uncorrected and corrected stability coefficients. Table 6.9 also provides the average stability coefficients for the three age groups. As the information in these tables demonstrates, the WIAT–II scores possess adequate stability across time, ages, and grades. Across all of the scores (from subtest to subtest, from composite to composite, and from age to age), the differences in scores between the first and second testing are relatively small. Generally, the differences are between 1 and 4 standard-score points.

Interscorer Agreement

The majority of the WIAT–II subtests are scored in a straightforward and objective manner. However, some of the subtests require more judgment in scoring. The Reading Comprehension, Written Expression, and Oral Expression subtests are more likely to result in scoring variability (see Chapters 3 and 4 for a discussion of scoring procedures and Appendix A of the supplements for scoring guidelines and examples). Therefore, two special studies were conducted to evaluate subtest score agreement between scorers.

For each study, a total of 2,180 examinees' responses (approximately 190 from each age in the 6–16 age range and 140 from the 17–19 age range) were scored independently by two scorers. The first study analyzed the dichotomously scored passage items in the Reading Comprehension subtest that require more judgment in scoring (as opposed to the Target Word items). The interscorer reliability coefficients between pairs of scores ranged from .94 to .98 across ages, with an overall reliability of .94.

Table 6.1.
Age-Based Reliability Coefficients of the Subtests and Composites

Subtests/Composites	Age in Years														Average r_{xx}[a]
	4	5	6	7	8	9	10	11	12	13	14	15	16	17–19	
Subtests															
Word Reading	.98	.99	.99	.98	.98	.98	.98	.97	.97	.96	.95	.94	.95	.95	.97
Numerical Operations		.85	.85	.81	.91	.88	.87	.90	.92	.93	.96	.90	.93	.95	.91
Reading Comprehension			.97	.96	.94	.96	.96	.94	.96	.96	.96	.91	.94	.93	.95
Spelling		.93	.94	.95	.93	.94	.94	.96	.95	.94	.94	.89	.90	.93	.94
Pseudoword Decoding			.98	.98	.98	.97	.98	.97	.98	.97	.96	.96	.96	.97	.97
Math Reasoning	.85	.92	.93	.92	.92	.93	.94	.93	.94	.95	.92	.89	.92	.94	.92
Written Expression			.87	.87	.87	.87	.81	.81	.81	.87	.87	.87	.87	.87	.86
Listening Comprehension	.71	.75	.83	.83	.82	.81	.78	.78	.82	.85	.81	.79	.78	.82	.80
Oral Expression	.89[b]	.89[b]	.89	.89	.89	.89	.83	.83	.83	.85	.85	.85	.85	.85	.86
Composites															
Reading			.99	.99	.99	.99	.99	.98	.99	.98	.98	.97	.98	.98	.98
Mathematics		.93	.93	.91	.95	.94	.94	.95	.96	.97	.97	.94	.96	.97	.95
Written Language			.94	.94	.94	.94	.93	.93	.93	.94	.94	.93	.93	.94	.94
Oral Language			.91	.91	.91	.91	.87	.87	.88	.90	.89	.86	.88	.87	.89
Total			.98	.98	.99	.98	.98	.98	.99	.98	.98	.98	.98	.98	.98

Note. The reliability coefficients are split-half correlations corrected by the Spearman-Brown formula. The coefficients for the composites were calculated with the formula for the reliability of a composite (Nunnally, 1978).

[a] Average reliability coefficients were calculated with Fisher's *z* transformation.

[b] For ages 4 and 5, the Oral Expression subtest was estimated based on data from age 6.

Table 6.2.
Age-Based Standard Errors of Measurement of the Subtests and Composites

Subtests/Composites	4	5	6	7	8	9	10	11	12	13	14	15	16	17–19	Average SE_M[a]
Subtests															
Word Reading	2.12	1.50	1.50	2.12	2.12	2.12	2.12	2.60	2.60	3.00	3.35	3.67	3.35	3.35	2.63
Numerical Operations		5.81	5.81	6.54	4.50	5.20	5.41	4.74	4.24	3.97	3.00	4.74	3.97	3.35	4.82
Reading Comprehension			2.60	3.00	3.67	3.00	3.00	3.67	3.00	3.00	3.00	4.50	3.67	3.97	3.38
Spelling		3.97	3.67	3.35	3.97	3.67	3.67	3.00	3.35	3.67	3.67	4.97	4.74	3.97	3.86
Pseudoword Decoding			2.12	2.12	2.12	2.60	2.12	2.60	2.12	2.60	3.00	3.00	3.00	2.60	2.52
Math Reasoning	5.81	4.24	3.97	4.24	4.24	3.97	3.67	3.97	3.67	3.35	4.24	4.97	4.24	3.67	4.20
Written Expression			5.41	5.41	5.41	5.41	6.54	6.54	6.54	5.41	5.41	5.41	5.41	5.41	5.71
Listening Comprehension	8.08	7.50	6.18	6.18	6.36	6.54	7.04	7.04	6.36	5.81	6.54	6.87	7.04	6.36	6.73
Oral Expression	4.97[b]	4.97[b]	4.97	4.97	4.97	4.97	6.18	6.18	6.18	5.81	5.81	5.81	5.81	5.81	5.55
Composites															
Reading			1.50	1.50	1.50	1.50	1.50	2.12	1.50	2.12	2.12	2.60	2.12	2.12	1.89
Mathematics		3.97	3.97	4.50	3.35	3.67	3.67	3.35	3.00	2.60	2.60	3.67	3.00	2.60	3.43
Written Language			3.67	3.67	3.67	3.67	3.97	3.97	3.97	3.67	3.67	3.97	3.97	3.67	3.80
Oral Language			4.50	4.50	4.50	4.50	5.41	5.41	5.20	4.74	4.97	5.61	5.20	5.41	5.01
Total	2.12		2.12	2.12	1.50	2.12	2.12	2.12	2.12	1.50	2.12	2.12	2.12	2.12	2.03

Note. The standard errors of measurement are reported in standard-score units for the subtests and composites. Standard errors of measurement were computed using the following formula:

$$SE_M = 15\sqrt{1 - r_{xx}}$$

where 15 is the population standard deviation and r_{xx} is the reliability coefficient from Table 6.1.

[a] The average SE_Ms were calculated by averaging the sum of the squared SE_Ms for each age group and obtaining the square root of the result.

[b] For ages 4 and 5, the Oral Expression subtest was estimated based on data from age 6.

Table 6.3.
Grade-Based Reliability Coefficients of the Subtests and Composites: Fall

Subtests/Composites	PreK (Age 5)	K	1	2	3	4	5	6	7	8	9	10	11	12	Average r_{xx}[a]
Subtests															
Word Reading	.98	.98	.98	.98	.98	.98	.98	.95	.96	.95	.94	.95	.97	.95	.97
Numerical Operations		.83	.71	.75	.90	.87	.89	.90	.91	.92	.94	.91	.95	.94	.89
Reading Comprehension			.89	.92	.93	.96	.96	.86	.96	.93	.92	.94	.90	.91	.93
Spelling		.90	.94	.94	.93	.91	.96	.93	.92	.93	.91	.90	.93	.93	.93
Pseudoword Decoding			.98	.98	.98	.97	.98	.97	.97	.96	.96	.95	.96	.97	.97
Math Reasoning	.91	.92	.90	.90	.93	.91	.95	.93	.94	.93	.91	.91	.94	.93	.92
Written Expression			.91	.91	.78	.78	.81	.81	.87	.87	.87	.88	.88	.88	.86
Listening Comprehension	.76	.76	.80	.84	.85	.82	.81	.83	.81	.82	.79	.76	.79	.82	.80
Oral Expression	.88[b]	.88[b]	.88	.88	.83	.83	.79	.79	.86	.86	.86	.84	.84	.84	.85
Composites															
Reading			.98	.98	.98	.99	.99	.97	.98	.98	.97	.98	.97	.98	.98
Mathematics		.92	.88	.90	.95	.94	.95	.95	.95	.96	.96	.95	.97	.96	.94
Written Language			.95	.96	.92	.91	.93	.92	.94	.94	.94	.94	.94	.94	.94
Oral Language	.88	.90	.90	.90	.88	.87	.87	.88	.89	.90	.88	.85	.86	.87	.88
Total	.98	.98	.98	.98	.98	.98	.98	.98	.98	.98	.98	.98	.98	.98	.98

Note. The reliability coefficients are split-half correlations corrected by the Spearman-Brown formula. The coefficients for the composites were calculated with the formula for the reliability of a composite (Nunnally, 1978).

[a] Average reliability coefficients were calculated with Fisher's z transformation.

[b] For Grades PreK (age 5) and K, the Oral Expression subtest was estimated based on data for Grade 1.

Table 6.4.
Grade-Based Standard Errors of Measurement of the Subtests and Composites: Fall

Subtests/Composites	PreK (Age 5)	K	1	2	3	4	5	6	7	8	9	10	11	12	Average $SE_M{}^a$
Subtests															
Word Reading	2.12	2.12	2.12	2.12	2.12	2.12	2.12	3.35	3.00	3.35	3.67	3.35	2.60	3.35	2.75
Numerical Operations		6.18	8.08	7.50	4.74	5.41	4.97	4.74	4.50	4.24	3.67	4.50	3.35	3.67	5.23
Reading Comprehension			4.97	4.24	3.97	3.00	3.00	5.61	3.00	3.97	4.24	3.67	4.74	4.50	4.15
Spelling		4.74	3.67	3.67	3.97	4.50	3.00	3.97	4.24	3.97	4.50	4.74	3.97	3.97	4.10
Pseudoword Decoding			2.12	2.12	2.12	2.60	2.12	2.60	2.60	3.00	3.00	3.35	3.00	2.60	2.63
Math Reasoning	4.50	4.24	4.74	4.74	3.97	4.50	3.35	3.97	3.67	3.97	4.50	4.50	3.67	3.97	4.19
Written Expression			4.50	4.50	7.04	7.04	6.54	6.54	5.41	5.41	5.41	5.20	5.20	5.20	5.73
Listening Comprehension	7.35	7.35	6.71	6.00	5.81	6.36	6.54	6.18	6.54	6.36	6.87	7.35	6.87	6.36	6.64
Oral Expression	5.20[b]	5.20[b]	5.20	5.20	6.18	6.18	6.87	6.87	5.61	5.61	5.61	6.00	6.00	6.00	5.87
Composites															
Reading			2.12	2.12	2.12	1.50	1.50	2.60	2.12	2.12	2.60	2.12	2.60	2.12	2.17
Mathematics		4.24	5.20	4.74	3.35	3.67	3.35	3.35	3.35	3.00	3.00	3.35	2.60	3.00	3.63
Written Language			3.35	3.00	4.24	4.50	3.97	4.24	3.67	3.67	3.67	3.67	3.67	3.67	3.80
Oral Language	4.74	4.74	4.74	4.74	5.20	5.41	5.41	5.20	4.97	4.74	5.20	5.81	5.61	5.41	5.21
Total	2.12	2.12	2.12	2.12	2.12	2.12	2.12	2.12	2.12	2.12	2.12	2.12	2.12	2.12	2.12

Note. The standard errors of measurement are reported in standard-score units for the subtests and composites. Standard errors of measurement were computed using the following formula:

$$SE_M = 15\sqrt{1 - r_{xx}}$$

where 15 is the population standard deviation and r_{xx} is the reliability coefficient from Table 6.3.

[a] The average SE_Ms were calculated by averaging the sum of the squared SE_Ms for each age group and obtaining the square root of the result.

[b] For Grades PreK (age 5) and K, the Oral Expression subtest was estimated based on data for Grade 1.

Table 6.5.
Grade-Based Reliability Coefficients of the Subtests and Composites: Spring

Subtests/Composites	PreK (Age 5)	K	1	2	3	4	5	6	7	8	9	10	11	12	Average r_{xx}[a]
Subtests															
Word Reading	.98	.97	.98	.98	.97	.97	.97	.98	.94	.96	.94	.95	.97	.95	.97
Numerical Operations		.83	.74	.83	.85	.85	.86	.92	.90	.94	.94	.91	.95	.94	.89
Reading Comprehension			.91	.91	.92	.89	.93	.95	.95	.96	.92	.94	.90	.91	.93
Spelling		.91	.89	.93	.93	.94	.93	.97	.93	.94	.91	.90	.93	.93	.93
Pseudoword Decoding			.97	.98	.98	.98	.98	.98	.97	.97	.96	.95	.96	.97	.97
Math Reasoning	.90	.89	.90	.92	.91	.92	.94	.94	.92	.93	.91	.91	.94	.93	.92
Written Expression			.91	.91	.78	.78	.81	.81	.87	.87	.87	.88	.88	.88	.86
Listening Comprehension	.72	.78	.81	.79	.79	.81	.71	.85	.85	.86	.79	.76	.79	.82	.80
Oral Expression	.88[b]	.88[b]	.88	.88	.83	.83	.79	.79	.86	.86	.86	.84	.84	.84	.85
Composites															
Reading			.98	.98	.98	.98	.98	.99	.98	.99	.97	.98	.97	.98	.98
Mathematics		.90	.89	.92	.93	.93	.94	.96	.95	.96	.96	.95	.97	.96	.94
Written Language			.94	.95	.92	.92	.92	.94	.94	.94	.94	.94	.94	.94	.94
Oral Language	.88		.90	.89	.88	.88	.83	.89	.90	.91	.88	.85	.87	.88	.88
Total		.98	.98	.98	.98	.98	.98	.98	.98	.99	.98	.98	.98	.98	.98

Note. The reliability coefficients are split-half correlations corrected by the Spearman-Brown formula. The coefficients for the composites were calculated with the formula for the reliability of a composite (Nunnally, 1978).

[a] Average reliability coefficients were calculated with Fisher's z transformation.

[b] For Grades PreK (age 5) and K, the Oral Expression subtest was estimated based on data for Grade 1.

Table 6.6.
Grade-Based Standard Errors of Measurement of the Subtests and Composites: Spring

Subtests/Composites	PreK (Age 5)	K	1	2	3	4	5	6	7	8	9	10	11	12	Average SE_M[a]
Subtests															
Word Reading	2.12	2.60	2.12	2.12	2.60	2.60	2.60	2.12	3.67	3.00	3.67	3.35	2.60	3.35	2.81
Numerical Operations		6.18	7.65	6.18	5.81	5.81	5.61	4.24	4.74	3.67	3.67	4.50	3.35	3.67	5.16
Reading Comprehension			4.50	4.50	4.24	4.97	3.97	3.35	3.35	3.00	4.24	3.67	4.74	4.50	4.13
Spelling		4.50	4.97	3.97	3.97	3.67	3.97	2.60	3.97	3.67	4.50	4.74	3.97	3.97	4.08
Pseudoword Decoding			2.60	2.12	2.12	2.12	2.12	2.12	2.60	2.60	3.00	3.35	3.00	2.60	2.56
Math Reasoning	4.74	4.97	4.74	4.24	4.50	4.24	3.67	3.67	4.24	3.97	4.50	4.50	3.67	3.97	4.28
Written Expression			4.50	4.50	7.04	7.04	6.54	6.54	5.41	5.41	5.41	5.20	5.20	5.20	5.73
Listening Comprehension	7.94	7.04	6.54	6.87	6.87	6.54	8.08	5.81	5.81	5.61	6.87	7.35	6.87	6.36	6.79
Oral Expression	5.20[b]	5.20[b]	5.20	5.20	6.18	6.18	6.87	6.87	5.61	5.61	5.61	6.00	6.00	6.00	5.87
Composites															
Reading			2.12	2.12	2.12	2.12	2.12	1.50	2.12	1.50	2.60	2.12	2.60	2.12	2.12
Mathematics		4.74	4.97	4.24	3.97	3.97	3.67	3.00	3.35	3.00	3.00	3.35	2.60	3.00	3.67
Written Language			3.67	3.35	4.24	4.24	4.24	3.67	3.67	3.67	3.67	3.67	3.67	3.67	3.80
Oral Language		4.74	4.74	4.97	5.20	5.20	6.18	4.97	4.74	4.50	5.20	5.81	5.41	5.20	5.20
Total	2.12	2.12	2.12	2.12	2.12	2.12	2.12	2.12	2.12	1.50	2.12	2.12	2.12	2.12	2.08

Note. The standard errors of measurement are reported in standard-score units for the subtests and composites. Standard errors of measurement were computed using the following formula:

$$SE_M = 15\sqrt{1 - r_{xx}}$$

where 15 is the population standard deviation and r_{xx} is the reliability coefficient from Table 6.5.

[a] The average SE_Ms were calculated by averaging the sum of the squared SE_Ms for each age group and obtaining the square root of the result.

[b] For Grades PreK (age 5) and K, the Oral Expression subtest was estimated based on data for Grade 1.

Table 6.7.

Stability Coefficients of the Subtests and Composites: Ages 6–9

Subtests/Composites	First Testing Mean	SD	Second Testing Mean	SD	r_{12}	Corrected r^a
Subtests						
Word Reading	100.56	12.97	102.62	13.46	.98	.99
Numerical Operations	98.09	11.67	100.26	12.45	.86	.92
Reading Comprehension	96.80	12.81	99.60	12.08	.95	.96
Spelling	102.12	13.02	103.47	13.28	.95	.96
Pseudoword Decoding	99.77	12.78	101.56	13.03	.96	.97
Math Reasoning	100.53	12.40	103.51	12.23	.94	.96
Written Expression	102.37	14.30	102.41	12.75	.86	.87
Listening Comprehension	102.78	12.96	107.46	13.17	.85	.88
Oral Expression	102.88	13.17	105.82	13.77	.85	.89
Composites						
Reading	97.64	13.33	100.61	13.85	.98	.98
Mathematics	98.65	12.36	101.69	12.91	.94	.96
Written Language	102.28	14.06	103.14	13.33	.95	.96
Oral Language	102.47	13.43	107.34	14.18	.90	.92
Total	99.75	12.93	102.13	12.79	.98	.98

Note. N = 123.

[a] Correlations were corrected for the variability of the standardization sample (Guilford & Fruchter, 1978).

Table 6.8.

Stability Coefficients of the Subtests and Composites: Ages 10–12

Subtests/Composites	First Testing Mean	SD	Second Testing Mean	SD	r_{12}	Corrected r^a
Subtests						
Word Reading	102.49	13.10	103.91	13.53	.96	.97
Numerical Operations	103.76	12.74	103.37	13.90	.88	.91
Reading Comprehension	106.24	11.00	108.64	10.21	.89	.94
Spelling	102.90	14.90	103.44	14.60	.96	.96
Pseudoword Decoding	103.63	13.26	103.49	12.42	.96	.97
Math Reasoning	102.54	14.81	105.40	15.54	.93	.93
Written Expression	102.60	14.87	103.48	14.32	.81	.81
Listening Comprehension	102.51	14.00	105.57	14.26	.92	.93
Oral Expression	101.14	14.35	102.37	12.68	.81	.83
Composites						
Reading	104.61	13.20	105.60	13.38	.97	.98
Mathematics	103.41	14.78	105.00	15.94	.93	.94
Written Language	103.55	15.91	104.15	15.07	.92	.91
Oral Language	101.94	14.60	104.06	13.93	.91	.92
Total	104.52	13.21	105.22	13.95	.97	.98

Note. N = 96.

[a] Correlations were corrected for the variability of the standardization sample (Guilford & Fruchter, 1978).

Table 6.9.

Stability Coefficients of the Subtests and Composites: Ages 13–19 and Averages for Ages 6–9, 10–12, and 13–19

Subtests/Composites	First Testing Mean	SD	Second Testing Mean	SD	r_{12}	Corrected r^a	Average[b]
Subtests							
Word Reading	101.70	13.37	104.11	12.94	.95	.96	.98
Numerical Operations	103.04	13.40	105.35	13.82	.91	.93	.92
Reading Comprehension	102.01	12.79	105.78	9.66	.85	.89	.94
Spelling	101.35	12.70	103.70	13.45	.96	.97	.96
Pseudoword Decoding	104.29	13.52	107.98	9.14	.84	.87	.95
Math Reasoning	101.27	12.57	104.01	13.65	.91	.93	.94
Written Expression	101.47	13.27	103.15	12.16	.84	.87	.85
Listening Comprehension	98.81	14.88	102.50	15.14	.90	.90	.91
Oral Expression	99.50	14.30	98.91	14.88	.83	.85	.86
Composites							
Reading	102.22	14.04	106.45	11.03	.92	.93	.97
Mathematics	102.62	13.31	105.48	14.62	.94	.95	.95
Written Language	101.57	13.46	104.30	13.11	.94	.95	.94
Oral Language	98.36	14.84	100.17	15.75	.92	.92	.92
Total	102.32	12.03	106.73	10.90	.98	.98	.98

Note. N = 74.

[a] Correlations were corrected for the variability of the standardization sample (Guilford & Fruchter, 1978).

[b] Weighted average of corrected correlations for all three age bands were obtained with Fisher's *z* transformations (*N* = 291).

The second study analyzed the Written Expression and Oral Expression subtests that are scored according to a set of multipoint criteria. To assess interscorer agreement, this study used a type of intraclass correlation that evaluates scorer leniency (Shrout & Fleiss, 1979). Before conducting the correlation analyses for the Written Expression subtest, responses to the two prompts for the paragraph and the two prompts for the essay were compared. Because no meaningful differences were found between the two sets of scores, the responses to Prompt 1 and Prompt 2 were combined and analyzed as a single group. The intraclass correlations between pairs of scores ranged from .71 to .94 across ages; the average Written Expression intraclass correlation was .85. The intraclass correlations between pairs of scores for the Oral Expression subtest ranged from .91 to .99 across ages, with an overall correlation of .96. The results show that although these subtests require more scoring judgment, they can be scored reliably.

Validity

Evidence of the validity of test interpretations should be based on information accumulated from numerous and diverse studies. Such evidence demonstrates the extent to which a test measures what it is intended to measure, and can be categorized by three traditional types: (a) content-related, (b) construct-related, and (c) criterion-related validity (*Standards for Educational and Psychological Testing*, 1985). More recently, the *Standards for Educational and Psychological Tests* (hereafter referred to as the *Test Standards*) suggests that the establishment of validity should not be discussed in terms of different *types* of validity, but instead in terms of providing lines of validity evidence (1999). The *Test Standards* emphasizes that there are degrees of validity; test validity requires evaluating the degree to which the instrument's results and interpretations are justified in accord with the body of supporting evidence. According to the *Test Standards*, the term *construct* should be used "broadly as the concept or characteristics that a test is designed to measure" (p. 5). The evidence for the validity of the WIAT–II interpretations is discussed following the guidelines specified by the *Test Standards*.

Evidence Based on Test Content

Validity can be evaluated by the degree to which the test items adequately represent and relate to the content that the test is designed to measure (Borg & Gall, 1989, p. 250). Two types of systematic information, expert judgments and empirical item analysis, were collected to provide content-related evidence of the validity of interpretations for each subtest and for the WIAT–II as an overall measure of achievement.

Content representativeness of the WIAT–II subtests and items was examined continuously during the development, tryout, and standardization phases of the project. One of the initial steps in ensuring content validity focused on determining the curriculum objectives within each of the domains, or curriculum areas, as specified in the Individuals with Disabilities Education Act Amendments of 1997. These curriculum objectives, in turn, defined the scope, or content, of the WIAT–II subtests. Details of these steps and the process used for selecting and developing each subtest and its items are presented in Chapter 5.

The most critical aspect of establishing content validity was to ensure that the items of each subtest correspond to the curriculum objectives represented in the subtest. Several steps were taken to ensure content validity. Following the development of the subtest blueprints, or specifications detailing the number and format of the items planned for each curriculum objective, curriculum experts in reading, mathematics, speech, and other language arts reviewed each subtest. The development team also compared the WIAT–II subtest designs, item formats, and content to those of the PAL–RW (Berninger, 2001). The proposed objectives and items of each subtest were subjected to thorough examinations including comparisons with school textbooks, other achievement tests and diagnostic instruments, emerging curricular trends, various state standards, opinions of nationally recognized experts including special education experts, national item tryouts, and teacher surveys.

After the curriculum objectives were determined and items drafted for each subtest, expert reviewers again examined each item for content coverage and relevance. For items in the Math Reasoning, Numerical Operations, and Reading Comprehension subtests, reviewers assessed the congruence between each item (content, format, and wording) and the curriculum objective it was designed to address. If a majority of the reviewers could not agree that an item was a measure of its intended curriculum objective, the item was deleted or revised. For items in the Word Reading subtest, reviewers evaluated each word for its phonemic characteristics and grade level (refer to the Skills Analysis section of Chapter 7). For the Oral Expression subtest, reviewers examined the pictorial prompts, the wording of each item, and the wording of each scoring criterion to ensure that the item addressed the expressive-language objectives represented in the subtest blueprint (e.g., ability to give directions). For the Written Expression subtest, reviewers examined the quality of the prompts and the wording of the scoring criteria. For the Oral Expression and Written Expression subtests, the responses of examinees from the tryout and standardization samples were examined to assess if the items elicited responses that were rich in fluency and structure and of sufficient length and variety to allow scorers to apply the subtest scoring criteria. In addition, extensive surveys were conducted with the examiners who participated in the pilot, tryout, and standardization phases of the WIAT–II. Examiners were asked to evaluate the administration directions, ease of administration, and item content. If an examiner perceived an item as biased, incongruent with the subtest, or unappealing to the examinees, the item was noted for further evaluation.

Although a discussion of content-related evidence of validity often emphasizes only the content representativeness of items, item analysis is often included as a criterion for evidence of validity (Kamphaus, Slotkin, & DeVencentis, 1990). Analyses of the data by both conventional and item response theory (IRT; Lord, 1980) methods were conducted during the development phases of the WIAT–II to document the degree to which each item was empirically consistent with the other items in the subtest. For example, item–total correlations were inspected for each subtest and each age. Any item for which the correlation was less than .20 was considered for revision and replacement. A 1-parameter IRT model (Rasch, 1980) was fit to the item-level data for the purpose of examining item difficulty and to indicate the correct item order within a subtest. Items with large IRT chi-square fit statistics were noted and examined for problems. Poorly fitting items were deleted from the test. Additionally, extensive item-bias studies were conducted on the data from the tryout and standardization phases (see Chapter 5). After the pilot and tryout phases, items were also reviewed by comparing the pattern of responses from examinees diagnosed with a learning disability to those without a learning disability ($p < .05$ level of significance). Any item noted as problematic according to the empirical criteria was evaluated for deletion.

Throughout the process of reviewing the subtests for content validity, the balance among the curriculum objectives addressed by each subtest was maintained by carefully evaluating the deletion of any items. Therefore, the WIAT–II subtests have internally consistent, content-representative sets of items that are free of significant gender and ethnic bias. Moreover, each resulting subtest is content-homogeneous. Subtest homogeneity is often described as an essential goal of test construction (Nunnally, 1978).

Construct-Related Evidence of Validity

Each WIAT–II subtest measures achievement in one of nine curriculum domains. The subtest score indicates the appropriate interpretations and inferences that can be made about the underlying dimension of academic skill that connects all of the curriculum objectives within the domain. For example, the Reading Comprehension score is an observable measure of the complex set of skills that form the construct of comprehension of reading passages. This section presents the evidence gathered to document the validity of construct interpretations based on the WIAT–II scores. The evidence includes intercorrelations of the subtests, correlations with the measures of ability, studies of group differences, and other evidence (e.g., correlations with other achievement tests).

Intercorrelations of the Subtests

Table K.13 in Appendix K presents the intercorrelations of the WIAT–II subtest scores for each age. The patterns of correlations confirm the expected relations between subtests and the domains they comprise (e.g., Math Reasoning and Numerical Operations; Oral Expression and Listening Comprehension). The intercorrelations also provide discriminant evidence of validity (Campbell & Fiske, 1959). The mathematics subtests tend to correlate more highly with each other than with the reading subtests, and the reading subtests tend to correlate more highly with each other than with the mathematics subtests.

Correlations With Measures of Ability

Table K.13 also presents the correlations between the WIAT–II subtest scores and the IQ scores of the Wechsler scales (WPPSI–R, WISC–III, and WAIS–III). As expected from other research on ability-achievement correlations (e.g., Sattler, 2001), most of the correlations range from .30 to .78 for the FSIQ scores. The high correlations between the Reading Comprehension subtest and ability, the Math Reasoning subtest and ability (for the WAIS–III and WISC–III), and moderately high correlations between the Numerical Operations subtest and ability (for the WPPSI–R) confirmed the expectation that these subtests address curriculum objectives that require a higher level of cognitive skill than the other WIAT–II subtests.

Group Differences

The grade-based normative table (Table C.1) and the age-based normative table (Table F.1) provide evidence of expected group differences. For any given subtest standard score, the tables indicate that as age and grade increase, raw scores (and subsequent score ranges) also increase. For example, to achieve a standard score of 100 on the Word Reading subtest, a 6-year-old needs to have a total raw score of 43, while a 7-year-old needs to have a total raw score of 63 to achieve the *same* standard score. Consistent differences of the same magnitudes, as those found for the age groups, are also found between the raw scores of examinees in Grades 1 and 2. An examinee in Grade 1 during the fall must have a Word Reading total raw score of 51 for a standard score of 100; an examinee in Grade 2 during the fall must have a Word Reading total raw score of 77 for a standard score of 100. The same pattern is found within grades from fall to spring. As expected, the differences between adjacent raw scores become increasingly smaller as the ages and the grades of the examinees increase. For example, to achieve a standard score of 100 on the Word Reading subtest, a 15-year-old needs to have a total raw score of 117–118 points and a 16-year-old needs to have a total raw score of 120 points. The adjacent-group differences in raw scores provide evidence that the WIAT–II scores are measures of the same constructs, with the same patterns of findings, as is commonly observed in other achievement tests designed to encompass the identical curriculum domains (Thorndike & Hagen, 1977).

A second approach to establish group differences is to compare the subtest total raw scores by age, grade, and season within grade (i.e., fall, winter, spring). The raw score means increase from age to age, grade to grade, and from fall to spring within grades. The largest adjacent-group differences occur between younger examinees and lower grades; adjacent-group differences decrease in size with older examinees and higher grades.

Other Evidence

Correlations between the WIAT–II scores and scores on other achievement tests provide evidence that the WIAT–II is a valid measure of achievement for constructs such as math reasoning (labeled "Mathematical Applications" in some achievement tests). The sizeable differences between the scores of the examinees in the standardization sample and those of examinees in the various clinical groups, such as examinees in gifted programs or examinees diagnosed with mental retardation, also verify the construct validity of WIAT–II interpretations.

Criterion-Related Evidence of Validity

Evidence of validity is criterion-related if it documents the relation between the test and independent criteria. Such criteria can include other test scores, indexes, diagnostic categories and other classifications, and other indicators that have been constructed without reference or connection to the test that is being evaluated. The independent criteria used for validity studies of the WIAT–II include scores on other achievement tests (both individually administered and group-administered), grades in school, and diagnostic classifications such as gifted, mentally retarded, and learning disabled.

Correlations With Other Individually Administered Achievement Tests

Correlations between the WIAT–II and other achievement tests are an indication of the similarity of constructs being measured, thus providing convergent evidence for the validity of the WIAT–II. Unless otherwise noted, the individually administered achievement test and the WIAT–II were administered within 60 days of each other.

Correlations With the WIAT

The WIAT–II and the WIAT were administered to a sample of 72 examinees aged 8–15 (M = 11 years). The sample was 49% female and 51% male. Table 6.10 presents the correlation coefficients, means, and standard deviations for the WIAT–II and WIAT subtest and composite standard scores. As expected, subtest correlations remained high for subtests such as Word Reading (.91) and Spelling (.93), in which there was little change in content from the WIAT to the WIAT–II. Subtest correlations were moderate for subtests in which content changed considerably from the first edition to the second edition (.48 for Written Expression and .62 for Oral Expression). Correlations for the Reading and Math Composites were high (.85 and .86, respectively).

Correlations With the PAL–RW

The WIAT–II and the PAL–RW (Berninger, 2001) were administered to a sample of 120 examinees aged 5–12 years (M = 8 years) in Grades K–6. The sample was 46% female and 54% male. The PAL–RW was designed as a companion to the WIAT–II and provides in-depth assessment of the processing skills that are necessary for the development of the academic skills measured by the WIAT–II. The PAL–RW Receptive Coding subtest requires the examinee to compare whole words, single letters, and letter groups to presented target words and the Expressive Coding subtest requires the examinee to spell selected parts of previously presented nonsense words. The PAL–RW Rapid Automatized Naming (RAN) tasks assess reading fluency of letters, words, and digits. The PAL–RW Note-Taking tasks require examinees to record critical information from an orally presented passage, then reconstruct the passage using their notes. The PAL–RW Rhyming, Syllables, Phonemes, and Rimes subtests assess related orthographic and phonological processes. For example, the examinee must divide words into phonological segments or produce rhyming words. The PAL–RW Word Choice subtest requires the examinee to distinguish the correct spelling of a word from misspelled distractors and the Story Retell subtest assesses listening and verbal skills. The PAL–RW Sentence Sense subtest assesses sentence-comprehension processes when reading for meaning under timed conditions and the Copying tasks assess the ability to copy information (near point) under timed conditions.

Table 6.10.
Correlations Between Selected WIAT-II and WIAT Subtests and Composites

WIAT-II	WIAT Total Group Subtests								WIAT Total Group Composites				WIAT-II	
	Basic Reading	Num Ops	Reading Comp	Spelling	Math Reason	Written Exp	Listen Comp	Oral Exp	Reading	Math	Writing	Lang	Mean	SD
Subtests														
Word Reading	.91												104.34	11.73
Numerical Operations		.81											107.22	14.14
Reading Comprehension			.74										101.06	10.43
Spelling				.93									104.86	11.22
Math Reasoning					.86								105.28	15.29
Written Expression						.48							103.39	13.84
Listening Comprehension							.68						103.41	11.35
Oral Expression								.62					104.07	11.42
Composites														
Reading									.85				102.18	12.41
Mathematics										.86			107.01	16.39
Written Language											.66		104.39	12.71
Oral Language												.66	103.25	10.74
WIAT														
Mean	106.44	105.78	104.22	105.49	108.67	99.63	103.56	114.25	104.60	107.18	102.71	110.82		
SD	12.89	13.79	12.52	11.41	14.78	15.26	14.74	10.31	13.47	15.70	15.35	14.41		

Note. N = 72.

Table 6.11 lists the correlation coefficients of the WIAT–II and of the PAL–RW subtests. Four of the PAL–RW subtests, Receptive Coding, Syllables, Phonemes, and Rimes, required grouping data for Grades K–3 and for Grades 4–6 because item sets for each subtest differed for these two groups. For Syllables, Grade K data were not included in analysis because the data were not normally distributed and the item set differed from Grades 1–3. The correlation coefficients by grade groupings were averaged and are reported in Table 6.11. The data in Table 6.11 demonstrates that the WIAT–II subtests that evaluate reading skills (e.g., Word Reading, Reading Comprehension, Pseudoword Decoding) are moderately correlated with the PAL–RW subtests that measure the processing skills of orthographic and phonological coding (e.g., Receptive Coding, Expressive Coding, Rhyming, Syllables, Phonemes, and Rimes). In addition, the correlation coefficients between the PAL–RW and the WIAT–II provide divergent evidence of validity; that is, the WIAT–II Math Reasoning subtest, which includes receptive and expressive reading components, tends to have higher correlations with the PAL–RW subtests than does the WIAT–II Numerical Operations subtest.

Correlations With the *Wide Range Achievement Test–Third Edition*

The WIAT–II and the *Wide Range Achievement Test–Third Edition* (WRAT3; Wilkinson, 1993) were administered to a sample of 37 examinees in Grades 8–12 (aged 13–17 years; $M = 14$ years). The sample was 65% female and 35% male. The WRAT3 Reading subtest contains letter- and word-reading items. The Arithmetic subtest contains paper-and-pencil computation items, most requiring the basic operations of addition, subtraction, multiplication, or division. The WRAT3 Spelling subtest is very similar to the WIAT–II Spelling subtest in that both require the examinee to write a word based on its meaning in a dictated sentence. Table 6.12 presents the correlation coefficients, means, and standard deviations, based on standard scores, for the corresponding WIAT–II and WRAT3 subtests. A strong correlation exists between the WIAT–II and WRAT3 Spelling subtests. Moderate correlations were found between the WRAT3 Arithmetic subtest and the WIAT–II Math Reasoning and Numerical Operations subtests. The correlations also indicate that the WRAT3 Reading subtest is closer in content to the WIAT–II Word Reading than to the Reading Comprehension subtest.

Correlation With the *Differential Ability Scales*

The WIAT–II and the *Differential Ability Scales* (DAS; Elliott, 1990) were administered to a sample of 27 examinees aged 6–9 and 12–14 years ($M = 7$ years). The sample was 56% female and 44% male. The interval between testings ranged from 1 to 117 days, with a median of 114 days. The DAS Word Reading, Basic Number Skills, and Spelling subtests generally parallel the structure and content of the WIAT–II Word Reading, Numerical Operations, and Spelling subtests. Table 6.13 presents the correlation coefficients, means, and standard deviations, based on standard scores, for these subtests. The mean scores vary slightly for corresponding pairs of subtests (DAS Basic Number Skills, $M = 101.11$, and WIAT–II Numerical Operations, $M = 102.48$), and the correlations for the corresponding pairs are low to moderately high. The WIAT–II Word Reading subtest includes letter recognition and phonological comparison items in addition to word reading items, which may in part explain the correlation of .28 between the WIAT–II Word Reading and the DAS Word Reading subtests. The score on the DAS Word Reading subtest, which focuses on the reading of individual words rather than passages, correlates in the expected moderate range (.38) with the WIAT–II Reading Comprehension score.

Table 6.11.
Correlations Between the WIAT-II and Selected PAL-RW Subtests

WIAT-II Subtests and Supplemental Scores	PAL-RW Subtests																
	Receptive Coding	Expressive Coding	RAN-Letters	RAN-Words	RAN-Digits	RAN-Words & Digits	Note-Taking Task A	Note-Taking Task B	Rhyming	Syllables	Phonemes	Rimes	Word Choice	Story Retell	Sentence Sense	Copying Task A (20" Score)	Copying Task B (90" Score)
Word Reading	.77	.80	−.78	−.54	−.73	−.72	.64	.65	.45	.47	.61	.48	.82	.07	.30	.60	.46
Numerical Operations	.66	.46	−.66	−.48	−.63	−.47	.48	.48	.46	.21	.52	.35	.82	.12	.35	.54	.42
Reading Comprehension	.65	.51	−.69	−.35	−.66	−.56	.28	.34	—	.43	.37	.47	.89	—	.38	.40	.54
Spelling	.77	.81	−.78	−.48	−.74	−.62	.58	.65	.50	.43	.59	.42	.79	.28	.26	.68	.56
Pseudoword Decoding	.69	.83	−.72	−.54	−.72	−.56	.54	.59	—	.49	.56	.52	.80	—	.28	.57	.32
Math Reasoning	.73	.77	−.75	−.57	−.69	−.57	.60	.60	.34	.42	.61	.42	.81	.20	.31	.60	.48
Written Expression	.69	.70	−.78	−.39	−.73	−.69	.46	.48	.49	.30	.50	.32	.75	.17	.31	.66	.61
Listening Comprehension	.51	.41	−.64	−.38	−.58	−.39	.57	.59	−.12	.30	.53	.19	.48	.13	.23	.59	.43
Oral Expression	.49	.56	−.35	−.32	−.32	−.21	.57	.60	.24	.20	.48	.21	.08	.67	−.02	.41	.26

Note. $N = 120$. For Receptive Coding, Phonemes, and Rimes, correlations were calculated separately for grades K–3 and 4–6, and then averaged using Fisher's z transformation. For Syllables, correlations were calculated separately for grades 1–3 and 4–6, and then averaged using Fisher's z transformation. For all other subtests, correlations were calculated separately by test order, and averaged using Fisher's z transformation.

Table 6.12.

Correlations Between Selected WIAT–II and WRAT3 Subtests and Composites

| WIAT–II | WRAT3 Total Group | | | WIAT–II | |
	Reading	Arithmetic	Spelling	Mean	SD
Subtests					
Word Reading	.75			102.19	12.58
Numerical Operations		.60		102.39	16.19
Reading Comprehension	.52			102.24	13.13
Spelling			.80	102.30	11.90
Pseudoword Decoding	.55			103.39	14.20
Math Reasoning		.65		103.41	11.97
Composites					
Reading	.77			100.84	12.98
Mathematics		.68		102.94	13.95
Written Language			.73	101.76	15.42
WRAT3					
Mean	101.97	102.24	101.14		
SD	11.72	10.88	11.56		

Note. N = 37.

Table 6.13.

Correlations Between Selected WIAT–II and DAS Subtests and Composites

| WIAT–II | DAS | | | WIAT–II | |
	Word Reading	Basic Number Skills	Spelling	Mean	SD
Subtests					
Word Reading	.28			96.78	10.59
Numerical Operations		.75		102.48	11.92
Spelling			.67	99.08	10.03
Composites					
Reading	.32			93.04	8.77
Mathematics		.64		100.15	9.97
Written Language			.47	97.50	8.43
DAS					
Mean	92.04	101.11	102.96		
SD	10.45	11.47	18.22		

Note. N = 27.

Correlations With the *Peabody Picture Vocabulary Test–Third Edition*

The WIAT–II and the *Peabody Picture Vocabulary Test–Third Edition* (PPVT–III; Dunn & Dunn, 1997) were administered to a sample of 65 examinees aged 4–7 years (*M* = 6 years), in Grades PreK– 2. The sample was 54% females and 46% male. The PPVT–III is primarily a measure of an examinee's receptive vocabulary for Standard American English and provides a single total score. The PPVT–III standard score was compared to the mean standard scores on the four WIAT–II subtests that tap similar skills: Word Reading, Reading Comprehension, Pseudoword Decoding, and Listening Comprehension. Table 6.14 presents the correlation coefficients, means, and standard deviations for the WIAT–II subtest standard scores and the PPVT–III total score. Note that the examinees in this study were relatively young (aged 4–7 years) with the limited range of reading-related skill expected for children of this age. The WIAT–II Listening Comprehension subtest score has a moderate but significant correlation with the PPVT–III total score (.44). This correlation most likely occurred because the WIAT–II Listening Comprehension subtest assesses sentence comprehension and receptive vocabulary in addition to expressive vocabulary. The correlation (.76) between the WIAT–II Reading Composite score and the PPVT–III total score provides construct-related evidence of validity, because the scope of an examinee's receptive vocabulary should correlate with his or her reading skills.

Table 6.14.
Correlations Between Selected WIAT–II Subtests and Composites and the PPVT–III

WIAT–II	PPVT–III Total Score	WIAT–II Mean	SD
Subtests			
Word Reading	.48	104.73	15.64
Reading Comprehension	.70	103.50	12.27
Pseudoword Decoding	.75	98.24	12.94
Listening Comprehension	.44	105.13	10.66
Composite			
Reading	.76	101.90	15.56
PPVT-III			
Mean	99.12		
SD	10.71		

Note. N = 65.

Summary of Studies of Individually Administered Achievement Tests

Two prominent trends were noted in the correlation studies between the WIAT–II and other individually administered achievement tests. First, correlation coefficients among the scores on the reading-related, mathematics, and spelling subtests of the WIAT–II and those of the corresponding subtests of the WIAT, PAL–RW, WRAT3, and DAS are highly consistent. For example, the WIAT–II Spelling subtest scores correlate from .67 to .93 across the corresponding spelling subtests in the WIAT, PAL–RW, WRAT3, and DAS. Second, the mean standard scores of the corresponding subtests are approximately equal. For example, the corresponding subtests of the WIAT–II and the WRAT3 have similar mean scores, despite the independent standardization samples that were collected 8 years apart. Therefore, the correlation data on individually administered achievement tests provides evidence of criterion-related and construct-related validity for the interpretation of the WIAT–II scores.

Correlations With Group-Administered Achievement Tests

Group-administered achievement test scores were obtained for a sample of examinees aged 6–18 years in Grades 1–12 who were also administered the WIAT–II. In addition to the WIAT–II, the examinees were administered one of the following achievement tests: the *Stanford Achievement Tests, Ninth Edition* (SAT9; Harcourt Educational Measurement, 1996; *N* = 148) and the *Metropolitan Achievement Tests, Eighth Edition*, (MAT8; Harcourt Educational Measurement, 1999; *N* = 153).

Four scores between the WIAT–II and the achievement test batteries were compared: (a) Reading Composite (called "Total Reading" in the group-administered tests), typically consisting of vocabulary and reading-comprehension subtests; (b) Math Composite (called "Total Math" in the group-administered tests), consisting of computation, concepts, and application subtests; (c) Language Composite consisting of paragraph and sentence composition, language expression, vocabulary, and reference skills; and (d) the Spelling subtest. The group-administered tests incorporate a multiple-choice item format, which measures a different aspect of achievement than the open-ended items of the WIAT–II. Performance on multiple-choice items in spelling, for example, reflects the skill of *recognizing* the misspelling and correct spelling of words, rather than the skill of *producing* (or writing) the correct spelling as is required by the WIAT–II.

Table 6.15 presents the correlation coefficients between the standard scores on the WIAT–II and the NCE scores on the SAT9 and the MAT8. For the SAT9 and WIAT–II analyses, correlations were calculated separately by testing order, then corrected for variability of the standardization

Table 6.15.
Correlations Between Selected WIAT–II and Group-Administered Achievement Test Subtests and Composites

| | WIAT–II | | | |
| | Subtest | Composites | | |
	Spelling	Reading	Mathematics	Written Language
SAT9				
Total Reading		.72		
Total Math			.75	
Language				.64
Spelling	.89			
N = 148				
MAT8 Levels 3–5				
(Grades 2–4)				
Total Reading		.72		
Total Math			.77	
Language				.61
Spelling	.80			
N = 57				
MAT8 Levels 6–10				
(Grades 5–9)				
Total Reading		.55		
Total Math			.68	
Total Language				.68
Spelling	.78			
N = 96				

sample. The MAT8 scores are reported according to the level groupings. The correlations demonstrate that the MAT8 Total Reading correlations range from .55 (Levels 6–10) to .72 (Levels 3–5), the MAT8 Total Math correlations range from .68 (Levels 6–10) to .77 (Levels 3–5). Spelling shows the strongest correlations, ranging from .78 for the MAT8 (Levels 6–10) to .89 for the SAT9. In summary, the results of these analyses show consistent similarity between these two group-administered achievement tests and the WIAT–II.

Correlations With *Academic Competence Evaluation Scales*

Another study that provided evidence for the validity of the WIAT–II was conducted using the *Academic Competence Evaluation Scales* (ACES; DiPerna & Elliott, 2000). The ACES is a standardized instrument that uses teacher ratings to measure academic skills (reading/language arts, mathematics, and critical thinking) and academic enablers (motivation, study skills, engagement, and interpersonal skills). The data for this correlational study were collected during the WIAT–II and ACES national standardization phases. Teachers completed ratings on the ACES for a sample of 97 students in Grades 1–12 who were administered the WIAT–II. The correlation coefficients between the WIAT–II subtest and composite standard scores and selected ACES Academic Skills subscales, along with means and standard deviations of the raw scores, are presented in Table 6.16. As expected, the strongest correlations occurred between the Academic Skills subscales of the ACES and their corresponding subtests on the WIAT–II. For example, moderate correlations exist between the ACES Reading/Language Arts subscale and the WIAT–II Reading Comprehension, Word Reading, Pseudoword Decoding, and the Reading Composite scores. Correlations were also moderate for the corresponding math scores between the ACES and the WIAT–II.

Table 6.16.
Correlations Between Selected WIAT–II Subtests and Composites and ACES Subscales

	ACES		WIAT–II	
WIAT–II	**Reading/Language Arts Subscale**	**Mathematics Subscale**	**Mean**	**SD**
Subtests				
Word Reading	.64		103.40	11.11
Numerical Operations		.54	102.09	12.19
Reading Comprehension	.52		102.46	12.06
Spelling	.48		102.51	12.92
Pseudoword Decoding	.52		101.09	12.61
Math Reasoning		.59	102.27	13.51
Written Expression	.45		102.80	11.81
Listening Comprehension	.55		103.41	12.24
Composites				
Reading	.68		101.10	12.44
Mathematics		.65	102.08	12.47
Written Language	.51		102.47	12.65
ACES				
Mean	37.03	25.38		
SD	8.66	6.09		

Note. N = 97.

Correlations With School Grades

Teacher-assigned grades were obtained for a sample of over 350 individuals in Grades 1–12 (aged 6–19 years; $M = 13$ years) who were administered the WIAT–II. The sample was 52% female and 48% male. The grades reflected a variety of scoring scales and were converted to a single numerical system (50–100) so that the data could be combined. Due to the variability in the criteria teachers use to assign grades, school grades are less reliable than standardized test scores, such as those from the WIAT–II. This unreliability, inherent in the criterion, may have affected the correlations.

Table 6.17 presents the correlation coefficients between the WIAT–II subtest and composite standard scores and the teacher-assigned reading, spelling, English, and mathematics grades. Generally, the reading, mathematics, and spelling grades were obtained for individuals in Grades 1–6, while mathematics and English grades were obtained for individuals in Grades 7–12. The table shows low correlations ranging from .16 between the WIAT–II Oral Expression subtest score and English grades to .56 between the WIAT–II Spelling and Written Expression subtest standard score and the spelling grades. The highest correlations occur between school grades and the WIAT–II subtests that assess similar constructs. For example, the mathematics grade correlates most strongly with the WIAT–II Math Reasoning subtest (.49); the English grade correlates most strongly with the WIAT–II Written Expression subtest and the Written Language Composite. The reading grade may represent an assessment of expressive skills related to reading, resulting in the higher correlations with the Written Expression, Listening Comprehension, and Oral Expression subtests than with the Reading Comprehension subtest.

Table 6.17.
Correlations Between School Grades and the WIAT–II Subtest and Composite Standard Scores

Subtests/Composites	n	Reading Grade	Spelling Grade	English Grade	Mathematics Grade
Subtests					
Word Reading	358	.41	.49	.23	.29
Numerical Operations	358	.40	.44	.31	.36
Reading Comprehension	354	.30	.28	.26	.19
Spelling	347	.49	.56	.34	.39
Pseudoword Decoding	267	.41	.46	.23	.30
Math Reasoning	355	.46	.46	.28	.49
Written Expression	330	.55	.56	.44	.39
Listening Comprehension	356	.48	.47	.24	.36
Oral Expression	336	.44	.42	.16	.32
Composites					
Reading	257	.42	.46	.29	.30
Mathematics	351	.44	.46	.32	.44
Written Language	316	.55	.57	.43	.40
Oral Language	330	.51	.50	.24	.37
Total	223	.56	.54	.35	.43

Note. N = 350.

Studies With Special Groups

Performance on the WIAT–II by individuals belonging to special groups (e.g., diagnosed with mental retardation, learning disability, ADHD) provides important evidence of the validity of the WIAT–II. Individuals within each group were matched with a control group of individuals from the standardization sample according to demographic characteristics including age and grade, sex, race/ethnicity, and PEL. The WIAT–II subtest and composite standard scores were compared between each special group and its matched control group. The descriptions and comparisons of scores refer to age-based subtest and composite standard scores.

Individuals in Gifted Programs

The WIAT–II was administered to a sample of 123 individuals, aged 6–17 years (M = 11 years), classified as gifted. The sample was 56 % female and 44% male. The individuals were classified on the basis of individual school criteria for giftedness. Table 6.18 presents the means and standard deviations of the WIAT–II subtest and composite standard scores for the clinical group and for the matched control group. The mean subtest standard scores for the gifted group range from 113.22 (Oral Expression) to 121.81 (Math Reasoning), with composite scores ranging from 118.32 (Oral Language) to 124.73 (Mathematics). This group's achievement level can be evaluated by comparing their achievement scores with those from the matched control group. Individuals in the gifted group had standard scores that were consistently higher than those in the matched control group across all subtests and composites. Subtest standard score differences ranged from 9.61 points (Reading Comprehension) to 15.33 points (Math Reasoning); composite standard score differences ranged from 12.59 (Oral Language) to 17.59 (Mathematics).

Table 6.18 also shows the percentage of individuals within each group whose standard scores fell at or above 130 points for each subtest and composite. For example, 15% of individuals in gifted programs had an Oral Expression standard score of 130 points or higher. In contrast, 2% of individuals in the matched control group had an Oral Expression standard score of 130 points or higher.

Individuals With Mental Retardation

The WIAT–II was administered to a sample of 39 individuals, aged 7–14 years (M = 10 years), diagnosed as mildly mentally retarded. The sample was 56% female and 44% male. The diagnosis of mild mental retardation was made by independent investigators and was based on standardized intelligence test FSIQ scores between 50 and 70, with both VIQ and PIQ scores below 70. Table 6.19 presents the means and standard deviations of the WIAT–II subtest and composite standard scores for the clinical group and the matched control group. For the subtests, the mean subtest standard scores range from 47.25 (Reading Comprehension) to 69.92 (Oral Expression); for the composites, the mean standard scores range from 49.71 (Reading) to 63.00 (Oral Language). All means are within the expected range for this group. The mean standard score differences between the two groups range from 24.92 (Oral Expression) to 51.92 (Reading Comprehension). The standard scores for examinees with mental retardation were lower than those for individuals in the matched control group across all subtests and composites. In addition, the majority of examinees with mental retardation had standard scores of 70 or less for all subtests and composites. The higher mean score on the Oral Expression subtest for individuals diagnosed with mental retardation may represent a relative strength for this group in expressive language, a skill that is less highly correlated with intellectual ability than are the other achievement domains; however, even the highest mean score was at least two standard deviations below the mean of the matched control group.

Table 6.18.
Mean Performance of Gifted Individuals and the Matched Control Group

Subtests/Composites	Gifted			Matched Control Group			Mean Difference of the Two Samples		
	Mean	SD	% With Score ≥ 130	Mean	SD	% With Score ≥ 130	Difference	t Value	p Value
Subtests									
Word Reading	118.17	7.13	3	104.15	12.92	1	14.02	10.53	< .01
Numerical Operations	119.70	11.81	20	106.84	12.81	3	13.11	8.35	< .01
Reading Comprehension	113.94	8.31	2	103.91	11.92	0	9.61	6.32	< .01
Spelling	120.11	8.94	11	106.72	12.86	3	13.36	9.39	< .01
Pseudoword Decoding	115.78	5.74	2	104.57	13.63	1	11.40	7.93	< .01
Math Reasoning	121.81	9.06	19	106.43	11.92	0	15.33	11.61	< .01
Written Expression	119.25	8.09	12	104.96	12.07	1	14.47	10.44	< .01
Listening Comprehension	117.19	9.21	9	107.57	10.98	3	9.79	7.64	< .01
Oral Expression	113.22	15.91	15	103.30	13.51	2	10.14	4.99	< .01
Composites									
Reading	120.46	8.24	11	103.43	13.89	2	17.30	10.08	< .01
Mathematics	124.73	10.81	27	107.32	12.73	3	17.59	11.32	< .01
Written Language	123.51	8.82	21	106.23	13.42	3	17.21	11.51	< .01
Oral Language	118.32	12.34	19	105.78	11.77	2	12.59	7.62	< .01
Total	124.48	6.41	18	105.36	11.97	2	18.68	12.14	< .01

Note. $N = 123$.

Table 6.19.
Mean Performance of Individuals With Mental Retardation and the Matched Control Group

Subtests/Composites	Mental Retardation			Matched Control Group			Mean Difference of the Two Samples		
	Mean	SD	% With Score ≤ 70	Mean	SD	% With Score ≤ 70	Difference	t Value	p Value
Subtests									
Word Reading	58.14	10.42	85	95.68	14.47	10	36.97	12.36	< .01
Numerical Operations	61.55	10.15	79	95.88	16.36	3	33.21	10.14	< .01
Reading Comprehension	47.25	11.30	59	96.24	16.44	8	51.92	13.20	< .01
Spelling	64.68	9.73	72	96.06	12.47	0	31.50	13.17	< .01
Pseudoword Decoding	68.76	4.76	56	96.91	17.56	8	28.87	8.01	< .01
Math Reasoning	56.16	9.64	90	95.73	12.86	3	39.58	14.65	< .01
Written Expression	62.81	7.69	69	93.95	15.17	5	31.38	9.85	< .01
Listening Comprehension	66.60	13.37	54	97.21	17.61	5	30.71	8.93	< .01
Oral Expression	69.92	9.73	56	94.97	14.28	5	24.92	8.87	< .01
Composites									
Reading	49.71	6.42	54	94.74	15.59	8	47.38	11.14	< .01
Mathematics	53.57	9.70	92	95.52	15.38	3	41.48	12.79	< .01
Written Language	58.41	8.94	74	93.83	13.56	3	36.10	11.71	< .01
Oral Language	63.00	9.75	74	94.74	16.70	5	31.86	9.99	< .01
Total	53.56	5.40	41	94.08	14.00	3	43.33	9.07	< .01

Note. N = 39.

Table 6.27 shows the percentage of individuals obtaining standard scores of 70 points or less on specific numbers of WIAT–II subtests. For individuals diagnosed with mental retardation, 100% had at least two subtests with standard scores of 70 points or lower, whereas only 12.9% of individuals in the matched control group had two or more subtests with scores within this range.

Individuals With Emotional Disturbance

The WIAT–II was administered to a sample of 85 individuals, aged 9–18 years (M = 15 years), diagnosed with emotional disturbance. These diagnoses were made by independent evaluators and were based on criteria defined in the *DSM–IV* (American Psychological Association [APA], 1994). The sample was 15% female and 85% male. Table 6.20 presents the means and standard deviations of the WIAT–II subtest and composite standard scores for the clinical group and the matched control group. The mean standard scores range from 85.48 (Numerical Operations) to 95.34 (Oral Expression) for the subtests, with a total composite score of 87.02. Note the relatively high mean scores (and relatively low mean score differences) for the Oral Expression and Listening Comprehension subtests, suggesting that expressive language of the pragmatic type (e.g., describing, giving directions) has been less affected than other skills by the emotional difficulties of these individuals.

While the scores for individuals diagnosed with emotional disturbance are typically lower than the scores in the matched control group, they do not indicate consistently low performance for all individuals in this group. The majority of individuals (78.8%) diagnosed with emotional disturbance had no more than one subtest with a score of 70 or less (see Table 6.27). In comparison, a total of 92.9% of individuals in the matched control group had no more than one subtest with a score of 70 or less.

Individuals With Learning Disabilities in Reading

The WIAT–II was administered to a sample of 123 individuals, aged 7–18 years (M = 11 years), diagnosed with a specific learning disability in reading. The diagnosis of a learning disability in reading was made by the individual's school district based on comprehensive assessment scores that met eligibility criteria within the district for learning disabilities. The sample was 28% female and 72% male. Table 6.21 presents the means and standard deviations for the subtest and composite standard scores for the clinical group and the matched control group. The mean standard scores range from 74.00 (Word Reading) to 91.92 (Oral Expression) for the subtests and from 73.75 (Reading) to 88.31 (Oral Language) for the composites. The differences between the clinical group and the matched control group are significantly large, particularly in the case of subtests relevant to reading (22.67 for the Reading Composite but only 11.05 for the Oral Language Composite). Because the expressive language skills being measured by the Oral Expression and Listening Comprehension subtests are less dependent upon reading skills, one would expect these areas to be less affected by a learning disability in reading, as shown in this study. Table 6.21 also presents the number of individuals whose subtest and composite standard scores are 70 or less. For individuals diagnosed with a learning disability in reading, 19% had Reading Composite scores of 70 or less. Eighteen percent of the individuals had subtest scores of 70 or lower in Reading Comprehension; 28% scored 70 or lower on Word Reading; and 24% had scores of 70 or less on Pseudoword Decoding. Only 9% had Math Reasoning scores of 70 or less.

An examination of the Reading Speed and Target Words supplemental scores indicates that individuals diagnosed with learning disabilities in reading take longer to read passages and demonstrate less accuracy in comprehension and reading words aloud than individuals in the matched control

Table 6.20.
Mean Performance of Individuals With Emotional Disturbance and the Matched Control Group

Subtests/Composites	Emotional Disturbance			Matched Control Group			Mean Difference of the Two Samples		
	Mean	SD	% With Score ≤ 70	Mean	SD	% With Score ≤ 70	Difference	t Value	p Value
Subtests									
Word Reading	89.37	16.67	13	98.71	13.29	4	8.62	4.23	< .01
Numerical Operations	85.48	16.68	16	96.80	16.40	7	10.75	4.75	< .01
Reading Comprehension	86.45	19.29	14	100.50	11.53	1	14.08	5.68	< .01
Spelling	89.33	15.97	8	98.20	14.10	4	8.85	4.06	< .01
Pseudoword Decoding	91.72	16.72	12	101.24	12.54	1	9.35	3.65	< .01
Math Reasoning	87.25	16.00	15	99.71	14.03	4	12.62	5.83	< .01
Written Expression	86.02	17.13	20	95.76	14.03	6	10.06	4.68	< .01
Listening Comprehension	93.15	15.63	6	98.48	13.27	2	5.24	2.66	< .01
Oral Expression	95.34	13.54	0	98.61	11.19	1	3.42	1.81	.07
Composites									
Reading	86.34	18.14	14	98.21	12.08	2	11.63	4.02	< .01
Mathematics	84.82	17.99	19	98.05	16.48	5	13.04	5.37	< .01
Written Language	85.84	17.60	18	96.18	14.22	4	10.79	4.74	< .01
Oral Language	92.73	14.28	2	97.56	12.20	2	4.67	2.46	< .05
Total	87.02	16.76	11	96.63	12.92	2	9.59	2.98	< .01

Note. N = 85.

Table 6.21.
Mean Performance of Individuals With Learning Disabilities in Reading and the Matched Control Group

Subtests/Composites	Learning Disabilities in Reading			Matched Control Group			Mean Difference of the Two Samples		
	Mean	SD	% With Score ≤ 70	Mean	SD	% With Score ≤ 70	Difference	t Value	p Value
Subtests									
Word Reading	74.00	10.67	28	100.30	13.24	1	25.89	17.01	< .01
Numerical Operations	86.03	14.00	9	102.75	13.09	2	16.58	10.07	< .01
Reading Comprehension	79.56	15.65	18	100.95	10.94	0	20.00	10.69	< .01
Spelling	77.77	9.52	18	99.58	13.09	0	21.48	14.98	< .01
Pseudoword Decoding	76.92	9.69	24	101.55	12.55	2	23.43	13.66	< .01
Math Reasoning	86.29	13.27	9	101.41	13.89	2	14.88	8.29	< .01
Written Expression	79.79	11.89	20	97.36	14.68	6	17.50	9.31	< .01
Listening Comprehension	89.12	16.05	11	101.12	14.35	2	12.22	6.67	< .01
Oral Expression	91.92	15.13	7	98.67	13.52	2	6.52	3.40	< .01
Composites									
Reading	73.75	11.81	19	99.94	12.08	0	22.67	11.23	< .01
Mathematics	84.56	13.30	12	102.19	14.43	2	17.97	9.73	< .01
Written Language	76.36	10.98	20	98.06	14.26	2	21.67	12.38	< .01
Oral Language	88.31	16.47	11	99.13	13.68	2	11.05	5.90	< .01
Total	78.63	10.54	11	99.71	12.93	1	18.96	8.37	< .01

Note. N = 123.

group. The mean scores for Reading Comprehension, Target Words, and Reading Speed (in seconds) are significantly lower for the reading disabled group than for the matched control group. For the WIAT–II, a higher Reading Speed score indicates reading that is slower. The clinical group had a mean Reading Speed of 120.15 seconds, while the matched control group had a mean Reading Speed of 100.95 seconds. The number of Target Words correctly read by the clinical group was 53.03, while the number of Target Words correctly read by the matched control group was 63.73. Individuals diagnosed with learning disabilities in reading demonstrate a distinct pattern of scores and overall performance on the WIAT–II, making the WIAT–II a useful tool in learning disability diagnosis.

Individuals With Learning Disabilities Not Specific to Reading

The WIAT–II was administered to a sample of 109 individuals, aged 7–19 years (M = 12 years), diagnosed with learning disabilities not specific to reading. The diagnosis of a learning disability was made by the individual's school district based on comprehensive assessment scores that met eligibility criteria within the district for learning disabilities. This clinical group included, for example, individuals diagnosed with learning disabilities in mathematics. The sample was 51% female and 49% male. Table 6.22 presents the means and standard deviations for the subtest and composite standard scores for the clinical group and the matched control group. The standard score differences between the two groups are significantly large. For individuals diagnosed with learning disabilities, the level of performance is low, particularly for those subtests that assess reading or mathematics achievement. The mean standard scores range from 73.23 (Reading Comprehension) to 90.67 (Oral Expression) for the subtests and from 71.29 (Mathematics) to 85.44 (Oral Language) for the composites. For the individuals diagnosed with a learning disability, 37% had Mathematics composite scores of 70 or less, 26% had Reading composite scores of 70 or less, but only 8% had Oral Language composite scores of 70 or less.

As with individuals diagnosed with mental retardation, expressive language may represent a relative strength for individuals diagnosed with learning disabilities, as indicated by the relatively high scores on the Oral Expression and Listening Comprehension subtests. The pattern of performance for this clinical group, while less distinct than that for the learning disability in reading group, still indicates that the WIAT–II can be useful in identifying achievement deficits among those with more generalized learning disabilities.

Individuals With ADHD

The WIAT–II was administered to a sample of 179 individuals diagnosed with ADHD as defined in the *DSM–IV* (APA, 1994). The individuals were aged 5–18 years (M = 12 years). The sample was 22% female and 78% male. Table 6.23 presents the means and standard deviations for the subtest and composite standard scores for the clinical group and the matched control group. All means are within the expected range for the clinical group, ranging from 91.95 (Written Expression) to 100.11 (Listening Comprehension). The lowest mean standard scores occur for the Written Expression and Spelling subtests and the Written Language composite. It is reasonable to hypothesize that the Written Expression and Spelling subtests require greater sustained effort, paired with concentration and attention to detail, and are thus more challenging for individuals with ADHD than are subtests such as Listening Comprehension.

Table 6.22.
Mean Performance of Individuals With Learning Disabilities not Specific to Reading and the Matched Control Group

Subtests/Composites	Learning Disabilities not Specific to Reading			Matched Control Group			Mean Difference of the Two Samples		
	Mean	SD	% With Score ≤ 70	Mean	SD	% With Score ≤ 70	Difference	t Value	p Value
Subtests									
Word Reading	76.24	14.48	34	98.30	15.64	6	20.98	9.86	< .01
Numerical Operations	74.98	11.63	30	97.80	16.20	8	22.31	11.42	< .01
Reading Comprehension	73.23	20.16	33	99.31	16.20	3	26.43	9.53	< .01
Spelling	77.41	10.78	25	99.59	13.97	0	21.57	12.37	< .01
Pseudoword Decoding	79.33	12.70	26	100.80	14.61	1	19.95	9.15	< .01
Math Reasoning	73.86	10.16	34	96.23	15.46	4	21.47	10.97	< .01
Written Expression	78.22	12.61	24	96.13	16.58	6	18.30	9.21	< .01
Listening Comprehension	86.04	13.62	13	99.02	13.64	3	12.41	6.90	< .01
Oral Expression	90.67	12.53	2	97.91	14.21	2	7.16	3.67	< .01
Composites									
Reading	74.73	14.94	26	99.64	13.38	0	24.15	9.34	< .01
Mathematics	71.29	10.10	37	96.21	15.51	6	23.48	11.98	< .01
Written Language	74.88	11.31	24	98.12	15.88	5	22.83	11.25	< .01
Oral Language	85.44	12.39	8	96.82	14.41	4	10.82	5.96	< .01
Total	74.96	8.22	15	99.00	13.28	0	23.97	9.82	< .01

Note. N = 109.

Table 6.23.
Mean Performance of Individuals With ADHD and the Matched Control Group

Subtests/Composites	ADHD			Matched Control Group			Mean Difference of the Two Samples		
	Mean	SD	% With Score ≤ 70	Mean	SD	% With Score ≤ 70	Difference	t Value	p Value
Subtests									
Word Reading	96.57	16.51	7	102.12	13.22	2	5.50	3.61	< .01
Numerical Operations	94.88	13.22	5	103.02	14.44	2	8.06	5.63	< .01
Reading Comprehension	95.22	18.83	7	101.70	13.41	2	6.09	3.53	< .01
Spelling	93.90	14.54	4	102.22	13.13	1	8.09	5.83	< .01
Pseudoword Decoding	97.16	15.04	4	103.75	13.40	2	6.52	3.53	< .01
Math Reasoning	95.82	15.16	3	102.61	14.24	2	6.78	4.62	< .01
Written Expression	91.95	14.71	6	100.53	14.98	2	7.87	4.71	< .01
Listening Comprehension	100.11	14.38	2	104.43	13.40	3	3.92	3.24	< .01
Oral Expression	98.14	14.00	2	100.04	13.21	2	2.01	1.49	.14
Composites									
Reading	95.41	17.07	4	101.56	13.71	2	5.91	2.97	< .01
Mathematics	94.18	14.21	7	102.84	14.94	2	8.42	5.74	< .01
Written Language	92.02	14.64	8	101.57	14.68	2	8.43	5.25	< .01
Oral Language	98.33	14.31	2	101.91	12.98	2	3.45	2.70	< .01
Total	94.54	13.73	2	102.14	12.19	0	6.76	3.65	< .01

Note. N = 179.

Differences in scores between individuals diagnosed with ADHD and the matched control group ranged from 2.01 (Oral Expression) to 8.09 (Spelling). With the exception of the Oral Expression subtest, all differences were significant. However, the differences in standard-score points are relatively small. Additional evidence indicates that the clinical group does not differ appreciably from the matched control group: 82.1% of individuals diagnosed with ADHD had all subtest scores above 70; 91.1% of individuals in the matched control group had subtest scores above 70 (see Table 6.27). Many individuals diagnosed with ADHD were receiving medication (e.g., Ritalin®) that may have mitigated the adverse effects of this disorder on learning and performance.

Individuals With Comorbid ADHD and Learning Disabilities

The WIAT–II was administered to a sample of 54 individuals, aged 7–18 years (M = 11 years), diagnosed with both ADHD and learning disabilities. The dual diagnosis of ADHD and a learning disability was made by the individual's school district based on comprehensive assessment scores that met eligibility criteria within the district for ADHD and learning disabilities. The sample was 26% female and 74% male. Table 6.24 presents the means and standard deviations for the subtest and composite standard scores for the clinical group and the matched control group. The mean standard scores range from 81.10 (Pseudoword Decoding) to 95.60 (Listening Comprehension) for the subtests and from 80.50 (Reading) to 91.74 (Oral Language) for the composites. The differences between the ADHD and learning disabilities group and the matched control group are significantly large, with the smallest differences found for the Listening Comprehension and Oral Expression subtest scores. For the clinical group, scores appear to be depressed, with the Oral Language composite scores being the least affected by disability.

Individuals With Hearing Impairments

The WIAT–II was administered to a sample of 31 individuals, aged 6–13 and 17 years (M = 11 years), who were diagnosed with a hearing impairment, ranging from mild to profound, at the time of testing. Thirty-five percent of the individuals were administered the WIAT–II using the aural method of communication. For the remaining 65%, administration procedures were adapted by implementing signed language (American Sign Language or signed English) either exclusively or in combination with the aural method. The sample was 71% female and 29% male. The WIAT–II was administered by examiners who are certified to test a hearing impaired individual. Table 6.25 presents the means and standard deviations for the subtest and composite standard scores for the clinical group and the matched control group. The mean standard scores range from 77.74 (Reading Comprehension) to 89.58 (Oral Expression) for the subtests and from 82.77 (Mathematics) to 84.00 (Written Language) for the composites. The use of signing for the majority of individuals would have altered the Listening Comprehension task sufficiently that it no longer assessed listening skills. Therefore, the Listening Comprehension subtest and Oral Language composite scores are not reported. In general, the scores of individuals diagnosed with hearing impairments are lower than those of the matched control group. Mean score differences, found in Table 6.25, indicate that individuals diagnosed with hearing impairments scored significantly lower than individuals in the matched control group.

Table 6.24.
Mean Performance of Individuals With Combined ADHD and Learning Disabilities and the Matched Control Group

Subtests/Composites	Combined ADHD With Learning Disabilities			Matched Control Group			Mean Difference of the Two Samples		
	Mean	SD	% With Score ≤ 70	Mean	SD	% With Score ≤ 70	Difference	t Value	p Value
Subtests									
Word Reading	81.10	14.48	19	104.74	13.90	4	23.88	8.63	< .01
Numerical Operations	86.46	16.27	20	107.38	13.51	0	21.79	7.28	< .01
Reading Comprehension	85.57	16.28	17	103.31	14.16	2	18.35	5.56	< .01
Spelling	81.22	10.51	9	106.59	13.70	2	26.44	10.28	< .01
Pseudoword Decoding	81.10	15.07	26	105.09	13.06	0	23.91	9.11	< .01
Math Reasoning	86.56	15.42	11	105.62	13.14	0	18.82	6.35	< .01
Written Expression	82.12	13.46	13	102.92	16.91	6	20.65	6.96	< .01
Listening Comprehension	95.60	16.88	6	104.42	14.21	4	8.22	3.03	< .01
Oral Expression	91.82	15.42	9	102.84	15.05	0	11.10	3.73	< .01
Composites									
Reading	80.50	14.31	15	103.91	14.47	2	24.19	7.11	< .01
Mathematics	84.98	15.78	15	107.37	14.17	0	22.92	7.35	< .01
Written Language	80.63	10.78	13	105.57	16.74	6	26.11	8.79	< .01
Oral Language	91.74	16.36	7	104.25	15.44	4	11.76	3.82	< .01
Total	82.69	10.50	7	104.46	15.09	4	23.23	6.98	< .01

Note. N = 54.

Table 6.25.
Mean Performance of Individuals With Hearing Impairment and the Matched Control Group

Subtests/Composites	Hearing Impairment			Matched Control Group			Mean Difference of the Two Samples		
	Mean	SD	% With Score ≤ 70	Mean	SD	% With Score ≤ 70	Difference	t Value	p Value
Subtests									
Word Reading	85.34	19.69	26	103.93	14.16	0	19.18	4.70	< .01
Numerical Operations	87.94	19.82	26	102.97	13.03	0	15.03	3.45	< .01
Reading Comprehension	77.74	23.99	32	97.33	16.43	3	20.40	4.82	< .01
Spelling	85.04	17.72	13	99.79	13.67	3	17.00	5.77	< .01
Pseudoword Decoding	87.57	15.87	16	108.09	12.87	0	20.13	3.69	< .01
Math Reasoning	81.65	18.84	29	99.27	14.44	3	17.67	4.54	< .01
Written Expression	87.04	20.65	19	99.71	13.14	0	15.23	3.61	< .01
Oral Expression	89.58	13.11	3	101.47	18.65	3	12.07	3.76	< .01
Composites									
Reading	82.82	21.85	16	103.81	13.58	0	17.62	3.54	< .01
Mathematics	82.77	21.04	32	101.62	12.98	0	18.69	4.30	< .01
Written Language	84.00	20.11	26	99.96	13.49	0	19.38	5.29	< .01
Total	83.08	17.91	10	101.15	11.62	0	17.18	4.12	< .01

Note. N = 31.

Individuals With Speech and/or Language Impairment

The WIAT–II was administered to a sample of 49 individuals, aged 5–8 years ($M = 7$ years), diagnosed with an expressive language disorder or a combination expressive and receptive language disorder. Individuals were required to have a PIQ, VIQ, or FSIQ score greater than 80 based on school records, and the diagnosis of a speech and/or language impairment was made by the individual's school district based on comprehensive assessment scores that met eligibility criteria within the district. The sample was 39% female and 61% male. Table 6.26 presents the means and standard deviations for the subtest and composite standard scores for the clinical group and the matched control group. The mean standard scores range from 86.24 (Reading Comprehension) to 95.89 (Numerical Operations) for the subtests and from 86.33 (Reading) to 91.09 (Written Language) for the composites. The differences in scores between individuals diagnosed with speech and/or language impairment and individuals in the matched control group vary: the largest difference is 16.29 for Pseudoword Decoding, followed by 15.10 for Reading Comprehension and 12.11 for Word Reading. The mean standard score for the Numerical Operations and Written Expression subtests did not differ between the two groups. For the most part, those subtests that did not require extensive phonological skills showed the smallest differences in scores between the clinical and matched control groups.

While achievement scores in reading are depressed for individuals diagnosed with speech and/or language impairment, they are not always extremely low. The proportion of individuals in the clinical group with Reading Comprehension subtest scores of 70 or less is 8%; the proportion with Pseudoword Decoding scores that fall in this range is 0%, as shown in Table 6.26. It is reasonable to hypothesize that because individuals diagnosed with speech and/or language impairments were receiving appropriate intervention, such action would improve performance in language-relevant subtests. It should also be noted that the membership of the speech and/or language impairment group was young children in the primary grades. It is likely that these children have not been in reading instruction long enough to begin to demonstrate a wide gap between their performance and that of their grade or age peers.

Table 6.26.
Mean Performance of Individuals With Speech and/or Language Impairment and the Matched Control Group

Subtests/Composites	Speech and Language Impairment			Matched Control Group			Mean Difference of the Two Samples		
	Mean	SD	% With Score ≤ 70	Mean	SD	% With Score ≤ 70	Difference	t Value	p Value
Subtests									
Word Reading	89.70	11.79	4	101.91	15.78	0	12.11	4.23	< .01
Numerical Operations	95.89	15.76	6	96.70	14.43	2	0.77	0.28	.78
Reading Comprehension	86.24	13.45	8	100.37	13.32	2	15.10	4.95	< .01
Spelling	90.69	14.54	8	100.71	13.28	2	9.81	3.21	< .01
Pseudoword Decoding	87.03	8.18	0	101.10	15.47	0	16.29	5.55	< .01
Math Reasoning	88.95	14.01	10	100.35	14.78	2	10.30	3.20	< .01
Written Expression	92.44	13.57	2	98.85	14.56	0	6.33	1.81	< .08
Listening Comprehension	91.76	16.57	6	101.94	15.82	4	9.91	2.78	< .01
Oral Expression	89.83	14.45	6	96.20	14.35	4	6.51	2.22	< .05
Composites									
Reading	86.33	9.99	4	103.78	17.97	0	19.16	4.40	< .01
Mathematics	90.35	15.02	8	98.50	13.67	0	7.28	2.26	< .05
Written Language	91.09	14.12	4	100.74	13.74	2	10.17	2.82	< .01
Oral Language	88.84	15.76	8	98.16	16.59	4	9.13	2.46	< .05
Total	89.74	11.34	0	103.08	14.32	0	14.70	1.90	.09

Note. N = 49.

Summary

The data on the internal consistency, test–retest stability, and interscorer reliability of the WIAT–II scores demonstrate a consistently high level of precision, especially for the composite scores, with a few exceptions (see Tables 6.1–6.9). The WIAT–II subtests, with the exception of the Listening Comprehension subtest, reveal very small practice effects, with test–retest scores differing by 2–3 standard-score points. The effect of error is greater on the differences between subtest scores than it is on the differences between composite scores.

The accumulated data from studies of the WIAT–II, including content-, construct-, and criterion-related evidence of validity, indicate that the subtests and composites adequately measure the achievement constructs that they were designed to measure. Correlations of the WIAT–II scores with other achievement test scores are moderate to high and consistent across a variety of individually and group-administered tests. In addition, the mean standard scores are consistent across a variety of samples administered the WIAT–II and other individually administered achievement tests. This pattern indicates that the level of performance of the WIAT–II standardization sample aligns well with performance on comparable tests and is in the expected range. Correlations in the range of .30 to .78 (see Table K.13) are typical of the relation between the WIAT–II scores and the scores on the Wechsler scales. Data on studies with clinical groups show expected patterns of mean standard scores, although the samples were relatively small and not intended as randomly stratified normative groups (e.g., for individuals diagnosed with hearing impairments). Data from the special group studies illustrate that the WIAT–II subtests are effective in identifying large percentages of individuals with these disabilities. The percentage of individuals in the clinical and matched control groups obtaining standard scores of 70 points or less on specific numbers of WIAT–II subtests are presented in Table 6.27. It is expected that independent research studies will be conducted with the WIAT–II, providing additional evidence of test validity and extending its clinical and research utility. The results of the current WIAT–II studies, although based on small clinical samples, suggest that the WIAT–II affords an excellent degree of accuracy in identifying individuals with learning disabilities.

Table 6.27.
Percentage of the WIAT–II Age-Based Subtest and Composite Standard Scores Less Than or Equal to 70 for the Clinical and Matched Control Groups

Subtests With Scores ≤ 70	Gifted[a]		Mild Mental Retardation		Emotional Disturbance		Learning Disability–Reading		Learning Disability	
	Clinical	Matched Control	Clinical	Matched Control	Clinical	Matched Control	Clinical	Matched Control	Clinical	Matched Control
0	48.0	87.8	0.0	76.9	57.6	84.7	43.2	87.8	20.2	83.5
1	25.2	9.8	0.0	10.2	21.2	8.2	19.5	9.8	21.1	9.2
2	17.1	2.4	2.6	2.6	8.2	2.4	14.6	1.6	18.3	0.9
3	6.5	0.0	2.6	10.3	3.5	3.5	7.3	0.8	17.4	4.6
4	1.6	0.0	12.8	0.0	2.4	0.0	8.9	0.0	10.1	1.8
5	1.6	0.0	12.8	0.0	1.2	1.2	4.1	0.0	8.3	0.0
6	0.0	0.0	17.9	0.0	1.2	0.0	1.6	0.0	3.7	0.0
7	0.0	0.0	30.8	0.0	3.5	0.0	0.0	0.0	0.9	0.0
8	0.0	0.0	15.4	0.0	1.2	0.0	0.8	0.0	0.0	0.0
9	0.0	0.0	5.1	0.0	0.0	0.0	0.0	0.0	0.0	0.0
n	123	123	39	39	85	85	123	123	109	109

Composites[b] With Scores ≤ 70	Gifted[a]		Mild Mental Retardation		Emotional Disturbance		Learning Disability–Reading		Learning Disability	
	Clinical	Matched Control	Clinical	Matched Control	Clinical	Matched Control	Clinical	Matched Control	Clinical	Matched Control
0	48.8	90.3	0.0	84.6	68.2	92.9	59.3	94.3	35.8	89.9
1	24.4	7.3	10.3	10.3	17.7	2.4	26.8	4.9	37.6	5.5
2	13.0	1.6	12.8	5.1	4.7	2.3	3.3	0.0	12.8	4.6
3	10.6	0.8	35.9	0.0	3.5	1.2	5.7	0.8	9.2	0.0
4	2.4	0.0	12.8	0.0	3.5	1.2	3.3	0.0	4.6	0.0
5	0.8	0.0	28.2	0.0	2.4	0.0	1.6	0.0	0.0	0.0
n	123	123	39	39	85	85	123	123	109	109

[a] Percentages based on subtests with scores ≥ 130.
[b] Composites include Reading, Mathematics, Written Language, Oral Language, and the Total Composite.

Table 6.27.

Percentage of the WIAT–II Age-Based Subtest and Composite Standard Scores Less Than or Equal to 70 for the Clinical and Matched Control Groups *(continued)*

Subtests With Scores ≤ 70	ADHD		Learning Disability/ADHD		Hearing Impairment		Speech/Language Impairment	
	Clinical	Matched Control	Clinical	Matched Control	Clinical	Matched Control	Clinical	Matched Control
0	82.1	91.1	46.3	92.6	51.6	93.6	77.6	89.8
1	6.7	3.9	20.4	1.9	3.2	3.2	12.2	8.2
2	4.4	3.3	14.8	1.8	6.5	0.0	0.0	0.0
3	3.9	1.1	3.7	3.7	6.5	0.0	2.0	0.0
4	1.1	0.6	9.3	0.0	19.3	3.2	8.2	2.0
5	0.6	0.0	1.8	0.0	12.9	0.0	0.0	0.0
6	0.6	0.0	3.7	0.0	0.0	0.0	0.0	0.0
7	0.6	0.0	0.0	0.0	0.0	0.0	0.0	0.0
8	0.0	0.0	0.0	0.0	0.0	0.0	0.0	0.0
9	0.0	0.0	0.0	0.0	0.0	0.0	0.0	0.0
n	179	179	54	54	31	31	49	49

Composites[a] With Scores ≤ 70	ADHD		Learning Disability/ADHD		Hearing Impairment		Speech/Language Impairment	
	Clinical	Matched Control	Clinical	Matched Control	Clinical	Matched Control	Clinical	Matched Control
0	86.6	94.9	64.8	94.4	58.1	96.8	79.6	93.9
1	7.3	3.4	20.4	0.0	16.1	3.2	16.3	6.1
2	3.3	1.7	11.1	1.9	9.7	0.0	4.1	0.0
3	1.7	0.0	1.9	3.7	6.4	0.0	0.0	0.0
4	1.1	0.0	0.0	0.0	9.7	0.0	0.0	0.0
5	0.0	0.0	1.8	0.0	0.0	0.0	0.0	0.0
n	179	179	54	54	31	31	49	49

[a] Composites include Reading, Mathematics, Written Language, Oral Language, and the Total Composite.

7 Interpretation

This chapter presents quantitative guidelines and procedures and qualitative approaches for interpreting the WIAT–II results. The first part of this chapter focuses on the general assumptions that underlie both quantitative and qualitative WIAT–II interpretation. The quantitative section that follows next includes a brief discussion of the types of derived WIAT–II scores available, information on the calculation of score differences, and the rationale and guidelines for conducting and analyzing ability–achievement discrepancies. The qualitative section provides suggestions and recommendations for conducting a skills analysis of the examinee's WIAT–II item responses. Included with this error analysis are suggested intervention strategies for addressing specific areas of concern. The chapter concludes with a recommended eight-step approach to basic interpretation of the WIAT–II results.

Assumptions Underlying the WIAT–II Interpretation

A fundamental assumption underlying the use of all assessment instruments, including the WIAT–II, is that prior to testing, the examiner determines whether or not the test is an appropriate instrument for answering the referral question or questions. Test attributes must be matched with the characteristics of the child and with the purposes for testing (Stone, 1995). Appropriate matching will provide a more accurate and valid measurement of the examinee's functioning. Also important is a reevaluation of the test's suitability during the interpretation of test results.

Guidelines for matching a test to test purposes (i.e., the referral questions) have been set forth in the *Standards for Educational and Psychological Testing* (1999). If the test user makes substantial changes in the administration, format, or mode of testing or applies the test results to a purpose for which the test was not designed or psychometrically validated, "the user bears special responsibility for validation" (p. 11). Further, "it is incumbent on the user to justify the new use, collecting new evidence if necessary" (p. 18). For example, if the examinee has a severe disability (e.g., blindness, paralysis) that interferes with perception of the test stimuli or completion of item responses, test scores may not be valid, unless effective adaptations of test procedures have been successful. In all cases, any change or adaptation of the standard administration procedures necessitates caution in the use of quantitative data such as the norms or other derived score information.

Recommendations for ethical test use, or "best practice suggestions," often state that test scores should not be interpreted in isolation from other information about the child. (Kamphaus, 1993; Sattler, 2001; Stone, 1995). The best interpretations incorporate all available information, including the examinee's developmental, medical, family, social, and academic history; information gained from observations (if possible) of the examinee's behavior in the classroom and his or her behavior and motivation during testing; other test results (including information from teachers, parents, or other family members); and any unusual characteristics or disabilities of the individual.

Proper interpretation of the WIAT–II results requires familiarity with measurement concepts (e.g., the characteristics of standard scores, the use of standard error of measurement) and selection of test scores (e.g., standard scores, percentiles, NCEs) that are appropriate for the purpose of test use. Reviews of these concepts are available in several excellent assessment texts available, such as those by Kamphaus (1993), Reynolds and Kamphaus (1990), Salvia and Ysseldyke (1991), and Sattler (2001).

Quantitative Interpretation of the WIAT–II Performance

Types of Quantitative Scores Available

Raw Scores

A raw score is the sum of all correct item scores or of the number of points earned for a subtest. The WIAT–II raw scores cannot be accurately compared to each other because each subtest has a different number of items and, therefore, a different range of possible scores. Comparisons between an examinee's scores and those of his or her peers are best based on derived scores, such as grade-based norms or age-based norms.

Derived Scores

The types of WIAT–II derived scores include standard scores (deviation scores, NCEs, and stanines), percentile ranks, quartile-based scores, decile-based scores, grade equivalents, and age equivalents. These derived scores vary significantly in the amount of information and the degree of psychometric precision or accuracy they provide. Table l.2 provides a description of the WIAT–II derived scores. Refer to the appendices in the *Scoring and Normative Supplement for Grades PreK–12* and the *Supplement for College Students and Adults* for tables of the WIAT–II derived scores.

Standard Scores

Standard scores are a normalized transformation of a distribution of raw scores and have a given mean and standard deviation. This transformation allows for a measurement in standard deviation units of how far an individual's score is from the mean or average score.

The distribution of the WIAT–II standard scores forms a normal curve. The apex of the curve, the mean (and median), is at a score of 100, and the scores have a standard deviation (*SD*) of 15. Approximately 68% of individuals in the standardization sample obtained scores between 85 and 115 (1 *SD* on either side of the mean of 100), and approximately 95% obtained scores between 70 and 130. These percentages are the same for the WIAT–II subtest standard scores and the composite standard scores. When an individual's scores are compared to scores obtained by others in the same grade, the grade-based norms (Appendix C) should be used. For examinees in Grades PreK (aged 5) through 8, the grade-based standard scores are reported separately for fall, winter, and spring. For Grades 9 through 16, these standard scores are reported for whole years. When an individual's scores are compared to scores obtained by others of the same age, the age-based norms (Appendix F) should be used. The WIAT–II age-based standard scores are reported by 4-month intervals for Ages 4:0 through 13:11 and in annual intervals for students aged 14 through 19. Standard Scores for adults are reported by five age bands: ages 17–19, ages 20–25, ages 26–35, ages 36–50, and ages 51–85. Annual intervals were deemed most appropriate for the older students because of the slow rate of academic growth from fall to spring and from grade to grade, as evidenced in the subtest and composite mean scores for the standardization sample.

For each subtest and composite, standard scores range from 40 to 160. This common metric enables direct comparisons between the subtest standard scores and the composite standard scores. The WIAT–II standard scores are also directly comparable to scores on the Wechsler intelligence scales. For comparisons of the WIAT–II standard scores to normalized standard scores from ability tests, the scores from the alternative test may need to be converted to the appropriate metric. Moreover, comparisons to scores from tests published by different developers should be conducted with caution, particularly when the tests have markedly different standardization dates. The characteristics of each test, the comparability of the psychometric qualities of each test, the comparability of the years in which the tests were standardized, and the characteristics of the standardization sample must be considered before direct comparisons are made. By definition, standard scores derive their meaning from the performances of individuals in the standardization sample for the specific test.

The conversion begins with the transformation of each score on the alternative test to a z-score metric (mean of 0, SD of 1). For this transformation, the mean of the alternative test metric is subtracted from the obtained score on the alternative test, and that result is divided by the standard deviation for the metric. For example, an IQ score of 84 from the *Stanford-Binet Intelligence Scale, Fourth Edition* (SB–IV; Thorndike, Hagen, & Sattler, 1986) corresponds to a z score of -1.0 because the SB-IV score metric has a mean of 100 and a standard deviation of 16:

$$\frac{84 - 100}{16} = {}^-1.0$$

The conversion of the z score for the alternative test to the WIAT–II standard score metric is completed by multiplying the z score by 15 and adding 100.

The WIAT–II standard scores can also be compared to other types of normalized derived scores, such as the subtest scaled scores from the Wechsler intelligence scales. For example, a WIAT–II standard score of 85 (1 SD below the mean) is comparable to a Wechsler subtest scaled score of 7 (which has a mean of 10 and a standard deviation of 3). The standard score of 85 is also comparable to a score of 40 in a normalized *T*-score metric (mean of 50, standard deviation of 10) and to a score of -1.0 in a normalized z-score metric (mean of 0, standard deviation of 1). See Table 1.2 for a comparison of standard scores, percentile scores, quartiles, NCEs, and stanines.

Normal Curve Equivalents

Normal curve equivalents, or NCEs, developed by Tallmadge and Wood (1978), were used in research and program evaluation as a means of quantifying the academic progress of groups of children who were participating in federally funded programs such as the Chapter 1 program. Thus, NCEs typically are not used for evaluating the progress of an individual but for evaluating the progress of groups of individuals (e.g., a class from spring to spring). NCE scores range from 1 to 99, with a mean of 50 and standard deviation of 21.06, and represent equally spaced units along the normal curve. NCE values of 1, 50, and 99 correspond to percentiles of the same value, but intermediate NCE values do not correspond to percentiles. For examinees in Grades PreK–12 or aged 4–19 years, the WIAT–II standard scores can be directly converted into grade-based NCE scores (Table D.3) or age-based NCE scores (Table G.3).

Stanines

A *stanine* ("standard nine") is the score that results from a conversion of an age-based or grade-based standard score to a 9-point scale. Stanines are normalized scores ranging from 1 to 9, with a mean of 5 and standard deviation of 2. Each stanine represents a range of standard scores. The use of stanines can help prevent the overinterpretation of small differences in scores. The WIAT–II scores can be converted into grade-based stanines (Table D.3) or age-based stanines (Table G.3).

Percentile Ranks

A percentile rank indicates the percentage of individuals in the standardization sample at a given age or grade who obtained scores less than or equal to a given *raw* score. Thus, a percentile rank indicates the standing of an individual relative to that of the individuals in the standardization sample. For example, if a child aged 6:0 attained a percentile rank of 70 on Word Reading, that child's score was higher than the scores of 70% of the 6-year-old children in the standardization sample.

Percentile ranks range from 1 to 99, with 50 always indicating median performance for an age or grade. Because percentile ranks are fairly easy to understand, they are often useful for explaining assessment results to parents and others who do not have an in-depth knowledge of psychometrics. However, as Kamphaus (1993) cautioned, when communicating results, the examiner must distinguish between percentile rank and the percent of items passed, because these are obviously very different scores.

Although percentile ranks can be compared across subtests, one important caution is that percentile ranks do not form an equal-increment scale. They tend to cluster near the median of 50, because more individuals obtain scores that fall near the center of the normal curve. Thus, for subtest raw scores near the median, a change of 1 raw-score point might translate into an increase of 8 percentile points. In other words, small score differences are unduly magnified. For subtest raw scores at either end of the normal curve, 1 raw-score point might translate into only 2 percentile points (and score difference are underemphasized). The WIAT–II standard scores can be converted into a grade-based percentile ranks (Table D.3) or age-based percentile ranks (Table G.3).

Quartile Scores

Quartile scores represent the distribution of percentile ranks divided into four equal parts. They are designated as the lower 25% (a quartile score of 1), 50% (a quartile score of 2, the median), 75% (a quartile score of 3), and upper 25% (a quartile score of 4) of the scores. For certain subtests of the WIAT–II, a finer categorization than quarters was calculated so that the lowest 5% of scores can be identified. In these cases, the lowest 5% of scores is given a quartile score of 0.

In the WIAT–II, supplemental scores for Target Words, Reading Speed, Written Expression Word Fluency, and Oral Expression Word Fluency are based on the quartile metric. The score for Reading Comprehension should be converted to a quartile-based score when calculating Reading Rate. Quartile-based scores (by grade) are provided in Appendix B; quartile-based scores (by age) are provided in Appendix E. Supplemental scores for Word Fluency, Word Count, Spelling Errors, and Punctuation Errors are also converted to quartile scores before they are added to the other item scores to calculate the subtest total raw score. This conversion ensures that the examinee's performance on the designated item receives the appropriate amount of credit added into the sum of scores for the subtest total raw score. For calculating the Reading Rate score, the total raw score for the Reading Comprehension subtest and the total raw score for Reading Speed must first be converted to grade-based quartile scores (Tables B.1 and B.3) or age-based quartile scores (Tables E.1 and E.3).

Decile-Based Scores

Decile-based scores represent the distribution of percentile ranks divided into ten equal parts and are designated in increments that correspond to 10%. The lowest decile-based score is 10 and includes scores between 0% and 10%; the highest decile-based score is 100 and includes scores between 90% and 100%. For the WIAT–II, the decile metric is used *only* for the timed alphabet writing task in the Written Expression subtest for examinees in Grades PreK through K. Tables B.4 (grade-based) and E.4 (age-based) provide decile scores for Alphabet Writing.

Grade Equivalents

A grade equivalent indicates the school grade and month of that grade for which a given total raw score is average or typical. For example, a grade equivalent of 4:2 for a Math Reasoning total raw score of 37 means that the score of 37 is at the center of the distribution of scores for students in the second month of Grade 4. Although grade equivalents were originally designed for tracking students' progress through an academic curriculum, the following technical attributes of this metric *significantly* limit its interpretive use.

First, grade equivalents are not directly comparable across subtests within the WIAT–II. For example, a grade equivalent of 5:2 for both Word Reading and Numerical Operations does not imply equal proficiency in the two curriculum areas because the student's percentile ranks for the two subtests may differ substantially.

Second, grade equivalents do not form equally spaced units throughout the scale. For example, the difference between fourth- and fifth-grade equivalent scores may not be the same as the difference between tenth- and eleventh-grade equivalent scores.

Third, a common belief is that children should be placed in the grade indicated by a grade equivalent or receive instruction for the grade indicated by the grade equivalent. This practice is a *misapplication* of these scores and is inaccurate because it involves an inappropriate comparison across normative groups. For example, a student in Grade 3 who obtains a grade equivalent of 5:1 on Numerical Operations shares with the average fifth grader *only the number of correct responses on the subtest*. The student in Grade 3 may not be able to work with the other mathematical elements such as fractions that appear in fifth-grade mathematics curriculum materials. Thus, the student's grade equivalent of 5:1 denotes a high total raw score for his or her grade, but it neither implies familiarity with Grade 5 material nor warrants the student's placement in Grade 5.

Fourth, grade equivalents at the extreme ends of the range are particularly difficult to interpret. On rare occasions, the grade equivalents for students in the middle grades range as low as 1:0 or as high as 12:9, scores indicating that the students are performing far below or far above average for their grade level. Such extreme equivalents do not mean that students should be presented with the curriculum content for that grade level. Sattler (2001) raised the following additional concerns regarding grade equivalents:

■ Grade equivalents, especially at the extreme ends of the range, are often obtained by interpolation and may not reflect the actual scores obtained by individuals in the standardization sample.

■ Grade equivalents are based on the assumption that academic growth progresses at a constant level throughout the school year. Research has not yet supported this assumption.

■ Grade equivalents at the upper levels will have limited meaning if applied to content that is not taught at those levels or content that is mastered at an early age.

In the WIAT–II, grade equivalents are available only at the subtest level. No grade equivalent scores are provided for composite scores because these scores are already corrected for grade. However, a grade equivalent for a composite score can be easily calculated: It is the average of the grade equivalent scores for the subtests that contribute to that composite score. For example, a grade equivalent for the Reading composite is the average of the three grade equivalent scores for Word Reading, Pseudoword Decoding, and Reading Comprehension. Table D.4 presents the WIAT–II grade equivalents.

Age Equivalents

An age equivalent is a derived score that indicates the age, in years and months, at which a given raw score is average or typical. Age equivalents have the same significant disadvantages as grade equivalents. Namely, comparisons between subtest age equivalents may be inaccurate; age equivalents do not form equally spaced units throughout the scale; a student should not be automatically assigned to an educational intervention strictly on the basis of age equivalency; and, extreme age equivalents (e.g., 5:0 or 17:0) may be misinterpreted as indicating that the student's performance is far below or far above average for his or her age. An extreme value does not mean that the student's performance resembles that of the extreme age group in every respect. Table G.4 presents the WIAT–II age equivalents. Age equivalent scores are not available for WIAT–II composite scores because these scores are already corrected for age. A composite age equivalent score is the average of the age equivalent scores of the contributing subtests.

Use of Subtest and Composite Scores

For many testing purposes, including the determination of learning disabilities, an examinee's profile of the WIAT–II subtest standard scores and percentile ranks will be the first interpretive step. An assessment of overall reading mastery, for example, should include an examination of as many components of the reading process as possible. Hence, the development of the Word Reading, Pseudoword Decoding, and Reading Comprehension subtests allows an evaluation of reading decoding (or word-attack skills), lexical access of sight words, reading comprehension, oral reading accuracy, and silent reading rate. Likewise, when an assessment of mathematical functioning is needed, math computation (Numerical Operations) should be assessed independently of Math Reasoning. Also, because proficient spelling requires the mastery of a complex set of rules, spelling performance should be examined separately from writing composition. Thus, the Spelling and Written Expression subtests measure both the mechanics and the quality of the writing response. Additionally, for purposes of screening for language-based learning difficulties, separate measurements of receptive and expressive language functioning can highlight problem areas. The Listening Comprehension and Oral Expression subtests can provide this kind of information.

In each of the Reading, Mathematics, Written Language, and Oral Language composites, multiple aspects of a curriculum area are merged (e.g., math calculation and math reasoning are represented in the Mathematics composite). Thus, the composite score is a broader, more global indication of academic achievement. At the same time, composite scores reflect many facets of the individual's achievement, within which there may be great variation. For example, an individual may demonstrate skills in Word Reading and Pseudoword Decoding that are commensurate with those of his or her grade-mates but have skills that are significantly below those of his or her peers in Reading Comprehension. As a result, the Reading composite score could mask specific deficits in comprehension. The total composite score provides a measure of an even broader, more general level of achievement. Thus, the total composite score should be interpreted with caution because of the diverse nature of the scores that it represents. Because of this diversity, the total composite score is not recommended for use in computing ability–achievement discrepancies.

Additionally, mixed comparisons of age-based and grade-based derived scores (standard scores, percentiles, stanines, etc.) should be conducted with caution. If a child is either young or old for his or her grade level, the child's age-based standard scores may differ from those based on grade norms. The reference groups for the two types of standard scores are quite different. The students in each grade in the standardization sample represented a heterogeneous mixture of ages, particularly in the upper grades. Therefore, a child's standing in a curriculum area, such as Spelling, may be significantly different when the comparison is made to the performance of peers of the same age (age-based norms) or to the performance of peers of the same grade (grade-based norms).

Score Differences

An important consideration in the quantitative interpretation of the WIAT–II results is the amount of difference between an examinee's own standard scores. Several comparisons can be made: between composite standard scores; between a subtest standard score and an average of subtest standard scores; and between single subtest standard scores. With this ipsative approach, the strengths and weaknesses identified are strengths and weaknesses relative to the individual's own achievement level. For example, a subtest standard score that is average in an absolute sense, that is, around 100, may still represent an area of weakness for an individual of extremely high achievement; conversely, a fairly low standard score may indicate a relative strength for an individual of generally limited achievement. The meaningfulness of the difference between two scores has two quite distinct aspects—the statistical significance of the difference and the base rate, or frequency, of the difference in the standardization sample.

The statistical significance of a difference between two scores (e.g., between the Reading and Oral Language composite standard scores or between the Word Reading and Reading Comprehension subtest standard scores) refers to the likelihood that the difference might occur because of chance variation or because of the unreliability of the scores. Expressed in another way, low probability levels (e.g., $p < .05$) associated with the difference between an examinee's standard scores indicate that such a difference is highly unlikely to be obtained if the "true" difference between the scores is zero.

The base rate of the difference between two scores refers to the incidence or frequency of such a difference in the standardization sample. Thus, the difference between an examinee's Reading composite and Oral Language composite standard scores can be significant in the statistical sense but not at all rare among individuals in the standardization group.

Data about the statistical significance of a difference between scores and about the rarity of the difference are not the same and have different implications for test interpretation. Payne and Jones (1957) and Silverstein (1981) have provided in-depth discussions of the distinction between statistically and clinically meaningful differences between scores.

Differences Between Composite Standard Scores

Statistical Significance of Differences

The minimum difference between any pair of the four composite standard scores required for statistical significance at two levels of confidence (.15 and .05) are provided for age-based and grade-based scores. The difference between scores required for significance is computed from the *standard error of measurement of the difference* ($SE_{M_{diff}}$). This statistic provides an estimate of the standard deviation of the difference between two obtained scores when the "true" difference is zero. Multiplying this value by an appropriate factor yields the amount of difference that is statistically significant at any given level of confidence. Tables K.1 and K.2 in the supplements present the data separately for each grade (by fall and spring, respectively), and Table K.3 presents the data separately for each age in the standardization sample. Although these differences vary slightly from grade to grade and from age to age, average values for all grades or all ages, which are given in the last row of the tables, are generally sufficient for the purpose of assessing the significance of differences between an individual's scores.

Frequency of Differences

The frequency of composite standard score discrepancies of various magnitudes that occurred in the WIAT–II grade-based and age-based standardization samples are also provided (Tables K.4 and K.5, respectively). The tables indicate the cumulative percentages of individuals whose standard scores on each pair of composites differed by the given amount or more, in the direction indicated. For example, according to Table K.4, 10% of the children in the standardization sample obtained a Reading composite standard score that was 18 points less than their Mathematics composite standard score, while only 8% obtained a Reading composite standard score that was 18 points greater than their Mathematics composite standard score. Also according to Table K.4, 18% of the children in the standardization sample obtained an Oral Language composite standard score that was 14 points greater than their Written Language composite standard score.

Differences Between a Single Subtest Standard Score and an Average of Subtest Standard Scores

The profile of an individual's subtest standard scores on the WIAT–II can show appreciable variability among those scores. The interpretation of a particular subtest score as especially high or low should be preceded by consideration of the statistical significance of the difference and the population base rates. A common procedure for evaluating the potential meaningfulness of a subtest standard score that appears especially high or low involves the comparison of that score to the individual's average of standard scores on all subtests (or group of subtests that includes the subtest in question). A single score that is significantly greater than the person's own mean score may reflect a relative strength, whereas one that is significantly less than the mean may indicate a relative weakness. Davis (1959) derived the basic procedures for testing such differences for statistical significance. Silverstein (1982) refined the procedure to account for the fact that several comparisons are being made simultaneously.

Tables K.6–K.8 in the supplements present the differences between single subtest standard scores and the averages of subtest standard scores required for statistical significance (at the .15 and .05 levels) and the cumulative percentages of various differences obtained by the grade-based and age-based standardization samples. Because the number of appropriate subtests that can be administered depends on the individual's age or grade, the calculation of the average of subtest standard scores varies. Single subtest scores are compared to the average of all nine subtest scores or to the average of the six subtest scores (for examinees in Grade K, aged 5 or 6), or to the average of four subtest scores (for examinees in Grade PreK, aged 4 or 5). For example, as indicated in Table K.8, a Word Reading standard score that is at least 8 points greater than or less than the examinee's average standard score on nine subtests is significantly different from that average score at the .05 level of confidence.

Frequency of Differences

A difference between a single subtest standard score and the average of a group of subtest standard scores may be statistically significant but not especially unusual in the population. Thus, the fact that an individual's standard score on a single subtest, for example, Word Reading, is significantly less than the examinee's average of scores on all nine of the subtests does not indicate that the difference is necessarily meaningful. The difference may call for careful interpretation. For this purpose, the frequency of such a difference, whether it is rare or common among examinees in general, is important.

Tables K.6–K.8 provide data on the frequency of differences for the WIAT–II standardization sample. The following example illustrates the use of this part of the table. Table K.8 indicates that 10% or less of the standardization sample obtained a difference of 13 points between the Word Reading score and the mean score of the nine subtests.

Differences Between Subtest Standard Scores

The difference between the standard scores on a particular pair of subtests may also be of interest. For example, an examinee's score on Word Reading may be 8 standard score points greater than the score on Reading Comprehension. An interpretation of that difference must take into account whether or not such a difference is statistically significant. Tables K.9–K.11 provide, for every possible pair of WIAT–II subtests, the differences significant at the .15 level of confidence (above the diagonal) and at the .05 level of confidence (below the diagonal). The values represent the average score differences across grades (Tables K.9 and K.10) and across ages (Table K.11). As indicated in Table K.10, a 7-point difference between Word Reading and Reading Comprehension is significant at the .15 level but not at the .05 level, for which a difference of at least 9.79 standard score points is required for significance.

Intersubtest Scatter[1]

Intersubtest scatter is the variability of a person's standard scores across the subtests. Such variability is frequently considered as diagnostically significant. As with other score comparisons, the frequency of the scatter is important for interpretation because it provides evidence that the scatter exhibited in a particular protocol is relatively uncommon in the population. Although various measures of scatter are possible, the index used in the WIAT–II is the easiest to obtain: the simple difference between the examinee's highest and lowest subtest standard scores. Table K.12 shows the percentages of individuals in the WIAT–II standardization sample whose subtest standard scores exhibited various degrees of scatter. Again, the data reflect that the number of subtests composing the battery depends on the age or grade of the examinee. An example illustrates the use of this table.

For a Grade 7 examinee, a difference between the highest and lowest subtest scores (scatter) of 40 points occurred in only 15.6% of the standardization sample. This percentage indicates that this degree of scatter is unusual. A scatter of 20 points, however, is not rare, as evidenced by its occurrence in 83% of the sample.

---

[1]Analyses of variance were conducted to establish whether or not the differences between the subtest standard scores and their respective WIAT–II averages of scores varied by age or sex. Again, occasional statistically significant ($p < .05$) differences were noted among certain subtest scores, but the magnitudes of differences did not exceed one-third standard deviation (the level of practical significance suggested by Tallmadge and Wood, 1978). Therefore, a single set of frequencies is reported in Tables K.6, K.7, and K.8.

Ability–Achievement Discrepancy Analysis

Since the release of the WIAT and its advantageous link to the WISC–III, a growing number of professionals have used the WIAT/WISC–III combination to compare an individual's general ability to his or her level of achievement. Despite its limitations, the discrepancy between ability and achievement continues to be a key element in establishing specific learning disabilities (Kavale & Forness, 1995). Assessment of both ability and achievement for the purposes of documenting discrepancies was a cornerstone in the Education for All Handicapped Children Act of 1975 (Public Law 94-142) and continues in the Individuals with Disabilities Education Act (IDEA) Amendments of 1997 legislation. The WIAT–II provides measures for each of the seven traditional areas of achievement assessed in the establishment of specific learning disabilities: mathematics calculation, mathematics reasoning, basic word reading, reading comprehension, listening comprehension, oral expression, and written expression. This section of the manual describes the methods employed during the development of the WIAT–II to provide the numerical tables needed for evaluating discrepancies between ability (as measured by the WPPSI–R, WISC–III, or WAIS–III) and achievement as measured by the WIAT–II.

Despite the widespread use of discrepancy analysis, the examiner is cautioned to read and reflect on the inherent complexities of establishing true discrepancies, the many sources of measurement error, and the conceptual difficulties with simply subtracting achievement scores from IQ (Kavale & Forness, 1995; Reynolds, 1990). The prediction of achievement from estimates of intelligence never produces a perfect correlation, and, therefore, users are encouraged to use methods such as the "predicted-achievement" approach presented here. Also, recent concern has emerged about the "slow learner" or the individual with complex attention disorders, who may pose difficulties during assessment and who may exhibit poor performance in both achievement and ability. Thus, guidelines for professional practice suggest the presentation of discrepancy information in the context of a complete assessment, including input from tests, teacher and home observations, clinical observations, and medical and scholastic history. Also, included should be a thorough review of each individual's behaviors and performance by a team of educators, assessment professionals, parents, and so on. The use of only a numerical discrepancy score for identification of learning disabilities is not recommended (Kavale & Forness, 1995; Salvia & Ysseldyke, 1991).

Quality of the Data Employed in Discrepancy Analysis

Criteria for the data used in discrepancy analysis were originally developed by Cecil Reynolds and the Special Education Programs Work Group on Measurement Issues in the Assessment of Learning Disabilities, sponsored by the U.S. Department of Education (Reynolds, 1985; 1990). These criteria were followed in the development of the WIAT and were applied to the WIAT–II:

1. **Individually administered and nationally normed measures of high quality and comparability should be employed.** The rigorous nature of the standardization procedures and representative quality of the samples for the WIAT–II and the various Wechsler scales are well documented and generally considered to be exemplary in the field of individual assessment (Reynolds, 1990, p. 584). Each normative sample for the linking studies is nationally representative. The WISC–III and WIAT–II have a common linking sample of 775 children aged 6–16, stratified by age, sex, ethnicity, geographic region, and PELs. A supplementary sample of 199 children (aged 4–6) was administered both the WIAT–II and the WPPSI–R. Another sample of 95 adolescents (aged 16–18) was administered the WIAT–II and the WAIS–III combination. Additional samples of 268 college students and 190 adults were administered the WIAT–II and the WAIS–III. All supplementary samples were stratified and included representative proportions

according to sex, ethnicity, and socioeconomic variables (see the linking sample description in Chapter 5 and in the *WIAT–II Supplement for College Students and Adults*).

2. **Correlations between achievement and ability should be based on appropriate samples.** For the WIAT–II and WISC–III combination, correlations, regression analyses, and other statistical data were tabulated either for the full sample of 775 or for subsamples of younger (Ages 6–11) and older (Ages 12–16) children. Data from the full sample were employed in the estimation of predicted achievement scores (reported in Appendix H) and for the calculation of frequencies of discrepancies (reported in Appendix I). The subsamples were relatively large ($n = 425$ for Ages 6–11 and $n = 350$ for Ages 12–16) and provided data for the stable estimation of correlations (standardized regression coefficients) used in the calculation of significant discrepancies. The WPPSI–R and WAIS–III supplemental samples were also of sufficient size ($n = 199$ [WPPSI–R], $n = 95$ [WAIS–III high school], $n = 268$ [WAIS–III college], and $n = 90$ [WAIS–III adult]) to provide statistical power in estimation of correlations.

3. **Measures should have high reliability.** Reliability coefficients employed in the various formulas for discrepancy analysis were based on the scores of the full standardization samples of the WIAT–II, WISC–III, WPPSI–R, and WAIS–III, and are widely recognized as exemplary for individually administered measures (most exceed .90).

4. **Other reliability and validity issues should be addressed and documented.** Extensive quantitative evidence of the reliability and validity of each component of the WIAT–II has been presented in Chapter 6. Similar evidence is presented in the respective manuals for the other Wechsler scales.

Use of the Linking Samples

The FSIQ means and standard deviations for the WPPSI–R, WISC–III, and WAIS–III linking samples were 102.94 (15.26), 102.86 (15.09), and 101.7 (13.41), respectively.[2] The higher means observed for WPPSI–R and WISC–III were expected because of the known inflation of norms over time (Flynn, 1984, 1987; Matarazzo, 1972). It is considered important that the ability–achievement discrepancy analysis be based on scores that are normed at the same point in time so that the means are comparable (Berk, 1984; Reynolds, 1990). Therefore, the current WPPSI–R and WISC–III linking samples were used to re-anchor the WISC–III and WPPSI–R IQ and Index scores to a mean of 100 and a standard deviation of 15.[3] After re-anchoring, the WPPSI–R and WISC–III FSIQ means and standard deviations were 99.45 (14.86) and 99.92 (15.02), respectively. These re-anchored scores were used for creating the predicted-achievement scores reported in Appendix H. Thus, the adjustment of the WISC–III and WPPSI–R ability scores is built into the tables. The examiner finds the examinee's obtained ability score, and the table reports the predicted achievement score, which is based on the re-anchored ability score that corresponds to that obtained ability score. This adjustment increases the technical accuracy of the prediction, and the arrangement of the tables obviates an extra step for the examiner.

---

[2] The values reported here include five WPPSI–R protocols that were weighted to adjust the standard deviation to near 15, and nine WAIS–III protocols that were weighted to adjust the mean and standard deviation nearer to 100 and 15, respectively.

[3] This procedure was not necessary for WAIS–III because that test was normed closer in time to the WIAT–II.

Methods and Formulas for Calculating Ability–Achievement Discrepancies

The first step in implementing discrepancy analysis is a thorough review of the quality, reliability, [2] and validity of the tests and testing procedures employed in the assessment of both ability and achievement. Is the professional satisfied that accurate and reliable scores are available and that a thorough understanding of the individual's context and the fairness of assessment have been considered? What are the local or state guidelines in the individual's location for evaluating discrepancies?

The second step in discrepancy analysis method is the selection of the appropriate metric for test scores. As numerous measurement experts have recommended (e.g., Kavale & Forness, 1995; Reynolds, 1990), grade equivalents, age equivalents, percentile ranks, and ratio IQ scores all have statistical limitations that eliminate them from serious consideration as metrics for discrepancy calculation. Only standard scores have been endorsed by experts (Kavale & Forness, 1995) as the acceptable metric for calculating discrepancies between ability and achievement (hence their selection for use in WIAT–II).

The third step in discrepancy analysis is the selection of a statistical approach for comparing ability and achievement. Methods vary by school, district, county, state or region, and the professional should be aware of acceptable practice in his or her local area. The method determines the calculations by which the two scores are contrasted. Two methods of discrepancy analysis are offered for the WIAT–II: the simple-difference and the predicted-achievement methods because of their widespread use.

Simple-Difference Method

With the simple-difference method, a WIAT–II standard score is subtracted directly from the ability IQ or Index standard score. The method is easy to use and widely employed but often criticized by psychometric researchers. As Braden and Weiss (1988) showed, with the simple-difference method, the correlation between the two scores is ignored and can thereby result in errors of classification. Also, if the simple-difference method is based on a multiple of the standard-score standard deviation (e.g., 1.5 times the standard deviation of 15), the measurement error and the statistical significance of the result is also ignored. Thus, the proper use of simple-differences requires consideration of statistical significance of the difference (statistically significant differences are presented in Appendix J). In addition, as recommended by assessment professionals such as Sattler (2001), the frequency of discrepancies in the norming or linking samples should be considered. In other words, "How often do discrepancies of this size occur?" These two considerations—significance and frequency of discrepancies—have been employed for years in the analysis of VIQ and PIQ differences in the various editions of the Wechsler scales (e.g., Wechsler, 1991). An evaluation of statistical significance provides an answer to the concern that measurement error in each test may produce a score difference by chance. The difference must be of sufficient size to minimize the probability that a difference occurred because of unreliability or chance errors in the assessment. An evaluation of the frequency provides an answer to the concern that certain magnitudes of difference may not be rare in the normative population (estimated by the linking-sample frequency of the calculated discrepancies for each examinee). The difference should be sufficiently large and relatively rare in the population.

The statistical significance of simple differences is determined by the following formulas:

Formula 1 $1.96\, SD\sqrt{2 - r_{xx} - r_{yy}}$ Formula 2 $2.58\, SD\sqrt{2 - r_{xx} - r_{yy}}$

In Formulas 1 and 2, the factors 1.96 and 2.58 are the critical values from the normal curve that define the boundaries of two-tailed significance tests. The standard deviation is 15, the population standard deviation for IQ and WIAT–II standard scores. The internal-consistency reliabilities of the ability and achievement tests, r_{xx} and r_{yy}, are the average reliabilities (calculated with Fisher's z transformation) for the two subsamples previously described: Ages 6–11 ($n = 425$) and Ages 12–16 ($n = 350$) Reliabilities for each score are listed in their respective test manuals. The statistically significant differences reported in Appendix Tables I.1–I.3 and Tables J.1–J.3 were calculated with Formulas 1 and 2.

In addition, Formulas 1 and 2 are identical to the classic formulas used for evaluating differences between two test scores. Specifically, the formulas employ the square root of the sum of the squared values of the two standard errors of measurement (based on $SD=15$) multiplied by the normal curve factor. Comparison of the results from these formulas and the results of various other formulas verified the accuracy of the tabled values for the WIAT–II.

For the calculation of the frequency of various discrepancy values (Appendices I and J), theoretical (normal curve) percentages were compared to percentages observed in the linking-sample data. Normal-curve percentages were estimated from the formula for the standard deviation of difference scores:

$$15\sqrt{2 - 2r_{xy}}$$

This value is divided into the difference value to create a normalized z score (Reynolds, 1985). This procedure resulted in the values reported in Appendices I and J and were nearly identical to the actual distributions of simple differences found for the WISC–III linking sample. The formula provided better estimates of simple-difference distributions for the WPPSI–R and WAIS–III because of the smaller linking samples and the resultant absence of certain numerical percentile points. Thus, the frequencies of differences were estimated with the formula and the correlations obtained for the linking samples for better generalizability.

Predicted-Achievement Method

The accuracy of discrepancy analysis is enhanced when the correlation between ability and achievement scores is taken into account. Shepard (1980) was one of the first advocates of the predicted-achievement method, and many other experts have since recommended its use (Braden & Weiss, 1988; Kavale & Forness, 1995; Konold, 1999). Technically, with this method, the ability score is used in a regression equation to predict the expected achievement score for an individual. The prediction of achievement from ability by regression methods has been employed for decades, and Thorndike (1963) explained the rationale: "It is necessary to define 'underachievement' as the discrepancy of actual achievement from the predicted value, predicted on the basis of a regression equation between aptitude and achievement" (p. 13).

For simplicity, both the ability and achievement scores are converted from actual standard scores (SS) to z scores with the following formula:

$$\text{Formula 3} \qquad z = \frac{SS - 100}{15}$$

The regression of ability on achievement may then be simplified to the correlation between the two scores (r_{xy}) multiplied by the z score of ability (z_{ab}), as shown in the following formula. Thus, predicted achievement, in z-score units, is z_p.

$$\text{Formula 4} \qquad z_p = r_{xy} z_{ab}$$

The z score for predicted achievement can then be converted back to standard-score units by the following formula, where SS_p is the predicted achievement in standard-score units, and z_p is the predicted achievement score in z-score units (as calculated with Formula 4), and 15 is the standard deviation of the scale.

$$\text{Formula 5} \qquad \text{SS}_p = 15 z_p + 100$$

The final step in the predicted-achievement method is the calculation of the regression-based discrepancy. The actual achievement standard score (SS_{ach}) is subtracted from the predicted standard score (SS_p):

$$\text{Regression-Based Discrepancy} = \text{SS}_p - \text{SS}_{ach}$$

Because the correlation between ability and achievement is considered moderately large in psychological research (e.g., in the range from .40 to .75, with a median of about .60), the correlation is nearly always statistically significant. Although error is inherent in the prediction, the size of the correlation indicates that the prediction will be accurate for most cases in a large group. The formulas for evaluating statistical significance of the predicted-achievement discrepancy thus employ the correlation between the measures as well as the reliability of each score. After extensive review of the literature on regression-based discrepancy formulas and consultation with experts, the formula used in the WIAT (The Psychological Corporation, 1992, p. 189) was used for assessing the statistical significance of the predicted-achievement discrepancies for the WIAT–II, as shown in Formulas 6, 7 and 8. These formulas provide the critical magnitudes of the standard error of the residual (SE_{resid}) from the regression method at the .05 and .01 levels of significance.

$$\text{Formula 6} \atop (p < .05) \qquad SE_{resid\,(.05)} = 1.96\, SD \sqrt{1 - r^2_{xy}} \, \sqrt{1 - r_{resid}}$$

$$\text{Formula 7} \atop (p < .01) \qquad SE_{resid\,(.01)} = 2.58\, SD \sqrt{1 - r^2_{xy}} \, \sqrt{1 - r_{resid}}$$

Formulas 6 and 7 were derived from the approved "Model 3" recommended by the original Work Group on Issues in Assessment of Learning Disabilities (Reynolds, 1985, Formula 10). The formulas employ the population standard deviation (15), the squared correlation between ability and achievement (r^2xy), and the reliability of the residual score (r_{resid}) as defined by the following formula.

$$\text{Formula 8} \qquad r_{resid} = \frac{r_{yy} + r_{xx} r^2_{xy} - 2 r^2_{xy}}{1 - r^2_{xy}}$$

The standard error of the residual from Formulas 6 or 7 will have slightly lower magnitudes than the critical values derived with the simple-difference method because the addition of the correlation adds information to the comparison of ability and achievement. The formulas produce values identical to those derived with the classic standard error formula. The classic formula employs standard errors of measurement as follows:

$$SE_{diff} = \sqrt{(r^2_{xy})SE_{M_x}^2 + SE_{M_y}^2}$$

$$\text{where } SE_M = 15\sqrt{1 - r_{xx}}$$

The formula was employed in several other ability–achievement batteries, such as the DAS (Elliott, 1990). Users of the WIAT will note the similarity of formulas presented here but also that the calculations of extreme discrepancies (The Psychological Corporation, 1992, p. 188) are no longer included, in favor of the more widely used standard error of the residual.

As in the simple-difference method, the frequencies of various residuals (differences between predicted and actual values) were estimated by formula for each of the linking samples, incorporating the observed correlations between ability and achievement. The standard deviation of the residuals is estimated by the well-known standard error of the estimate (Kavale & Forness, 1995; Reynolds, 1985):

$$SD\sqrt{1 - r^2_{xy}}$$

Application of the Formulas to IQ and Index Scores

New in the WIAT–II is the inclusion of a wide variety of IQ and Index scores employed in the discrepancy analysis. Increasing evidence of the validity of the Index scores and the four-factor structure of the WISC–III (Keith & Witta, 1997; Roid & Worrall, 1997) has supported the inclusion of the Verbal Comprehension Index (VCI) and Perceptual Organization Index (POI) scores. Konold (1999) also showed the predictive power of the WISC–III Index scores in the prediction of WIAT achievement. However, the Index scores are not jointly used, as investigated by Konold, because of the complexity of applying a regression-weighted composite in prediction and because of the need for continuing the tradition of hand-scoring in the WIAT–II. The greater variety of scores is provided as a service to informed users, for special cases in which, for example, communication disorders or recent-immigration status interfere with the fair assessment of verbal ability with the Wechsler scales (or other accommodations to disabilities are required). Users of ability scores other than the FSIQ, however, should be warned that the definition of *ability* is changed by the selection of an alternate ability score. Great caution should be exercised in the evaluation of specific learning disabilities with alternative ability scores.

Kaufman and Lichtenberger (2000) noted that the FSIQ is the most reliable score on the WISC–III (with an average split-half correlation of .96 and an average test–retest correlation of .94) and that it should be considered first for any discrepancy analysis unless there is a significant discrepancy between VIQ and PIQ scores or there is too much scatter among the subtest scores. According to Flanagan and Alfonso (1993), when a significant and meaningful VIQ–PIQ discrepancy exists, the FSIQ is misleading; therefore, the VIQ should be used because it has higher predictive validity with achievement than does the PIQ. The VIQ may also be the best estimate of ability for individuals with significant motor difficulties or for those who are unable to perform well under time pressure (Kaufman, 1979). At the same time, the PIQ may be a more appropriate measure of ability in other cases, such as for individuals who are culturally disadvantaged, of limited English proficiency, hearing impaired, or speech-language impaired. Nonetheless, Flanagan and Alfonso warned that the VIQ and PIQ should be used as the ability measure with caution, especially for the purposes of special education eligibility decisions, because they are somewhat less reliable than the FSIQ at certain ages. In fact, Flanagan and Alfonso recommended that the replacement of the FSIQ with the VIQ or PIQ should be limited to these special circumstances and that these substitute scores should never be used for the sole purpose of making eligibility decisions.

Prifitera, Weiss, and Saklofske (1998) have provided guidance for determining when a score other than FSIQ should be used in calculating ability–achievement discrepancies. The VCI score is a better estimate of verbal reasoning ability than the VIQ score when the Arithmetic subtest scaled score is significantly different from the individual's mean score (at $p < .05$) on the five subtests that contribute to the VIQ composite (i.e., Information, Similarities, Vocabulary, Comprehension, and Arithmetic). Also, when the Digit Span subtest is substituted for the Arithmetic subtest, and the Digit Span score is significantly different from the individual's mean score on the five Verbal subtests, the VCI score is a better indicator of verbal reasoning ability than the VIQ score. In either circumstance, the report on the individual's performance might include the following statement:

This student's verbal reasoning abilities are most appropriately characterized by his score on the Verbal Comprehension Index.

Similarly, when the Coding subtest scaled score is significantly different from the individual's mean score (at $p < .05$) on the five subtests that contribute to the PIQ composite, the POI score is a better indicator of nonverbal reasoning ability than the PIQ score. The PIQ composite includes the Picture Completion, Coding, Picture Arrangement, Block Design, and Object Assembly subtests. When Symbol Search or Mazes is substituted for Coding and if the scaled score on either of those subtests is significantly different from the individual's mean score on the five Performance subtests, the POI, rather than the PIQ score, is the better indicator of nonverbal reasoning ability.

In summary, the WIAT–II subtest and composite standard scores predicted from the WPPSI–R, WISC–III, and WAIS–III scores are provided in Appendix H. The FSIQ is the recommended ability measure for predicting achievement on the WIAT–II except in those cases where the VIQ or PIQ is a more appropriate representation of the examinee's true ability (e.g., when there is a statistically significant discrepancy between VIQ and PIQ). The VCI score may be more appropriate than the VIQ in cases where the Arithmetic (or Digit Span) subtest score is significantly lower than the mean score on the other Verbal subtests. The POI score may be more appropriate than the PIQ in cases where the Coding (or Symbol Search or Mazes) score differs significantly from the mean score on the other subtests that make up the PIQ composite.

Application of the Formulas to Non-Wechsler Ability Scores

Alternative ability measures should be used with extreme caution for the reasons stated earlier (see "Quality of the Data Employed in Discrepancy Analysis"). When other ability measures are used, significant discrepancies can be calculated by either the simple-difference or predicted-achievement method with Formulas 1–8.

Criteria for determining ability–achievement discrepancies, especially critical values, vary from state to state and may be mandated by the state's education authority. Examiners are reminded, however, that the final step in conducting the discrepancy analysis is a determination of the statistical significance of the differences between ability and achievement (Tables I.1–I.3 and Tables J.1–J.3) and the frequency of such differences obtained by various percentages of individuals in the standardization linking sample (Tables I.4–I.16 and Tables J.4–J.16).

Qualitative Analysis of the WIAT-II Performance

A qualitative analysis of an individual's performance should be conducted on two different fronts: first, behavioral and qualitative observations and, second, skills analysis.

Behavioral and Qualitative Observations

The examiner is encouraged to note on the record form any unusual or atypical behaviors of the examinee during testing. Behavioral observations are an important part of the assessment process in that they provide information that can serve as a cross-check on the validity of the examinee's scores (Glutting, Oakland, & Konold, 1994). Further, information gained from behavioral observations can help the examiner better understand how the examinee arrived at an answer and identify effective and ineffective approaches to problem solution. Glutting et al. suggest that examiners should be keenly alert to factors that could have a positive or adverse effect.

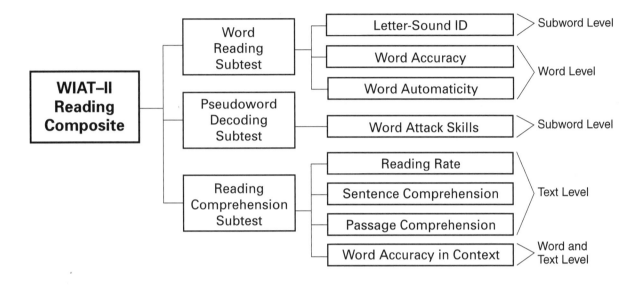

Figure 7.1.
WIAT–II Reading Subtests as Measures of the Subword, Word, and Text Levels

Qualitative Observations

Following administration of the Word Reading, Numerical Operations, Reading Comprehension, Spelling, and Math Reasoning subtests, the examiner is instructed to rate the frequency of specific behaviors observed during subtest administration. Frequency of a behavior is rated as *Never, Seldom, Often,* or *Always.* A rating of *Not Observed* is also included.

The frequent occurrence of targeted behaviors provides useful information that can guide the examiner in the interpretation of subtest scores and in the planning of intervention. For example, during the Spelling subtest, an examinee may make several attempts at writing the dictated word, commenting that "it doesn't look right." This approach to spelling is highly dependent on visual, or orthographic, rather than phonetic clues. Also, the examinee's performance on Pseudoword Decoding would reveal whether decoding skills are grade or age appropriate. An examinee who makes "spatial" rather than calculation errors when solving multi-digit multiplication problems (e.g., Numerical Operations) might find that using graph paper or lined notebook paper turned sideways helpful but might not benefit from additional drill and practice for math facts.

Skills Analysis

In addition to noting behaviors, the examiner should conduct a second qualitative analysis of the examinee's errors as they relate to specific skills. The WIAT–II subtests have been grouped together to measure various components of a construct. For example, reading proficiency is measured by three different subtests (Word Reading, Pseudoword Decoding, and Reading

Comprehension), with each providing unique information for the assessment of reading. Further, each subtest includes sets of items that measure a specific skill or set of skills.

Reading Subtests

The examinee's performance on each of the reading subtests can be interpreted separately, but a more well-rounded picture of the examinee's reading abilities is provided by a comparison of scores that take into account the types of skills that each subtest measures at all levels of language. Figure 7.1 illustrates how the WIAT–II measures reading at the subword, word, and text levels of language. A discussion of skills analysis and interventions specific to the domain of reading follows.

Table 7.1.
Skills Measured by the Word Reading Subtest

Approximate Grade Level	Skill	Items
PreK–1	Matching alphabet letters	1–3
	Identifying alphabet letters	4–29
	Identifying rhyming words	30–33
1–2	Identifying beginning sounds	34–36
	Identifying ending sounds	37–38
	Blending phonemes into words	39–41
	Matching sound to symbol	42–47
3+	Recognizing words	48–131

Word Reading

The Word Reading subtest measures a variety of decoding skills ranging from letter identification to the reading of familiar words. The record form provides space for indicating when the examinee self-corrects and when the reading of a single word is not automatic. Table 7.1 identifies the component skills of word reading measured by the Word Reading items.

Letter Identification and Phonological Awareness

Before students can read text, they must master letter identification, and phonological and phonemic awareness. Knowledge of the entire alphabet (lowercase letters) is measured in Word Reading by the 26 letter items (Items 4–29). Three components of phonemic awareness, the ability to focus on and manipulate phonemes in spoken words, are measured: skills in phonemic identity (Items 42–47), skills in phonemic categorization (Items 34–38), and skills in phonemic blending (Items 39–41). Phonological awareness, the more encompassing awareness of larger spoken units, such as syllables and rhyming words, is measured by Items 30–33. The phonological awareness items precede the phonemic awareness items because tasks that require the manipulation of spoken units larger than phonemes are easier for beginning readers than tasks requiring phoneme manipulation (Liberman, Shankweiler, Fischer, & Carter, 1974).

An examination of responses can reveal whether the examinee has difficulty with particular consonants or consonant combinations or with the various syllable types (see Berninger, 1998). Any pattern of errors should, however, be confirmed from additional observations or discussions with the student's teacher in order to verify the presence of a specific skill deficit. Individuals who perform poorly on these items might benefit from the administration of the PAL–RW subtests (Berninger, 2001) that include items that measure phonological awareness and phonemic manipulation (e.g., Rhyming, Syllables, Phonemes, and Rimes).

Many resources are available for instruction in phonological awareness. *Phonemic Awareness in Young Children: A Classroom Curriculum* (Adams, Foorman, Lundberg, & Beeler, 1998) and the PAL–RW (Berninger, 1998) include classroom and small-group activities for children beginning in kindergarten. Lists of reading books with repetitive rhyming patterns are found in *Assessment and Instruction of Reading and Writing Disability:An Interactive Approach* (Lipson & Wixson, 1997) and in "Using Children's Literature to Enhance Phonics Instruction" (Trachtenburg, 1990). The annotated bibliography, "Read-Aloud Books for Developing Phonemic Awareness" (Yopp, 1995), is also a good resource.

Word Reading Accuracy and Automaticity

Words were selected for the word-reading list based on their frequency of use in reading texts or inclusion on standard word lists, such as *The Reading Teacher's Book of Lists* (Fry, Polk, & Fountoukidis, 1984) and the *Spectrum Dolch Basic Sight Word Activities* (SRA/McGraw Hill, 1992). The Word Reading subtest score represents word-reading accuracy.

It is also important to know whether the individual recognizes words automatically, a skill referred to as *automaticity*. Skilled readers read words accurately, rapidly, and effortlessly. Individuals who do not develop this type of fluency continue to read slowly and with great effort. Moreover, the development of efficient word-recognition skills is associated with improved reading comprehension (Herman, 1985; Stanovich, 1985).

Beginning readers may be accurate in word recognition, but the process may be slow and laborious. With increased practice and exposure to the words, the individual would maintain accuracy in word recognition but would improve in the speed and ease with which he or she reads. Continued reading practice helps make the word-recognition process increasingly automatic. Although word-reading accuracy is a significant part of the reading process, it is not sufficient to ensure fluency, and without fluency, an individual's comprehension is likely to be hindered. When the word-recognition task is difficult, decoding the words may require all available cognitive resources and thereby leave little or no resources available for comprehending what is being read (Berninger, 1998).

During the scoring of the examinee's responses to the Word Reading items, the examiner may elect to identify words that were read accurately but not automatically (space is provided on the record form). The examiner should note when an examinee read words as accurately as others in his or her age or grade group, as represented by a Word Reading standard score in the average range, but read several words slowly, without automaticity. On the Reading Comprehension subtest, this individual's lack of word-recognition automaticity could be a contributor to a lower score. For example, he or she might exhibit a similar lack of automaticity when reading sentences aloud.

Pseudoword Decoding

By the second half of first grade, children should be screened for purposes of determining whether they are acquiring grade-appropriate knowledge of the alphabet principle. The Pseudoword Decoding subtest can be used as a means of evaluating whether the phonological decoding mechanism is developing in an age-appropriate manner (Berninger, 2001). Frequently, older students who are struggling in reading will demonstrate nonmastery of the alphabet principle because they are unable to decode unfamiliar words. It is possible for an individual to score in the average range on Word Reading but score below average on Pseudoword Decoding because he or she must rely solely on word-structure knowledge and phonological abilities to decode the novel nonwords. A comparison of error patterns on Pseudoword Decoding and decoding errors in Word Reading can provide useful information about deficits in the examinee's knowledge and skills. The development of phonological and phonemic awareness and practice in applying the alphabet principle can improve a student's skill in decoding new words (Berninger, 2001).

Reading Comprehension

The process of reading requires the coordination of the separate skills of word recognition and word attack, or decoding, as well as comprehension. The Reading Comprehension subtest standard score represents the examinee's ability to understand what has been read. This score can also represent "Accuracy" when Reading Rate is calculated. Table 7.2 lists the types of comprehension skills measured by the subtest items. The identified skills are widely recognized and frequently used as curriculum objectives; therefore, a student's weakness in any one of these areas should translate directly into interventions suggested in numerous textbooks and specialized reading materials.

Research has demonstrated that readers must be taught comprehension strategies, including the monitoring of their own understanding as they read. In fact, the recent report by the National Reading Panel (2000) states that "active interactive strategic processes are critically necessary to the development of reading comprehension" (p. 4–1). Readers normally acquire strategies for active comprehension informally, but explicit instruction of effective strategies is believed to lead to better understanding and use of information. Therefore, strategy instruction should include direct instruction of a specific skill, modeling of the skill, guided practice, and evaluation of the effectiveness of the strategy for the reader.

Teachers and peers can model comprehension strategies through reciprocal teaching activities. For example, picture cues found in magazines can assist in vocabulary development. Another way of increasing word knowledge is semantic feature analysis. With this strategy, students explore what

Table 7.2.
Skills Measured by the Reading Comprehension Subtest

Skill	Items
Matching pictures with words	1, 2, 3, 4, 5, 9
Recognizing stated detail	7, 10, 11, 16, 17, 19, 20, 23, 34, 36, 41, 44, 45, 46, 51, 55, 56, 57, 59, 71, 72, 75, 77, 89, 100, 103, 107, 109, 111, 119, 124, 138
Recognizing implied detail	27, 43, 98, 102, 106, 114, 115, 121, 125, 131
Predicting events and outcomes	12, 63, 110, 112, 122, 135
Drawing conclusions	13, 28, 33, 48, 49, 58, 76, 92, 97, 126
Using context to determine word meaning	14, 24, 32, 38, 47, 52, 64, 73, 80, 83, 85, 88, 93, 94, 104, 108, 117, 118, 127, 129, 136
Recognizing stated cause and effect	21, 29, 87, 90
Recognizing implied cause and effect	22, 31, 54, 60, 61, 66, 82, 105, 134, 137, 138
Identifying main idea	25, 74, 91, 116, 130, 132
Sequencing	30, 62, 123
Identifying fact or opinion	35
Making inferences	37, 39, 69, 70, 78, 79, 95, 96, 133, 139, 140

they already know about a word or topic and determine what associations can be made with that knowledge. Sequencing can be taught with cartoon strips or with visual story boards created as passages are read. Students can practice identifying the main idea by creating headlines for news articles, by brainstorming appropriate titles for stories, and by semantic mapping, by which main ideas are drawn in relationship to supporting details. A possible strategy for identifying specific details is self-questioning. With this strategy, the student identifies important points as he or she reads and organizes that information by using an outline, semantic map, or other visual organizer. This strategy can be even more effective when the reader determines prior to reading what information he or she would like to gain from the passage. *Strategies for Instruction: Handbooks of Performance Activities* (Harcourt Educational Measurement, 1996) includes classroom and individual activities for a number of the curriculum objectives for reading at several levels. For example, the reading handbook for Grades 7–12 includes activities for building vocabulary (i.e., word meanings, synonyms, and context clues), improving listening comprehension (i.e., initial understanding and interpretation), and increasing comprehension of various types of reading passages (i.e., initial understanding, interpretation, critical analysis, and strategy awareness).

The ability of the student to draw inferences or to fill in gaps in a text to resolve ambiguities often depends on the reader's prior knowledge of the topic. Discussions about a topic, prior to reading about it, can guide the reader and expand the knowledge base of classmates. Another skill, drawing conclusions, can be taught through instruction in the strategy of making predictions about what will happen next. Lessons might include modeling of the process: thinking aloud about possible outcomes, explaining the reasons for that prediction based on what the reader already knows about the subject, and checking the accuracy of the prediction at the conclusion of the reading exercise (see *Developing Reading Strategies: Insights*, Steck-Vaughn, 1991).

The supplemental score for Target Words from the Reading Comprehension subtest represents the examinee's ability to read words at grade level or above by using context cues. A comparison of this score to the Word Reading subtest score can reveal whether or not these skills are commensurate. Errors in reading words from a list and in context of a reading passage can yield helpful information for purposes of designing appropriate interventions. For example, an examinee who can read words in context at grade level but who performs below average when reading from a list of words without context might benefit from guided oral reading procedures, which tend to improve word recognition, fluency, and comprehension (National Reading Panel, 2000).

Fluent readers can read with speed, accuracy, and proper expression; however, readers with good reading accuracy are not necessarily fluent. The Reading Comprehension subtest instructions encourage the examinee to employ a *rauding* process, which requires lexical accessing, semantic encoding, and sentence integrating. According to Carver (1990) rauding is "attending to each consecutive word in sentences and comprehending each consecutively encountered complete thought in a passage; operating the rauding process and comprehending about 75% or more of the thoughts in a passage" (p. 467). When the process is carried out effectively, the reader is able to integrate the words in each sentence of the passage into the complete thought the author intended to communicate and to answer correctly questions about what has been read. This process is representative of natural, normal, typical, or ordinary reading. In fact, it is reported that the rauding process is used about 90% or more of the total time spent reading (Carver, 1990).

Reading speed, however, should be analyzed in relationship to what the examinee can accurately comprehend. The WIAT–II Reading Rate measures the examinee's average silent reading speed across multiple passages; however, this measure should not be used if the reader appears to be skimming or obviously cannot read the passage. The Reading Comprehension subtest total score represents comprehension accuracy. Reading Rate is represented in the record form by a graph of the relation between reading accuracy (represented by the quartile-based score for Reading Comprehension) and silent reading speed (represented by the quartile-based score for Reading Speed).

Areas of the graph are shaded to help the examiner identify specific areas in need of remediation or intervention. The darkest shading represents scores that range from below average to far below average for both reading comprehension accuracy and reading speed. When an individual's score falls in these lower areas, scores on Word Reading and Pseudoword Decoding can reveal whether the examinee has a problem with reading accuracy or automaticity at the word level. Likewise, the Target Words score from the Reading Comprehension subtest can indicate whether or not the problem is with reading sentences or words in context. Low scores on these measures suggest that intervention directed at increasing decoding skills (i.e., training phonological processing abilities), developing automaticity of word recognition, and addressing reading fluency through activities like repeated readings could be beneficial (Berninger, 1998). Additional testing with the PAL–RW (Berninger, 2001) RAN tasks could provide a better understanding of how rapid, automatized naming might affect the examinee's reading skills. Several researchers (i.e., Berninger, 2001; Bowers, 1988; Samuels, 1988; Sunseth & Bowers, 1996) who have investigated the effect of deficits in both phonological awareness and naming-speed processes have recommended that direct instruction in decoding skills and extended practice in reading be provided.

For those individuals whose Reading Rate scores fall in the shaded areas indicating far below average to below average reading speed but average to far above average reading comprehension, instruction directed at increasing reading fluency has been recommended. Samuels (1988) noted that "when a person is accurate but not automatic at word recognition, considerable amounts of mental energy or effort are required." As a result, the goal for fluency must be "beyond accuracy to automaticity" (p.759). Techniques that can improve reading fluency include repeated reading and guided repeated oral reading. These procedures require students to read and reread text until a prescribed level of proficiency has been reached. Increasing time spent in oral reading practice through the use of paired reading, tutors, and read-alongs with audiotapes can also improve fluency (Berninger, 1998).

When the Reading Rate score is in the shaded area that indicates average to far above average reading speed but far below average to below average comprehension, attention should be directed at comprehension strategy instruction. Materials listed in the previous section on Reading Comprehension are recommended.

Math Subtests

Numerical Operations

Math calculation skills are measured by the Numerical Operations subtest. Table 7.3 identifies the skills measured by each item. Skills are ordered by level of difficulty and the most common order of instruction. Item-level analysis will be especially important if math concepts are taught in a slightly different order. As shown in Table 7.3, each item can be categorized by the type of number it contains (multiple digits, single digits, fractions, or decimals) and the operation and complexity of the process (e.g., addition with no renaming, subtraction with regrouping). Performance on this subtest should be compared to that on Math Reasoning because some individuals are able to learn math facts and the sequential procedures associated with calculation but are not able to generate a problem-solving strategy when confronted with a real-life or stated problem.

To communicate information about an examinee's ability to solve computational problems, the examiner can note the types of items to which the examinee responded correctly. Because skills are listed in a primarily hierarchical order, the examiner should be able to determine where an examinee's skills lie along the continuum of skill acquisition.

Table 7.3.
Skills Measured by the Numerical Operations Subtest

Skill	Items
Number discrimination	1, 2
Identifying missing number in rote count	3
Writing single and double digit numbers	4, 5
Counting to 8 by rote	6
Writing number to correspond with rote counting	7
Addition – basic facts	8, 9, 11
Subtraction – basic facts	10, 12
Addition – multi-digits – no renaming	13
Subtraction – multi-digits – no regrouping	14
Addition – multi-digits – with renaming	15, 17, 27
Subtraction – multi-digits – with regrouping	16, 18, 19
Subtraction – with regrouping using decimals	20, 31
Multiplication – basic facts	21, 22
Multiplication – multi-digit and single digit	23
Division – basic facts	24
Division – using single digit divisor – no regrouping	25
Division – using single digit divisor – with regrouping	26
Addition – using single digit decimals	28
Subtraction of simple fractions with common denominators	29
Subtraction of simple fractions with different denominators	30
Multiplication- multi-digits	32
Multiplication – simple fractions	33
Division – using multi-digits – with regrouping	34
Calculating with exponents	35, 36, 52
Multiplication – using decimals	37
Calculating square root	38
Addition of negative integers	39
Calculating percent	40, 51
Division – using simple fractions	41
Solving simple algebraic equations	42, 43, 49
Calculating pi	44
Multiplication of simple fractions and whole numbers	45
Division of simple fraction by whole number	46
Calculating after applying order of operations	47
Division with decimals	48
Solving complex algebraic equations	50
Calculating square root of exponents	53
Using basic geometry	54

Math educators continue to emphasize the value of teaching the concepts and thinking processes underlying math calculation. Thinking or problem solving aloud is encouraged as individuals learn a new process or skill. At the conclusion of the WIAT–II administration, the examiner may wish to return to items missed during administration of Numerical Operations and ask the examinee to talk through the computation. This form of error analysis can be especially useful in determining more precisely where the mathematical process breaks down.

For some examinees, an appropriate intervention will include additional drill and practice with number facts so that the process becomes automatic. Others may need instruction and guided practice in the sequential steps required to solve more complex problems. Calculation "recipes" that identify and order each required step may be very helpful for such examinees. For those examinees who demonstrate directional or spatial difficulties when solving multi-digit problems (i.e., Items 26, 32, and 34), instructional modifications, such as the use of graph paper, might be most beneficial. Several math-based interventions are recommended in *Learning about Learning Disabilities* (Wong, 1991). The instructions include modeling (i.e., demonstrating how to perform a skill), shaping (i.e., reinforcing successive approximations of the desired skill), and direct instruction that includes both (telling the student what he or she needs to do and then checking and monitoring performance). Individuals should also be provided feedback when performance is correct or incorrect, and feedback should be provided shortly after a skill is used.

Individuals with math deficits frequently benefit from the use of manipulables, especially when a skill is first introduced. For example, counting rods, beads, blocks, clothespins on a string, and the abacus can be used as counters. Some math experts believe that students must progress from the concrete (i.e., hands-on manipulables) to the representational (e.g., pictures, tallies), to the abstract (e.g., numerals; Baroody, 1987; Bigge & Stump, 1999).

Older individuals who are experiencing difficulty in mastering math facts can benefit from various strategies. "Count ons" requires the student to start with the higher number and then to count the number of times indicated by the second number. For example, for 4 + 9, the student starts with 9 and counts on four numbers—10, 11, 12, 13. "Doubles" (e.g., 5 + 5) are generally among the first facts mastered and can be used to help the student to think of the double nearest the problem and then to count on to solution. For example, for 7 + 8,—the student starts with 7 + 7 and then adds one more. "Count bys" is a strategy that helps with multiplication and division. For example, the student counts by 3s when solving a multiplication problem involving a three, such as 3 x 7. *Teaching Mathematics to the Learning Disabled* (Bley & Thornton, 1989), *Curriculum, Assessment, and Instruction for Students With Disabilities* (Bigge & Stump, 1999), and *Children's Mathematical Development: Research and Practical Applications* (Geary, 1994) are all good resources for planning effective interventions.

Math Reasoning

Performance on the Math Reasoning subtest is based on the individual's ability to solve stated problems by (a) discriminating essential from nonessential information, (b) identifying the required math process(es), (c) setting up the calculation problem for solution, and (d) correctly calculating the answer. The Math Reasoning page of the record form includes a column that lists the skill(s) addressed by each item. The patterns of correct and incorrect responses for items measuring similar skills can be helpful in the identification of an individual's strengths and weaknesses. Table 7.4 identifies the skills measured by each Math Reasoning item and groups the skills by instructional objectives. Items that require multistep solutions are in bold type. For example, under the objective for *Use patterns to solve problems*, Items 17 and 18 require the examinee to extend pictorial patterns, Item 50 measures the skill of using patterns to make predictions or generalizations, and Items 23 and 37 require the examinee to use patterns to skip-count.

Another way the examiner can conduct math skills analysis involves observing the strategies employed by the examinee, watching him or her solve problems, listening for spontaneous verbalizations, and reviewing any "scratch paper" used by the examinee for problem solution. Incorrect responses may be the result of miscalculations or an inappropriately selected process. Steps may be omitted in a multistep solution or performed in an incorrect sequence. Possible strategies that might be observed include the examinee's guessing with or without checking, drawing pictures or

Table 7.4.
Skills Measured by the Math Reasoning Subtest

Skill	Items
Use whole numbers to describe quantities	
Count with 1:1 correspondence and use sum to compare quantities	1, 2, 3, 8, 11
Order numbers	12, 14, 15, 19, 32
Use geometric and spatial reasoning to solve problems	
Identify, compare and contrast shapes, solids, lines, angles	4, 5
Identify the results of rotations and reflections	45, 51
Create and solve addition and subtraction problems using whole numbers	
Recall and apply basic addition and subtraction facts and procedures	9, 13, **26**, 31, **35**, **44**
Create and solve multiplication and division problems using whole numbers	
Recall and apply basic multiplication and division facts and procedures	38, **39**, 48, **49**, **58**, **64**
Use quantities less than a whole	
Use fraction words to name parts of a whole object or set	29, 40, 46, 53
Compare and order fractions	47
Relate fractions to decimals	57
Solve addition and subtraction problems using fractions and decimals	43, 55
Solve multiplication and division problems using fractions and decimals	**61**
Use patterns to solve problems	
Extend pictorial patterns	17, 18
Use patterns to make predictions or generalizations	50
Use patterns to skip-count	23, 37
Use non-standard and standard units to measure	
Use attributes such as length, weight, or capacity to compare and order objects	16
Select and use appropriate formulas to solve problems involving length, area, capacity, and weight	41, **62**
Tell time and use time to compare and order events	21, 22, 28, 33, 52
Use grids and graphs to make comparisons, draw conclusions, or answer questions	6, 7, 10, 24, 25, 36, 42, 59
Solve problems using or related to money	
Use words and numbers to describe the values of individual coins	20, 27
Determine the value of a collection of coins	30
Apply calculation skills using decimals to solve problems involving money	**44**, **54**, **60**, **63**, **65**
Use theoretical and experimental probability to draw conclusions, answer questions, and make predictions	34, 56, **66**, 67

Note. Numerals in **bold type** denote items that require a multistep solution.

tables, developing or recording a formula, estimating an answer and working backwards, and talking through alternative procedures. The Qualitative Observations at the end of the Math Reasoning section of the record form can assist the examiner in noting the frequency of the use of common strategies.

Montague and Bos (1986) suggested an eight-step process that can help adolescent students with mathematics reasoning deficits. The student

1. reads the problem aloud and makes sure that he or she knows all the words,
2. paraphrases the problem aloud and identifies the question being asked,
3. visualizes the problem (the student may want to "draw" it),
4. states the problem again and underlines all important information,
5. hypothesizes a solution strategy,
6. estimates the answer,
7. calculates the answer, and
8. checks his or her work for accuracy.

Written Language Subtests

Like the Reading subtests, the WIAT–II written language subtests, Spelling and Written Expression, were designed to measure all levels of written language. Figure 7.2 illustrates how writing is measured at the subword, word, and text levels. As a result, emphasis has shifted from the WIAT focus on the writing *product* to a new focus on the writing *process*.

Spelling

The Spelling items were designed to be dictated so that an examinee's written response could be evaluated. The first item measures the examinee's ability to write his or her first and last names. This skill is an early writing skill that is typically introduced at the beginning of the kindergarten year. Items 2–12 measure the examinee's understanding of sound–symbol relationships; for these

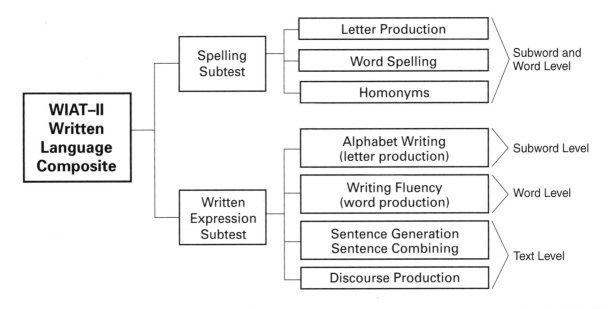

Figure 7.2.
WIAT–II Written Language Subtests as Measures of the Subword, Word, and Text Levels

items, letter sounds are verbalized and the examinee identifies the matching letter or letters. Because only a sampling of letter sounds are included, the results can only suggest hypotheses about possible skill deficiencies. At a later time, a full range of letters and sounds can be dictated, and the examiner can then review the results in consultation with the teacher to identify or confirm specific deficiencies.

An analysis of spelling errors can provide instructional clues for improving an individual's spelling. Reliability of errors is important, and recommended instructional interventions should be based on patterns of errors that occur repeatedly. The examiner is also urged to analyze patterns of errors on the Written Expression subtest to evaluate whether patterns of errors occur across contexts. Spelling errors can be classified according to seven broad categories, or, for more detailed analysis, according to the specific types of errors found within each category. Table 7.5 presents a structure for the analysis of spelling errors based on these categories and includes examples of the WIAT–II misspellings and recommended intervention activities. Additional spelling activities are provided in the *Strategies for Instruction: Handbooks of Performance Activities* (Harcourt Educational Measurement; 1996) and *Talking Letters* (Berninger, 1998).

Written Expression

The evaluation of the examinee's writing performance should occur at the subword, word, sentence, and text levels because an individual's skills in producing words, sentences, and text can vary in relation to each other. Research conducted by Berninger and others (Berninger, Mizokawa, Bragg, Cartwright, & Yates, 1994; Whitaker et al., 1994) has demonstrated that an individual's word skill did not predict the individual's sentence or text skills; moreover, an individual's sentence skills did not predict the individual's text skills. In other words, specific writing abilities can develop at uneven rates. Therefore, the examiner must determine specific skill deficits in order to plan appropriate intervention.

The timed alphabet-writing task can be especially diagnostic for children who have not automatized letter formation or who have difficulty recalling the alphabetical sequence. Low scores may be the result of slowed performance, as is the case when the examinee is able to produce only a few letters within the time limit. Low scores can also be the result of poorly constructed letter formations. The scoring guidelines in the *Scoring and Normative Supplement for Grades PreK–12* can help the examiner identify error types. Also, allowing the examinee to write the complete alphabet or to work toward that goal until a 5-minute time limit expires will provide more comprehensive information about his or her letter-writing proficiency or deficits, including sequential errors, letter reversals, and confusion of similar letters (*b/d, p/q, n/u, m/w*). Generally by the end of first grade, children should be able to produce all 26 letters. Second graders should be writing letters automatically. When a second grader or older student continues to have difficulty with letter formations, guided practice in letter automaticity is warranted so that the student is free to focus on writing content (see Berninger, 1998).

Word Fluency items appear in both the Written Expression and the Oral Expression subtests. Both items measure the examinee's ability to generate a variety of words that fit a specific category within a 60-second time limit; however, the Written Expression Word Fluency task is the more demanding one. An evaluation of the quality of an examinee's responses is based on whether or not the words are on target, varied, and imaginative. Bonus points are awarded for polysyllabic written responses. An overall poverty of words could be indicative of limited exposure or lack of experience or a language deficit. A comparison of performance on these items to performance on other language tasks is important especially for examinees with limited English proficiency. A low score,

Table 7.5.
Structure for Analysis of Spelling Errors

Types of Errors	Examples	Intervention Recommendations
Pre-Alphabetic Principle Stage		Phonemic awareness tasks such as identifying the names of pictures that begin with the same sound and blending onset-rime units into real words. Systematic phonics instruction through tutoring, small groups, and classroom instruction.
Produces random letters rather than attempting representation of speech	utody (jumped)	
Represents speech at a phonetic level, but is only partially phonemic	ubr (under) ridn (riding)	
Letter Production Errors		Activities to increase handwriting automaticity[a]
Letter reversals	maq (map)	
Letter inversions	me (we)	
Phonological and Orthographic Processing Errors		Phonemic awareness tasks such as: blending phonemes into real words, deleting a phoneme and saying the word that remains, segmenting words in phonemes, and blending phonemes into non-words. Instruction in the alphabet principle and its alternations in the direction of phonemes to a 1- or 2-letter spelling unit.[b]
Phonemes omitted	/r/ in pinsibl (principal)	
Phonemes inserted	abpsens (absence)	
Phonemes transposed	tow (two)	
Phonemes confused and similar ones substituted	beg (big) ondr (under)	
Mixed phonological errors	pharmasudical (pharmaceutical)	
Produces an implausible spelling unit given conventional phoneme-spelling correspondences	rithed (right)	
Word-Specific Orthographic Processing Errors		Instruction in the alphabet principle and its alternations in the direction of phonemes to a 1- or 2-letter spelling unit. Guided practice in spelling a target word in a dictated sentence.
Produces a plausible but incorrect phoneme-spelling correspondence	cairless (careless) riet (right)	
Incorrect letter for schwa sound	sovaran (sovereign)	
Omitted silent letter	ges (guess)	
Morphological Processing Errors		Morphological awareness training. Guided practice in spelling a target word in a dictated sentence.
Suffix or stem change for tense	jumpt (jumped)	
Produces an incorrect prefix	adcitement (excitement)	
Produces an error in a derivational suffix	prestigous (prestigious) subsidice (subsidize)	
Produces an error in the stem morpheme	soveregn (sovereign)	
Spelling Rule Errors		Systematic and explicit instruction of spelling rules.
Failure to double final consonant before adding another morpheme	acommodate (accommodate) begining (beginning)	
Error in changing y to i	easyer (easier)	
Error in forming a contraction	theyr'e (they're)	
Failure to add final e for soft c or g	charg (charge)	
Phonological/Orthographic/Morphological Confusion		Guided practice in spelling a target word in dictated sentences so that context must be taken into account.
Inappropriate use of homonym	their (they're) write (right)	

[a] see Berninger (1998) *Process Assessment of the Learner: Guides for Intervention: Handwriting Lessons*

[b] see Berninger (1998) *Process Assessment of the Learner: Guides for Intervention: Talking Letters*

based on a limited number of words, could also be the result of difficulty in accessing words in the memory store or a rate-based problem (i.e., the examinee writes slowly). Performance on other rate-based items, such as automaticity for Word Reading, Reading Speed, and Alphabet Writing, can provide support for this inference. The examinee may also have trouble employing a categorizing strategy to search for words and thereby produce words at random. Poor performance can also be due to loss of set, with the examinee's producing words that are outside of the specified category, or to lack of self-monitoring to avoid repeating words. Appropriate intervention strategies might include vocabulary-building activities, sorting activities that incorporate concrete objects or pictures, "What doesn't belong" activities, direct instruction in categorizing lists of words according to common characteristics, and brainstorming games in which students model the generation of as many words as possible to fit an assigned category.

The Sentence items of the Written Expression subtest allow for the evaluation of the examinee's ability to create grammatically correct sentences in response to semantic, visual, or verbal cues. The examinee must follow appropriate punctuation and capitalization rules in order to receive full credit. Content errors may occur when an examinee is unable to combine or summarize multiple pieces of information into a single, concise statement. Direct instruction in sentence combining, including the teaching of particular, definable structures, can help individuals improve the effectiveness of their writing during revision (Combs, 1976; Gregg, 1983).

Both analytic and holistic scoring methods for the Paragraph and Essay items are discussed in detail in Chapter 4, and examples of scored responses are included in Appendix A.2 of the supplements. The two methods can complement one another. Holistic scoring provides a rapid estimate of the overall quality of the writing, whereas analytic scoring provides more specific information that can be used for isolating deficiencies. The paragraph-writing sample is scored analytically according to a scoring rubric that includes vocabulary, organization, and mechanics. The essay is also scored according to theme development. The discussion by Berninger, Fuller, and Whitaker (1996) of the developmental progression of text structure in the developing writer can aid in the interpretation of responses.

Vocabulary

The use of vivid and specific words is a key part of good writing. Word choice is often an important step that follows idea generation. A low score may result from the lack of fluency in formal writing, such as classroom assignments or tests. The examinee may need specific instruction in the differences between informal language and that required in written communication (DiStefano, Dole, & Marzano, 1984). Errors such as the omission of articles, prepositions, verbs, or word endings may be indicative of specific writing disorders (Gregg, 1983).

Alternatively, a low score for vocabulary may result from a lack of specificity. The examinee might use general words such as *big*, *a lot*, and *nice*, without stopping to think of words that are more precise. Practice in identifying specific, vivid words in advertising materials, as well as an introduction to the use of a thesaurus may be helpful in teaching the effective use of words in written discourse. Instruction should also include demonstrations in how to select powerful words to use in persuasive writing tasks such as "letters to the editor" or campaign speeches. Learning to use figures of speech such as metaphor and simile can help students add interest and spark to their writing.

Organization

Difficulties with organization may result from poor prewriting or planning skills. Alternatively, the individual may have a plan but in the initial drafting stage becomes distracted from the central idea or theme so that the writing lacks unity or coherence. Organization should be evident at the sentence level in both syntax and the logical ordering of ideas. A paragraph should include examples or reasons that support the position taken by the author. Transitional expressions such as *first*, *next*, and *for example* link ideas for the reader. In essays, paragraphs should flow from one to another with transitional phrases such as *in addition, furthermore, on the other hand,* and *in conclusion*. Essays should have introductory sentences, or an introductory paragraph, as well as concluding statements.

Examples, or models, of well-organized writing can help individuals learn how to order ideas. Instruction in prewriting activities can help individuals become better planners. Using semantic organizers or maps and outlines prior to composing a first draft can help the writer stay focused and on topic. Direct instruction in the use of transitional words and phrases can demonstrate their effectiveness. Activities such as unscrambling word cards to create complete, grammatically correct sentences can direct the beginning writer to formulate more complex sentences. Prewriting, composing, and editing activities are included in the *Strategies for Instruction: Handbooks of Performance Activities* (Harcourt Educational Measurement, 1996).

Theme Development

Only essays are scored according to theme development. Because the prompt requires the examinee to produce a persuasive argument, the essay should include clear and concise statements that identify and support the writer's position. An argument can be bolstered by the inclusion of examples, personal experiences, facts and figures, or the employment of a point—counter-point approach. A low score might be the result of poor prewriting skills, weak organization, limited idea generation, or lack of interest in the topic. Direct instruction in persuasive writing that includes the use of effective vocabulary, the employment of organizational strategies that build an argument, and opportunities to argue for a position in areas of interest to the writer can lead to more effective written communication.

Mechanics

The score for mechanics includes tabulation of spelling and punctuation errors. The types of errors and the frequency and consistency of their occurrence can be diagnostic and useful in instructional planning. The most common punctuation errors are likely to occur in the use of commas. The examiner should note whether the spelling error score (which is converted to a quartile score) is commensurate with the examinee's performance on the Spelling subtest and whether spelling errors occurred more or less frequently in written discourse. The examiner can also monitor misspellings to determine if they are consistent or if the writer misspelled randomly (e.g., used *they're*, *their*, and *there* indiscriminately).

Research has shown that the writing products of students with writing disabilities contain numerous spelling, punctuation, capitalization, and handwriting errors. Their writing also tended to be inordinately brief, poorly organized, and weak in theme development (Houck & Billinglsey 1989; Lane & Lewandowski, 1994; Myklebust, 1973; Poplin, Gray, Larsen, Banikowski, & Mehring, 1980; Poteet, 1978; Thomas, Englert & Gregg, 1987). Although the calculation of the Word Count supplemental score is optional on the WIAT–II, there was a statistically significant difference in Essay Word Count by examinees with learning disabilities and a matched group of peers without learning disabilities.

A variety of activities are available for teaching spelling and writing mechanics. Generally, individuals who are struggling in the area of mechanics benefit from direct instruction that is functional rather than drill and practice. For example, given newspapers or magazines, individuals can be asked to highlight all of the capital letters and to discuss the reasons for their capitalization.

Computers offer another instructional strategy. The individual composes and prints a passage on the computer. Next, the individual uses the spell-check feature to correct the passage, prints the corrected passage, and then compares the two to identify errors that were corrected. Daily journal writing, for which the individual responds to a prompt or generates writing on a topic of choice, can increase writing fluency (the number of words written). Strategies for identifying possible spelling and mechanical errors and improving sentence quality can help individuals improve the editing process.

Oral Language Subtests

The oral language subtests of Listening Comprehension and Oral Expression were designed to measure the examinee's ability to understand and produce oral language. Few educators would dispute the importance of the role of listening and speaking, either in or out of school. Instruction in these skills is commonplace in the language arts curriculum, and the verbal communication skills of listening, speaking, reading, and writing are the hallmarks of modern language arts instruction.

Listening Comprehension

Children typically develop listening comprehension earlier than they develop reading ability (Sticht & James, 1984). In fact, the average child enters school with a listening vocabulary of about 6,000 words and a speaking vocabulary from 2,000 to 5,000 words. This listening–speaking vocabulary bank, coupled with skills in listening comprehension, provides the basis for reading and all other instruction in the early grades. For these reasons, any skill deficiencies in listening may have a cumulative effect on learning difficulties.

The Listening Comprehension subtest measures three types of listening activities: Receptive Vocabulary, Sentence Comprehension, and Expressive Vocabulary. Although the three activities do not yield individual scores, the examiner can determine if one activity is more difficult than another is or if performance is poor in all areas. More than likely, poor performance on the Sentence Comprehension items will be followed by a low score on the Oral Expression subtest because both are measures of the pragmatic use of language. A low score on the Sentence Comprehension items can also result from the examinee's not listening for specific details. Each item is heavily "language-loaded"; in other words, the task requires the listener to process every word and its relationship to the other words in the sentence in order to select the correct picture. If an examinee does poorly, the examiner may wish to consult with the teacher or parent(s) to determine if the performance is typical of day-to-day interactions. Poor performance on the Receptive Vocabulary items may be a result of poor vocabulary development, lack of exposure to or experience with the words, or a receptive language disorder. Poor performance on the Expressive Vocabulary items might also reflect poor vocabulary development or lack of exposure or experience, but it might also be a result of an expressive language disorder. When an examinee obtains a low score, the examiner should note the examinee's score on the Oral Expression subtest, which measures the pragmatic aspects of language, that is, the way the examinee uses language to communicate.

Instruction in listening comprehension is often implicit. For individuals who are experiencing difficulty, however, more direct instruction in listening skills may be warranted. Individuals can be taught to listen for the main idea, for specific details, for cause and effect, for elements of contrast and compare, and for other types of information targeted by the comprehension objectives. Storytelling, listening games (i.e., "Simon Says"), and following multiple verbal directions can add an element of fun to instruction.

Oral Expression

As noted previously, the Oral Expression subtest measures the pragmatic uses of language or how the examinee uses language to communicate effectively. The Oral Expression items are primarily expressive in nature, requiring the examinee to produce oral language to recall and repeat, categorize, describe, and inform. Occasionally, an examinee may perform poorly on an expressive language task because of the receptive difficulty associated with comprehending task directions. Such individuals may ask to have instructions or prompts repeated multiple times or may produce a response that is only partially related to the prompt.

The Sentence Repetition items require verbal memory span and short-term memory. Performance on the shorter sentences (Items 1–5) is more dependent on memory span, whereas, the longer sentences require short-term memory. An examinee's verbatim repetition of the shorter sentences but omission of words in the longer sentences can indicate a reduced memory span. Likewise, omissions on the shorter sentences but correct responses on the longer sentences can indicate inattentiveness or lack of interest. In addition, some examinees with language problems may have difficulty on these items due to the linguistic demands or syntactic construction of the sentences. Errors of this type can result in meaningless sentences or syntactically irregular sentences.

Guided practice in the verbatim recall of words, lists of words, and sentences of varying length can help students develop their verbal memory span. Mnemonic strategies such as visualization or silent verbal rehearsal can help students develop short-term memory.

Two Word Fluency items are included in the Oral Expression subtest. As discussed previously, these items measure the examinee's ability to generate words quickly in response to a verbal prompt. Performance on the easier item (Item 2) should be compared to performance on the more difficult item (Item 10) and to that on the Word Fluency item in Written Expression. Because quartile-based scores are available for all three items, the comparison is direct. Poor performance on all of the items may be the result of poor vocabulary development, lack of exposure to or experience with the category, or lack of interest in the task. Average or better performance on Item 2 (the generation of nouns) but poor performance on Item 10 (the generation of verbs) may indicate semantic or grammatical difficulties. Average or better performance on the Oral Expression items but poorer performance on the Written Expression item may be a result of a writing disorder, lack of automaticity in writing, or low motivation on writing tasks. Games that teach word categories or that require the player to describe an object while others guess its name (e.g., "I Spy") can aid in the development of oral fluency.

The Visual Passage Retell items elicit natural, spontaneous language from the examinee. Responses must be recorded verbatim and reviewed prior to evaluation and scoring. In general, the score for these items is based on the inclusion of the essential story elements: main idea, descriptive details, characters, setting, plot, sequence of events, and a conclusion or resolution. Each story should include a "twist" that defines the story plot. Poor performance could be a result of inexperience with or lack of exposure to story elements, the inability to process sequential visual information into a meaningful whole, a lack of interest in the task, or the inability to use language effectively to communicate information. The responses of some examinees will not reflect the inference required for the complete development of the story plot. This omission is appropriate for younger students but should be present in stories from examinees in the intermediate grades and above. The responses from skilled storytellers will be more descriptive and entertaining and will enable the listener to understand the entire story even without benefit of pictures.

Many activities that help individuals develop a sense of story and the ability to create or retell stories are included in the language arts curriculum. The use of puppets, role-play, drama, story time, or oral reading of age-appropriate books to the class can improve students' listening and oral expression skills while they learn about the essential elements of a story.

The Giving Directions items measure the examinee's ability to generate sequential, essential directions for performing a common task. The examinee who does well on this item should be able to describe the specific process in enough detail so that the listener could follow the instructions and perform the task without benefit of pictures. Poor performance could be a result of the examinee's difficulty in interpreting the meaning of the visual cues, inability to sequence visual information or to translate it into verbal communication, lack of interest, or lack of experience with or exposure to the task. The examinee's performance on Item 14, which includes visual clues, should be compared to his or her performance on Item 15, which requires the examinee to generate his or her own visual clues. For examinees who can perform the first task but not the latter, testing of the limits is recommended. Examinees are asked to draw out their instructions first and then to proceed, using their own visual clues. From this exercise, the examiner may be able to determine if difficulties are the result of the examinee's inability to visualize detailed information or to sequence or communicate the information effectively.

Integrated language arts activities that require individuals to use research skills, listening, reading, speaking, and writing to complete "project" assignments can be especially beneficial to individuals who might be struggling with any component of the communication process. For example, an environmental issue in the local community can be chosen as a topic for the project. The individual or the team then finds printed resources, interviews local officials, prepares a speech accompanied by visual displays, and writes a report. Such activities integrate oral expression into a total context of a "real life" problem that is interesting and exciting for students to explore.

Eight Steps for Basic Interpretation of WIAT-II Performance

The basic interpretation of WIAT–II performance follows an eight-step process. Interpretation begins after subtest raw scores and composite scores have been calculated and converted into standard scores.

Step 1: Determining Whether the Test Results are Representative and Whether They Answer the Referral Question(s)

To determine if test results are representative of the functioning of the examinee, the examiner should evaluate the degree to which the examinee was able to understand instructions, the extent to which the tasks held his or her attention, and his or her motivation to give correct responses. Test performance should be compared to the examinee's level of functioning as reported by teachers or others and to the results of other tests administered to the examinee, particularly ability tests (e.g., Wechsler scales).

Step 2: Comparing the Total Composite Standard Score to the Ability Score

If the conclusions reached in the first step were positive, the second step is an evaluation of the overall composite standard score. First, the examiner should compare the obtained composite achievement score to the score predicted from the examinee's ability score. Next, the examiner should determine if this level of achievement is representative of an overall similar level of achievement across skills (e.g., subtests) or if the examinee's performance across skills varied significantly.

Step 3: Interpretation of the Differences Between the Composite Standard Scores

Next, the examiner can determine whether the difference between any pair of the four composite standard scores is statistically significant at the desired level of confidence (.15 or .05; see Tables K.1–K.3). For any differences that are statistically significant, the examiner can check the cumulative percentages of the standardization sample that obtained similar composite score discrepancies (see Tables K.4–K.5)to determine if the differences are typical or rare.

Step 4: Interpretation of the Differences Between the Subtest Standard Scores

The profile of an examinee's subtest standard scores on the WIAT–II can show appreciable variability among those scores. The interpretation of a particular subtest score as especially high or low should be preceded by consideration of the statistical significance of the difference and the population base rates. The examiner should compare any subtest standard score that appears to be especially high or low to the examinee's average of standard scores on all subtests (or group of subtests that includes the subtest in question) and determine if a discrepancy is significant (see Tables K.6–K.8). A single score that is significantly greater than the examinee's own mean score may reflect a relative strength, whereas one that is significantly less than the mean may indicate a relative weakness.

A difference between a single subtest standard score and the average of a group of subtest standard scores may be statistically significant but not especially unusual in the population. The difference may call for careful interpretation. For this purpose, the frequency of such a difference, whether it is rare or common among individuals in general, is important. Data on the frequency of differences for the WIAT–II standardization sample is also provided in Tables K.6–K.8.

The difference between standard scores on a particular pair of subtests may also be of interest. Differences of any given amount between two subtest standard scores may occur because of chance fluctuation; therefore, the examiner must determine whether the difference is statistically significant. Tables K.9–K.11 also shows, for every possible pair of WIAT–II subtests, the differences that are significant at the .15 level of confidence (above the diagonal) and at the .05 level of confidence (below the diagonal).

Step 5: Interpretation of Intersubtest Scatter

Intersubtest scatter is the variability of an examinee's standard scores across the subtests. Such variability is frequently considered diagnostically significant. As with other score comparisons, the frequency of the scatter is important to interpretation, and the examiner should have evidence that the degree of scatter exhibited in a particular protocol is relatively uncommon in the population. Intersubtest scatter is the simple difference between the examinee's highest and lowest subtest standard scores. The percentages of the WIAT–II standardization sample whose subtest standard scores exhibited various degrees of scatter in those subtests contributing to the age- or grade-appropriate battery are provided in Table K.12.

Step 6: Interpretation of an Ability–Achievement Discrepancy

The first step in implementing this discrepancy analysis is a thorough review of the quality, reliability, and validity of the tests and testing procedures employed in the assessment of both ability and achievement. Because the WIAT–II was designed to be used in tandem with the Wechsler intelligence scales, the following discussion is based on the assumption that test selection includes those instruments.

The second step in the ability–achievement discrepancy analysis is the selection of the appropriate metric for test scores. Standard scores are recommended.

The third step in the analysis is the selection of a statistical approach for comparing ability and achievement: the predicted-achievement method, whereby the actual achievement score is subtracted from the achievement score predicted from the ability score, or the simple-difference method, whereby the actual achievement score is subtracted from the ability score. For the various reasons explained earlier in this chapter, the predicted-achievement method is recommended. Next, for either method, the ability score that will be used for the discrepancy analysis must be selected. Except in the circumstances previously discussed in this chapter, the FSIQ score is the best measure of ability and is recommended.

Tables of the WIAT–II subtest and composite standard scores predicted from the WPPSI–R, WISC–III, and WAIS–III scores are located in Appendix H.

Appendix I provides the differences between actual and predicted WIAT–II subtest and composite standard scores required for statistical significance based on the predicted-achievement method. The tables present the differences according to the ability test used: WPPSI–R (Table I.1), WISC–III (Table I.2), and WAIS–III (Table I.3). Appendix J provides similar information for discrepancy analysis based on the simple-difference method.

For any statistically significant difference, the frequency of that difference indicates its clinical meaningfulness. Appendix I reports the differences between actual and predicted WIAT–II subtest standard scores and composite standard scores that were obtained by the various linking samples. Appendix J provides similar information for discrepancy analysis based on the simple-difference method.

Step 7: Interpretation of the Qualitative Observations

The examiner should note the frequency of targeted behaviors and use their qualitative descriptors to identify possible learning or problem-solving strategies employed by the examinee. Patterns of behaviors can provide clues that help explain the examinee's performance. Inconsistencies in behaviors from subtest to subtest may provide information about examinee's effort or level of interest during testing and can provide direction for error analysis.

Step 8: Subtest Error Analysis

Considerable guidance in the procedures of error analysis is provided in the preceding discussion in this chapter. It is important for the examiner to extract as much information as possible from the test protocol and the testing session about the examinee's errors as they relate to identified skills. The information from this type of analysis can then be used in the design of an instructional plan or a specific intervention for the examinee.

WIAT–II Examiners, Reviewers, and Participating Schools and Districts

Examiners

Alabama

Birmingham
Sharon Fowler, BA
Kathy Noell, BS
Mary Woods, BA

Dothan
Kathy King
Leighann Smith, MS
Yolanda Vincent, MA

Florence
Joyce Elliott, EdS
Cheryl McAnalley, MA

Huntsville
Annie Wells, PhD

Jasper
Ann Wilson, MA

Madison
Debra Fleming, BS

Mobile
Susan McConnell, MA

Northport
Debbie Phares, EdS

Opelika
Vera Goodman

Tuscaloosa
Alicia Caputo, BA
Mesha Ellis, BA
Lauren Hawkins, BS

Peggy Renner, MA
Jean Spruill, PhD

Tuskegee
Ardelia Lunn, MEd

Valley
Virginia Tompkins, MA

Alaska

Juneau
Stacey Seitz, MS

Arizona

Flagstaff
Margaret Boatright, MA
James Connell, BA
R. Carol Cordero, MA
Kerry Kain, MA
Mary McLennan, PhD
Leah Nellis, PhD

Glendale
Frymet Hare, MEd
Ellen Hughson-Hale, MS

Marana
Joanne Weber, MA

Peoria
Shirley Simpson, MS

Phoenix
Yvette Alvarez-Rooney, MA
D.J. Gaughan, PhD

James F. Scooler, MC
Cheri Vetter, MEd

Scottsdale
Sumer Statler Aeed, EdD
John Stapert, PhD

Tempe
Karen Behm
Heather V.A. Hoover, MA

Tucson
Mary Jo Bates, MS
Susan Cooper, MA
Janet Eddins, MS
Brenda Evans, MS
David Federhar, PhD
Pam Moore, MS
Cynthia Randall, AA
Ann Ritter

Arkansas

Benton
Vanessa Edwards, MS

El Dorado
Joy Daymon, MSE

Glenwood
Carol Hokanson, MSE

Jonesboro
Cara Kriehn, MRC

Oden
Brenda Ledbetter, MSE

Rudy
Paula Testerman, MS

California

Alhambra
Alexandra Kaminski, BA
Valerie Kolone, MS

Aliso Veijo
Rajko Strizic, PhD

Arcadia
Maryam Golestani, MS
Carrie Li, MS

Aromas
Jacqueline Palmer, MEd

Calumet City
Joseph Kovach, PhD

Camarillo
Kathy True, MA

Carlsbad
Lori Magnusson, PhD

Chino Hills
Maureen Bosanko, MA

Claremont
Doron Dula, PsyD

Del Mar
Hallie Ben-Horin, MA

Diamond Bar
Joyce Robinson, MS

Encino
Joseph Vanek, MA

Eureka
Mark Winter, PhD

Fallbrook
Lynda Brooks, MA

Fresno
Lori Jern, MA

Galt
Lynn Thull, PhD

Grass Valley
Marc La Fleur, MA

Hemet
Ruben Lopez, MS

La Mesa
Leslie Faris, PhD

Los Angeles
Marylin Calzadilla, PhD

Oakland
Joanne Crawford

Ontario
Barry Sandoval, MA

Pasadena
Fallynn Cox, MS

Placerville
Clare Gavin, MA

Riverside
James Simonds, PhD

San Bernadino
Marty Milligan, MA

San Diego
Jonell Blevins
Janie Ferguson
Rebecca Hopewell
Mildred Hutcherson
Heidi Kennedy, MS
Ali Linnert, MS
Barbara Mason, MS
Todd Pizitz, MA
Hideo Shimizu, MA
Linda Simmons, BA
Linda Sunderman, MSE
Walter Wells
Donna Yeaman

San Francisco
Vicki Nielsen Strotz, MS

San Ramon
Tine deMateo, MS

Santa Ana
Blancarosa Craig, BA

Santa Barbara
Maria J. Alvarez, PhD
Michael Furlong
Robin Kracker, BA
Sujin Rhee

Santa Rosa
Connie Freeman, MA

Sebastopol
Kathleen Holland, MA

Sherman Oaks
Martha Ottina, PhD

Sierra Madre
Lori Buckley, BA
Lisa Harris, PhD

Sun Valley
Susan Sheldon, PhD

Sunland
Lyle Peterson, EdD

Temecula
Jerry Spadafore, PhD
Sharon Spadafore, MEd

Thousand Oaks
Elizabeth Cook, BA
Julie Porto, MS

Walnut
Susan Coats, MS

Whittier
Holly Brunton

Colorado

Arvada
Lisa Fischer-Valuck, EdS
Paula Jeane, PhD
Susan Valero, PD, NC

Aurora
Phyllis MacCartney, PhD
Jack McInroy
Phillip Thomsen, PsyD

Canon City
Pat Draper
Dorothy Williams, BS

Denver
William Boyd, PhD
Ellen Cashman, PhD
Victor Cordero, PsyD
Norman Dewhurst, EdD
Suzanne Hamm, PhD
Warren Knepper, EdD
Sue Verbiscus, MA

Fort Collins
Mark Luoma, BA

Fort Morgan
Heather Schulte

Grand Junction
Judith Wicker, MEd

Greenwood Village
Barbara Vicory

Lakewood
A. Barney Alexander, PhD
Rebecca Bell, BA
Robert Kooken

Conneticutt

East Hampton
Doreen Johnson

Naugatuck
Donna Passabet, CAGS

Old Greenwich
William Savage, MS

Delaware

Wilmington
Heidi Gomez, MA

Florida

Daytona
Nancy Long, EdD

Daytona Beach
Jennifer Riccitiello, MFA

Gulfport
Anna Eissfeldt, MA

Holiday
Rob Dusseau

Hollywood
Agnes Shine, PhD

Jacksonville
Pauline Gregory, MA

Kissimmee
Michael Monaco, BS
Julie Rauch, BA

Miami
Cary Ballesteros, MS
Christine Collado, BA
Maria De La Sierra, MA
Christina Ruiz, MS

North Miami
Naheed Jawed, MS

New Port Richey
Marijana Filomarino, MA

Ormond Beach
Cecile Ropelis Jurgensen, EdS

Panama City
Gloria Dumas, EdS, NCSP
Janice Shipbaugh, EdS

Plantation
Lisa Aronowitz, MS
Allan Ribbler, PhD

Georgia

Albany
Deborah Moore, EdM

Atlanta
Frank Batkins
Ros Byrd, MEd
W. Jean Heinrich, PhD
Dana Henderson, PhD
Tony Levitas, PsyD
Mary Ann McGrath, PsyD
Hamid Mirsalimi, PhD

Camilla
Deborah Murphy, MA
College Park
Betsy Box, PhD
John Coody, BS

Columbus
Rosetta Demming, EdS

Cordele
Chris Sumner, EdS

East Point
Shannon Allen, BS
Eugene Emory
Seymour Shaye
Melanie Winstead, MEd

Fayetteville
Kathleen Collins, BS
Jennifer Duncan, BS

Jefferson
Robert Covi, PhD

Leesburg
Ron McGhee, EdD

Lithia Springs
Alan Brue, BA

Marietta
Patricia Harbin, BS

Mc Donough
Jack Teague, BS

Stockbridge
Lynne Milam, MEd

Tucker
Karen Hike, MA

Warner Robbins
Chris Ceretti, MA

Hawaii

Aiea
Letitia Bailey, JD

Honolulu
Gary Turvold, EdD

Mililani
Jayne Asakura

Idaho

Blackfoot
Jenene Anderson, MEd
Debra Hamilton, EdS

Garden Valley
Laura Ropelis, MS

Lewiston
Gail Price, BS

Moreland
Bobbi Jo Alvarez, MEd

Moscow
Rebecca Barnes, MEd
Sharon Fritz, PhD
Brian Hastings, MS
Steve Saladin, PhD
Stacy Vickrey, MS
Catherine Weeks, EdS

Illinois

Arlington Heights
Nicole Hoffman, PsyD
Robin S. Johnstone, PhD

Calumet City
Pam Stipanich, MA

Chicago
Nikki Bishop, MS
David Boley, MA
Loren Chernoff, MEd
Francis Feeley, MA
David Finch, MA
Winston Hall
Reginald Hill
Norma Johnson, MA
Christine McGreevy, BS
Alice Murata, PhD
Randa Sabbagha, MA
Deborah Starkus, MSEd
Carolyn Trevino, BA
Gloria Washington, EdS

Des Plaines
Marianne Pfeiffer, BS

Evanston
Kerry Kennelly, MA

Geneva
Donna Pyshos-Burg, MA

La Grange
Dianne Stevenson, PsyD
Sue Szumigalski, MA

Lemont
Judith Drong, MA

Libertyville
Frances Pacheco, PhD

Long Grove
Julianne Kraut, PsyD
Michelle Navarro, PsyD

Mattoon
Sally Ryan, BA

Mount Prospect
Deborah Biwer

Oak Forest
Lois Paxton, MA

Palatine
Nana Brooks, MA

Pittsburgh
Melissa Ryner

Rockford
Paula Hougan, MS

Tinley Park
Alan Johnson, MA

Wilmette
Carole Dale

Indiana

Anderson
Colleen Garner, MA
Rebecca Reese, MA

Beech Grove
Dawn La France, BS

Berne
Douglas Lunn, MA

Carmel
Louanne Davis, PsyD

Fishers
Jacqueline Wall, MSE

Franklin
Alison Westerkamm, EdS

Gary
Myra Akins, MS

Greencastle
Charity Pankratz, MA

Indianapolis
Nathan Anderson, BA
Daniel Brown, PsyD
Hope Gawlowski, BA
Gail Kibiger, MA
Geoffrey Putt, MA

Lagrange
Theresa Nelson, MA

Middletown
Bonnie Huxford, MS

Muncie
Peter Duggan, MA

Ellen Fuscus, MA
Betty Gridley, PhD
Andrea Kelly, BS
Marci Kipfer, MA
Melanie Plunkett, MSE

Shelbyville
Heike Minnich, PsyD

Sheridan
Victoria Stumm, BA

Kansas

Iola
Stephanie Larson, MA

Lyons
Cindy Hogan, EdS
Elaine Flory Stefany, PhD
John Stuever, MEd

McPherson
Kathy Turner, MS

Norwich
Tara Ayres

Wellington
Debi Jones, MS

Wichita
Howard Babb, EdS
Linda Hickerson, MS

Kentucky

Ashland
Michael Sherman, MA

Bowling Green
Pamela Kielty, EdS

Lexington
Teresa Belluscio, MSE

Louisville
Denis Cambron, PhD

Mt. Sterling
Daniel Fasko, PhD

Richmond
Keith Feck, BS
Clarence Stapleton, BS
Rebecca Stigall, PsyD
Amy Szarlowski, MS

Louisiana

Baton Rouge
Mary Byrd, MS
Joanne Hotard, MEd
Meta Johnson, MEd
Gail Knecht, MS
Sherry LeBlanc, MA
Shirley Lewis, MEd
Erin Redlich, MEd
Ginger Speer, MEd
Linda Talbot, EdSP

Mandeville
Rachel Ogg, MA

New Iberia
Karen Declouet, MS

New Orleans
Sarah Ducey, PhD

Shreveport
Paula Lyrse, MS

Zachary
Katherine Leming, MS

Maine

Blaine
Terrie Brewer, MA

Bridgten
Loraine Spenciner, PhD

Lebanon
Karen Knight, MS

Portland
R. Peter James, PhD

Scarborough
Nancy Jones, MS, CCC-SLP

Windham
Catherine Kelso, MS, NCSP

Maryland

Baltimore
Gregory Ford, BA

Bethesda
Mary Silverman, MA

Camdenton
Diana Vogt, MSE

Landover
Bertha Henderson, MS

Largo
Sondra Kelley, BA

Silver Spring
Alicia Benn, BS
Cynthia Henderson, MSW

University Park
Bonnie McClellan, MA

Massachusetts

Acton
Kathleen Donnellan, MA

Amherst
Jack Horrigan, MEd

Boston
Fatima Aydin, PhD
Leon Brenner, PhD
Amy K. Heim, MA

Brookline
Joan T. Abramson, EdD
Christine Hutchinson

Charlestown
Samuel Sokol, PhD

Concord
Carole Donlon, CAGS

Harvard
Donna Burgess, MS

Lexington
Jana Bennett, MEd

North Billerica
Christine Newton, MA, CAGS

North Easton
Laurel Silverman, CAES

Somerville
Jessica Tredeau

Waban
Lydia Kenin, PsyD

Walpole
Caroline Wandle, PhD

West Townsend
Dennis Young, MEd

Williamstown
Linda Crowe, MEd

Michigan

Ann Arbor
Wendy Cheng

Beverly Hills
Elaine Swenson

Bloomfield Hills
Nicholas J. Bodoin, PhD

Dearborn
Dwayne Evans
George Garcia, MA, LLP
John Sczomak, PhD

Detroit
Carla Lee, MA
Brant MacLean

Grand Rapids
Kathy Barnett, EdS

Harper Woods
Anne E. Jackson, PhD

Huntingdon Woods
Beth Avadenka

Milford
Kathy Nelson

Niles
Donna Turner-Campbell, PhD

Okemos
Emmelyn McKillips, EdS
Brenda Washington, MA

Plymouth
Jennifer Harms, MA, CCC-SLP

Rochester Hills
Roxanne Alfsen, EdSP

Southfield
Samuel Goldstein, PhD
Rody Yezman, PhD

Tuecumseh
Carol Tapp, MA

West Bloomfield
Lorraine Goldberg

Minnesota

Brooklyn Park
Leanne Goth, MA

Duluth
Judith Bromen, MEd
Penny Cragun, MSE

Egan
Diane Grinnell, MS

Granite Falls
Theresa Ziebarth-Moritz, BA

Maplewood
Timothy Kellen, BS

Mississippi

Baldwyn
Deborah Nemit, MEd

Mendenhall
Rosalind Rhodes-Lee, MA

Missouri

Bolivar
Katrina Douthit, BS

Columbia
Shawn Roberson, MA
Molly Stebbins, MA

Festus
Melissa Lane, MEd

Gladstone
Janet Hurst, MA, SPE

Higginsville
Janet Oetting, MA

Kansas City
Michael Chapman
Connie Nielson

Lebanon
Millie Gann, MEd
Linda Pickering, BA

La Rita Pope, MS
Rebecca Simpson, BSE
Jennifer Snyder, MA

Liberty
Myra Angel

Republic
Ruth Ann Wood-Humiston, PhD

Richland
Barbara Yearsley, MS

Rogersville
Rhonda Smith, MS

Springfield
Matthew Awad, BS
Steve Capps, PhD
Douglas Greiner, PhD
Hayden Haller, BA
Craig Johnston, BS
Jennifer Keet, BS
Lori Lingenfelser, MS
Alix McLearen, BS
David Richard, PhD
Martaun Stockstill, BS

St. Louis
Patricia Ligon, MS
John Siebel, PhD

St. Peters
Claudia McClarran, MA

Stafford
Keith Bendure, BA

Warrensburg
David Dai, PhD
Nicole Nickens, PhD
Johnathan Smith, PhD

Webb City
Linda Wilson, MA

Montana

Billings
Kimberly Paulsen, EdD
Mark Taylor, MA

Great Falls
Robin Treptow, PhD

Havre
Lorraine Larson, MEd

Nebraska

Bellevue
Lorene Ruuska, PhD

Crete
Jennifer Wagner

Doniphan
Janet Blake, EdS

Gothenburg
Gwen Fecht, EdS

Lincoln
Barbara Newell, MA
Judy Parmelee, MEd
Martin Wiese, PhD

McCook
Dennis Radford, EdSP

Norfolk
Mark R. Claussen, EdS

Ogallala
Linda Lund, EdS

Omaha
John Downs
Victoria Porter, EdS
Christine Pratt, BS

Nevada

Las Vegas
Lenise Dudman, BA
Susan Shaver, BS

New Hampshire

Chesterfield
Donna Borynack, MEd, CAGS

Londonderry
Patricia Isopo, CAGS

Plaistow
Shana Healy

Portsmouth
Terry Karnan, MA

Raymond
Ellen Kelsall, MEd

New Jersey

Birdgeton
Patricia Kenelia, MA

Clifton
Lynn Sullivan, MA

Hampton
Annie Culp Lawrence, EdS

Midland Park
James F. Battaglia, PhD

Ridgewood
Stacy Mathiesen, BA

Wenonah
Kenneth Solem, MA

West Paterson
Patricia Urgo, MA

New Mexico

Albuquerque
Rochelle Cordova, MA
Robert Wengrod, MEd

Clovis
Michael Shaughnessy, PhD

Las Cruces
Jennifer Castro, BA
Authur Montgomery, MA

Sapello
Shirley Jones, MA

New York

Auburn
Pat Carberry, MS
Christina Smith, MS

Bronx
Cleveland Campbell, MS
Carla Tellez, BA

Brooklyn
E. Dinos
Michael Homsey
M. Lachman
P. McGrath

Chantee McKinney, MS
B. Milano
A. Milonopoulas
Effie Noufrios
J. Ribellino
R. Ribellino
F. Stingo
W. Vitiello

Burnt Hills
Paula Taylor, MEd

Clarence Center
Miriam Carey

Cortland
Joanne Finn, MS

Deansboro
Kathleen Wright, PhD

Dobbs
Ferry Selma Thackeray, MS

Geneseo
Joan Ballard, PhD

Hamburg
Linda Boulange, MS

Laurelton
Anita Lee, MS

Melville
Yvette Frumkin Feis, PhD

New York
Erin K. Elto, PsyD
Shana L. Levine, PsyD
Donna Paul, MS
Bonnie Seiler, PD

North Babylon
Norma Scanlon, MS

Plattsburgh
Cynthia Pollock, BA
Tracy Van Auken, BA

Port Jefferson Station
Michelle Kees, MA

Rochester
Susan Shonk, PhD

Saratoga Springs
Kimberly Dellis

Scott Dellis

South Hampton
Alan Roberts

Staten Island
Janet Juliano
Carole Schaffer

Troy
Janet Gorsky, PhD

North Carolina

Durham
Asenath Devaney, EdS

Fayetteville
Patricia Heath, MEd
Donna Major, PhD
Kathie Mathews, MA

Greensboro
Robert Mitchum, PhD

Kernersville
Sally Cannon, MA

Lumberton
Jacqueline Hunt, EdS

Ohio

Avon Lake
Elizabeth Walker, MSE

Concord
Peggy Young, PhD

Elida
Florence Shepps, MS

Ironton
Edward Kittinger, Jr., MA

Jackson
John Lehew, MS

Lima
Jennifer Jacobs, PsyD

Mayfield Heights
Anthony Goff
Harvey Sisler, PhD

Mentor
Gary Silbiger, MA

Richmond Heights
Johnathan Steinbach, BA

Stow
John Yovich, MA

Struthers
Alycia Muto, EdS

Toledo
Jane McCloskey, BS

Washington City
Stephanie Yerian, PsyD

Willow Wood
Panda Powell, BA

Oklahoma

Norman
Melissa Engleman, MEd

Oklahoma City
Marti Long, BS
Monica McGuire, MA
Mona Ryan, MS
Linda Walters, MS

Shawnee
Ann Ahern, MEd

Tulsa
Cindy Eland, MA

Oregon

Hillsboro
Jennifer Felker, PsyD

Portland
Emily Allen, BA
Marilyn Baer, BA
Joann Cordes, BA
William Hartwig, BA
Denise Peloquin, MS
Becky Swanson, BA

Pennsylvania

Allentown
Frederick Hahn, MEd
Lori McCann, MA

Coplay
Stephen Matulevicius, MSEd

Dresher
Sally Rosenwasser, MEd, CCC-SLP

Erie
Douglas Della-Toffalo, MSE

Harrisburg
George Schmidt, PhD

Huntingdon Valley
Gail Reichman Mancini, MA

Johnstown
Janice Deetscreek, MEd

Kingston
Frank Bozek, MA

Lake City
Kathleen Hanson, MA

Malvern
Linda Bonsall, MEd

Montoursville
Eve Hilsher, MEd

Orrtanna
Joan Reeve, MEd

Philadelphia
Umar Abdullah-Johnson, MS
Donna Wilson, PhD
Gang Xie, MEd

Pittsburgh
Eleanor Shirley, MA

Schnecksville
Deborah Thomas, MEd

Scranton
Maryann Burne, MEd

Shippenville
Peter Nachtwey, PhD

Wallingford
Diane Coffin, MS

Whitehall
Lynda Strohl, MSEd

Wyncote
Catherine Fiorello, PhD

Wyoming
Ann Kane, MS

Rhode Island

Cranston
Pamela Esten, MEd

North Kingstown
Alicemarie O'Connor, MEd

Rumford
Kathryn A. Lockwood, PhD

Warren
Anne McGloin, CAGS

Warwick
Annmarie McKenna, MA

South Carolina

Greenville
Lesa Seibert, MEd
Amy Streeter, MEd

Greer
Reggie Harrison, MS
Elisabeth Norris, MEd

Summerville
Janet Hansen, BS

South Dakota

Aberdeen
Joanna Dejong, MA
Lisa Ducheneaux, BA
Kristie Erickson, BS
Pamela White, BS

Mission
Kathy Chauncey, MA
Laurie Chauncey, BA
Alisha Van Dyke, BA

Norris
Lori Schmidt, AA

Sioux Falls
Vickie Bain, MA

Tennessee

Bartlett
Andrew Yu, MS

Clarksville
Comfort Asanbe, PhD
Cheryl Grieve, MS
Frederick Grieve, PhD
Maureen McCarthy, PhD
Chris Newton, MA

Franklin
Edwina Chappell, PhD
Mira Fleischman, MSE
Anne Nussle, MEd
Diane Wood, MSE

Goodlettsville
Tammy Ruff, MEd

Knoxville
John Chohanin, MA

Memphis
Evelyne Greer, MS
Laura Murphy, EdD

White House
Sherrie Mitchell, MS

Texas

Abilene
Janet McLennan, MEd

Arlington
Brenda Taylor, MEd

Austin
Carol Byrne, MSE
Kevin Hair, BA
Carmen Hendrickson, MEd
Kerry Owens, BSA
Amy Peterson, MEd
Alexandria Rankovic, MS
Tracy Sloan, MA
Surabhi Talesara, MA, CAGS
Jean Tanous, EdS
Deena Wright, MEd
William Yeatts, MA

Baytown
Donna Denny, MA

Beckville
Brenda Greer-Jennings, EdSP

Bryan
Doris Hermann, MEd

Canyon Lake
Jerry Trice, MA
Janice Vickers, MA

Converse
Lorraine Huffaker, MA

Corpus Christi
Wendy Atkins-Sayre, MA
Marynelle Davis, MEd
Jackie Ganschow, MA

Corrigan
Elwanda Stricklen, MEd

Cypress
Judy Brumer, MA

Dallas
Linda Atwill, PhD
C. Gary Barnes, PhD
M. Eileen Beiler, PsyD
Maria Cianforne, MS
Mark Foster
Shelley Lurie, PsyD
David O'Brien, PhD
Kathryn Quest, MS, LPC
Eric Smernoff

Duncanville
Renee Nelson, MEd

El Paso
Ann Romer, EdS

Ennis
Brenda Hogue, MEd

Fair Oaks Ranch
Jessica Gombert, MA

Fort Worth
Devette Robinson, MS
Fara Raines, MEd
Donna Stockdale, MA

Granbury
Judith Klein, BA

Harker Heights
Ann Budke, MEd

Hillsboro
Frieda Grigsby, MS

Houston
Katherine Bell, MA

Anna Forey, BS
Cheryl Gabriel, MEd
Linda Harms, EdS
Cynthia Olson, MS

Hurst
Monica Freeman

Irving
Lana Holland, PhD
Ellen Wells, MEd

Laguna Vista
Elizabeth Neck, MA

Lockhart
Joanne Pike, MA

Los Fresnos
Susi Clark, MEd

New Braunfels
Anita Barsalou, MEd
Laura Schulte, MS

Orange
Nell Pence, BS

Pampa
Donna Anderson, MEd

Plano
Jennifer Doran, MA
Mary Ann Morris, MEd
Michael Novotny, MEd

Plattsburgh
Ron Dumont, EdD

Richardson
Erin Owen-Salters, PhD

Round Rock
Yvonne Demsky
Brenda Stady, MEd

San Angelo
Margaret Altom, BS
Dee Chesser, MEd
Billie Jean Thoma, BS
Tina Tucker, MEd
Michelle Williams, BA

San Antonio
Rana Afeiche, BA
Alison Arnatt, BA
Cynthia Bailey, MS
Liza Baker, BA
William Baker, MA
Brandi Barnard, BS
Nicole Boyer, MA
Amy Cassata, MA
Mary Castillo, BSW
Jennifer Catron, BA
Meghan Chance, BA
Kristan Dixon, MA
Gay Duncan
Kerry Farris, MEd
William Franklin, MEd
Annie Garza-Gutierrez
Teresa Giustino, BA
Vivian Harrington, MA
Cilla Holmes-Stultz, MA
Edward Howarth, MA
Diana Jasnau, MA
Marilyn Jones-Oliver, BA
Maria Juarez, MA
Sandra Kaiser, BA
David Kenny, BS
Diana Kenny, BA
Amber King, BA
Sheree Lenhart Kreusel, MEd
Judith Longfellow, BA
Jeff Majors, MA
Kim McIntyre, BA
Ashley Nelson, MA
Patricia O'Sullivan, MA
Joan Patteson, MS
Cherry Procter, MEd
Laura Reagan, BA
Veronica Rodriguez, BA
Jennifer Rohn, BA
Jacquelyn Rumpf, MA
Sylvia Saucedo, MA
Pam Sauls, MEd
Susan Shires, MA
Charlie Sims, MEd
Judith Smith, EdD
Yvonne Soucie, BS
Jason Stewart, BS
Lynn Thompson, MEd
Stephanie Tong, MA
Smaranda Valescu, BA
Tina Wehner, MEd
Sandra Westbrook, MA
Lauren Woolley, MA
Ray Zurcher, PhD

San Marcos
Gaylynn Clevenger, MA

Scroggins
Shay Blakeway, MEd

Spring
Debora Gnatzig, MEd

Spring Branch
Dawn Magers, MEd
Paulette Pilsner, MEd

Universal City
Donna Cantu, BA

Wake Village
Manaleta March, MEd

Witchita Falls
John Conway

Utah

Salt Lake City
Shufeng Zheng, MEd

Woodland Hills
Galen Downing, MSE

Vermont

Chittenden
Stacy Shortle, MS

Virginia

Alexandria
Virginia Lindahl, BA

Arlington
Catherine Martin, BA

Falls Church
Rose Rice, MS

Farmville
Jill Lewis, MA

Richmond
Tracey Brown, BA
Ann Capell, MS
Shyla Ipsen, PhD

Vienna
Elizabeth Anderson, MS

Washington

Bremerton
Carole Bergman, MA

Clallam Bay
Donna Smith, EdS

Clarkston
Teri Rust, PhD

Fort Louis
Angelia Jennen, MA

Pullman
Tammie Rogers, BS

Seattle
Michael Moretsky, MEd

Shoreline
Donna Ahron

Spokane
Mary Hoekzema, MS

Tacoma
Sandy Benson, MA
Annette Kloeppel, MEd

West Virginia

Huntington
Yvonne Stroud, BA

Hurricane
Farah Jalali, MA
Linda Reber, MA

St. Albans
Vicki Horn, BA

West Hamilton
Teresa Feller, MA

Wisconsin

Brookfield
Mike Schmitz, MS

Fond Du Lac
Dave Davenport, MS
Craig Ferch, MEd

Green Bay
Anne Coleman, PhD

Milwaukee
Irene Panagopoulas, MS

Spring Green
John Humphries, MS

Stoddard
Milton Dehn, EdD

Wyoming

Afton
G. Nohl Sandall, PhD

Reviewers

Robert Abbott, PhD
Virginia Berninger, PhD
Lupe Chavez, BA
Deborah Crockett, PhD
Steve Graham, PhD
Betty Gridley, PhD
Jan Longfellow, MA
Ronald Palermo, PhD
Carrie Perez, MEd
David Ramirez, MEd
Nancy Robinson, PhD
Gale Roid, PhD
Don Saklofske, PhD
Brenda Vavricek, MS
Richard Venezky, PhD
Susan Vogel, PhD

Participating Schools and Districts

Aberdeen Catholic School, Aberdeen, SD
Adelphi Academy, Brooklyn, NY
Adler School of Professional Psychology, Chicago, IL
Advent House Ministries, Lansing, MI
Amphitheater Middle School, Tucson, AZ
The Bedford School, East Point, GA
Believer's Academy, San Antonio, TX
Benavides Learning Center, San Antonio, TX
Blocks To Books, Raymond, NH
Body of Christ Ministries, San Antonio, TX
Booth-Fickett Magnet School, Tucson, AZ
Brookside School, Sea Girt, NJ
Butte College, Oroville, CA
Calvary Christian School, Baton Rouge, LA
Cambria County Christian School, Johnstown, PA
Carden School, Tucson, AZ
Chicago Department of Aging, Chicago, IL
Church of Acts-Royal Point Academy, San Antonio, TX
City College of Los Angeles, Los Angeles, CA
Columbia College, Sonora, CA
Community College of Allegheny County, Pittsburgh, PA
Cosumnes River College, Sacramento, CA
Crafton Hills College, Yucaipa, CA
Cross Road Kindergarten, Dover, NH
Dover Day Care, Dover, NH

Participating Schools and Districts *(continued)*

East Pennsboro Public School, Enola, PA
Emmanuel Lutheran School, Tempe, AZ
Frank Garrett Center, San Antonio, TX
Gavilan College, Gilroy, CA
Grace Lutheran School, Portland, OR
Higgs, Carter, King, San Antonio, TX
High Street Christian Academy, Philadelphia, PA
Houston Academy, Dothan, AL
Hurray For Me! School, Shoreline, WA
Lamb's Gate Preschool, Tucson, AZ
Lancaster County School District, Lancaster, SC
Lutheran High School of Indianapolis, Indianapolis, IN
Madonna Day Care, San Antonio, TX
Marri-Lee Childcare Center, Lee, NH
Millercreek Township School District, Erie, PA
North Kansas City School, Kansas City, MO
Northside ISD, San Antonio, TX
Northeast ISD, San Antonio, TX
Northside Learning Center, San Antonio, TX
Nosotros Alternative School, Tucson, AZ
Orchard Hill School, Tinley Park, IL
Palomar College, San Marcus, CA
Peace Lutheran School, Holiday, FL
Roebuck Park Christian School, Birmingham, AL
Sacred Heart Catholic School, Austin, TX
San Antonio, ISD, San Antonio, TX
Scotch Plains Public School, Scotch Plains, NJ
Sierra College, Rocklin, CA
Sierra Vista Methodist School, San Angelo, TX
Small Creations Daycare, Warrensburg, MO
South San Antonio ISD, San Antonio, TX
Southwestern College, Chula Vista, CA
St. Luke's School, Schenectady, NY
St. Margaret Mary, San Antonio, TX
St. Martin's Hall, San Antonio, TX
St. Paul Lutheran School, Austin, TX
Steppin' Out Dance Academy, Kingston, NH
Southern Vermont College, Bennington, VT
Summitview Elementary School, Tucson, AZ
Sunshine Cottage, San Antonio, TX
Suny Genesco, Department of Psychology, Genesco, NY
Suny Plattsburgh, Plattsburgh, NY
Temple University, Philadelphia, PA
The Nurturing Place, Springfield, MO
Triangle Park Research, Research Triangle Park, NC
Tri-City Christian Academy, Summersworth, NH
Tucson Regional Ballet, Tucson, AZ
Tufts University, Boston, MA
Tzu-Chi Academy, Monrovia, CA
Westfield State College, Westfield, MA
Winston School, San Antonio, TX
Yucaipa Calimesa Jt. Unified School District, Yucaipa, CA

References

Adams, M. (1990). Beginning to read: Thinking and learning about print. Cambridge, MA: MIT Press.

Adams, M., Foorman, B., Lundberg, I., & Beeler, T. (1998). *Phonemic awareness in young children: A classroom curriculum.* Baltimore: Brookes.

Adams, M., & Henry, M. K. (1997). Myths and realities about words and literacy. *School Psychology Review, 26*(3), 425–436.

Alexander, A., Andersen, H., Heilman, K., Voeller, K., & Torgesen, J. (1991). Phonological awareness training and remediation of analytic decoding deficits in a group of severe dyslexics. *Annals of the Orton Society, 41,* 193–206.

American Psychiatric Association. (1994). *Diagnostic and statistical manual of mental disorders* (4th ed.). Washington, DC: Author.

Balmuth, M. (1992). *The roots of phonics: A historical introduction.* Baltimore, MD: York Press.

Barenbaum, E., Newcomer, P., & Nodine, B. (1987). Children's ability to write stories as a function of variation in task, age, and developmental level. *Learning Disability Quarterly, 10,* 175–188.

Baroody, A. J. (1987). *Children's mathematical thinking: A developmental framework for preschool, primary, and special education teachers.* New York: Teachers College Press.

Berk, R. A. (1984). *Screening and diagnosis of children with learning disabilities.* Springfield, IL: Charles C. Thomas.

Berninger, V. (1989). Orchestration of multiple codes in developing readers: An alternative model of lexical access. *International Journal of Neuroscience, 48,* 85–104.

Berninger, V. (1998). *Process assessment of the learner. Guides for intervention: Reading and writing.* San Antonio, TX: The Psychological Corporation.

Berninger, V. (2001). *Process assessment of the learner–Test battery for reading and writing.* San Antonio, TX: The Psychological Corporation.

Berninger, V., Cartwright, A., Yates, C., Swanson, H., & Abbott, R. (1994). Developmental skills related to writing and reading acquisition in the intermediate grades: Shared and unique variance. *Reading and Writing: An Interdisciplinary Journal, 6,* 161–196.

Berninger, V., Fuller, F., & Whitaker, D. (1996). A process model of writing development across the life span. *Educational Psychology Review, 8*(3), 193–218.

Berninger, V., Mizokawa, D., Bragg, R., Cartwright, A., & Yates, C. (1994). Intraindividual differences in levels of written language. *Reading and Writing Quarterly, 10,* 259–275.

Berninger, V., Yates, C., Cartwright, A., Rutberg, J., Remy, E., & Abbott, R. (1992). Lower-level developmental skills in beginning writing. *Reading and Writing: An Interdisciplinary Journal, 4,* 257–280.

Bigge, J. L., & Stump, C. S. (with Spagna, M. E., & Silberman, R. K.). (1999). *Curriculum, assessment, and instruction for students with disabilities.* Belmont, CA: Wadsworth.

Bley, N. S., & Thornton, C. A. (1989). *Teaching mathematics to the learning disabled* (2nd ed.). Austin, TX: Pro–Ed.

Borg, W. R., & Gall, M. D. (1989). *Educational research: An introduction* (5th ed.). New York: Longman.

Bowers, P. G. (1988, November). *Naming speed and phonological awareness: Independent contributors to reading disabilities.* Paper presented at the meeting of the National Reading Conference, Tucson, AZ. (ERIC Document Reproduction Service No. ED 301 871).

Braden, J. P., & Weiss, L. (1988). Effects of simple difference versus regression discrepancy methods: An empirical study. *Journal of School Psychology, 26,* 133–142.

Bradley, L., & Bryant, P. E. (1978). Difficulties in auditory organisation as a possible cause of reading backwardness. *Nature, 271,* 746–747.

Bransford, J. D., Brown, A. L., & Cocking, R. R. (1999). *How people learn: Brain, mind, experience, and school.* Washington, DC: National Academy Press.

Bryant, D. P., Bryant, B. R., & Hammill, D. D. (2000). Characteristic behaviors of students with LD who have teacher-identified math weaknesses. *Journal of Learning Disabilities, 33*(2), 168–177.

Campbell, D. T., & Fiske, D. W. (1959). Convergent and discriminant validation by the multitrait–multimethod matrix. *Psychological Bulletin, 56,* 81–105.

Carver, R. P. (1990). *Reading rate: A review of research and theory.* San Diego, CA: Academic Press.

Combs, W. (1976). Further effects of sentence-combining practice on writing ability. *Research in the Teaching of English, 10,* 137–149.

Davis, F. B. (1959). Interpretation of differences among averages and individual test scores. *Journal of Educational Psychology, 50*(4), 162–170.

DiPerna, J. C., & Elliott, S. N. (2000). *Academic Competence Evaluation Scales–Manual K–12.* San Antonio, TX: The Psychological Corporation.

DiStefano, P., Dole, J. A., & Marzano, R. J. (1984). *Elementary language arts.* New York: Wiley.

Dunn, L., & Dunn, L. (1997). *Peabody Picture Vocabulary Test–Third Edition.* Circle Pines, MN: American Guidance Service.

Education for All Handicapped Children Act of 1975, Pub. L. No. 94–142, 89 Stat. 773 (1977).

Elliott, C. D. (1990). *Differential Ability Scales.* San Antonio, TX: The Psychological Corporation.

Flanagan, D. P., & Alfonso, V. C. (1993). WIAT subtest and composite predicted-achievement values based on WISC–III Verbal and Performance IQs. *Psychology in the Schools, 30,* 310–320.

Flynn, J. R. (1984). The mean IQ of Americans: Massive gains 1932 to 1978. *Psychological Bulletin, 95*(1), 29–51.

Flynn, J. R. (1987). Massive IQ gains in 14 nations: What IQ tests really measure. *Psychological Bulletin, 101*(2), 171–191.

Fry, E., Polk, J., & Fountoukidis, D. (1984). *The reading teacher's book of lists.* Englewood Cliffs, NJ: Prentice Hall.

Geary, D. C. (1994). *Children's mathematical development: Research and practical applications.* Washington, DC: American Psychological Association.

Gelman, R., & Gallistel, C. R. (1978). *The child's understanding of number.* Cambridge, MA: Harvard University Press.

Glutting, J. J., Oakland, T., & Konold, T. R. (1994). Criterion-related bias with the guide to the assessment of test-session behavior for the WISC–III and WIAT: Possible race/ethnicity, gender, and SES effects. *Journal of School Psychology, 32*(4), 355–369.

Gough, P. B., & Tunmer, W. E. (1986). Decoding, reading, and reading disability. *Remedial and Special Education, 7*(1), 6–10.

Graham, S., Berninger, V. W., Abbott, R. D., Abbott, S. P., & Whitaker, D. (1997). Role of mechanics in composing of elementary school students: A new methodological approach. *Journal of Educational Psychology, 89*(1), 170–182.

Gregg, N. (1983). College learning-disabled writer: Error patterns and instructional alternatives. *Journal of Learning Disabilities, 16,* 334–338.

Guilford, J. P., & Fruchter, B. (1978). *Fundamental statistics in psychology and education* (6th ed.). New York: McGraw–Hill.

Harcourt Educational Measurement (1996). *Stanford Achievement Tests, Ninth Edition.* Sa TX: Author.

Harcourt Educational Measuremen *Metropolitan Achievement Te Standardization Edition. S* Author.

Harcourt Educational Me *for instruction: A H Activities.* San Ar

Henry, M. K. (199 *spelling instr structure.*

Herman, P. *readi acc 553–5

Holmes, D. R., specific seria dyslexics. *Cortex, 1*

Houck, C. K., & Billingsle 5. (1989). expression of students with and without learni disabilities: Differences across the grades. *Journal of Learning Disabilities, 22*(9), 561–572.

Individuals With Disabilities Education Act Amendments of 1997, 20 U.S.C. 1400 *et seq.* (Fed. Reg. 64, 1999).

Jorm, A. F. (1979). The cognitive and neurological basis of developmental dyslexia: A theoretical framework and review. *Cognition, 7,* 19–33.

Jorm, A. F. (1983). Specific reading retardation and working memory: A review. *British Journal of Psychology, 74,* 311–342.

Kamphaus, R. W. (1993). *Clinical assessment of children's intelligence: A handbook for professional practice.* Boston: Allyn & Bacon.

Kamphaus, R. W., Slotkin, J., and DeVencentis, C. (1990). Clinical assessment of children's academic achievement. In C.R. Reynolds & R.W. Kamphaus (Eds.), *Handbook of psychological and educational assessment of children: Intelligence and achievement* (pp. 552–568). New York: Guilford Press.

Kaufman, A. S. (1979). *Intelligent testing with the WISC–R.* New York: Wiley.

Kaufman, A. S., & Lichtenberger, E. O. (2000). *Essentials of WISC–III and WPPSI–R assessment.* In A. Kaufman, & N. Kaufman (Serial Eds.), Essentials of Psychological Assessment Series. New York: Wiley.

Kavale, K. A., & Forness, S. R. (1995). *The nature of learning disabilities. Critical elements of diagnosis and classification.* Mahwah, NJ: Erlbaum.

Keith, T. Z., & Witta, E. L. (1997). Hierarchical and cross-age confirmatory factor analysis of the WISC–III: What does it measure? *School Psychology Quarterly, 12,* 89–107.

Konold, T. R. (1999). Evaluating discrepancy analyses with the WISC–III and WIAT. *Journal of Psychoeducational Assessment, 17,* 24–35.

Kuhn, M., & Stahl, S. (2000). Fluency. A review of developmental and remedial practices (CIERA Report #2–0008). Ann Arbor: University of Michigan, Center for the Improvement of Early Reading Achievement.

Lane, S.E., & Lewandowski, L. (1994). Oral and written compositions of students with and without learning disabilities. *Journal of Psychoeducational Assessment,* 12, 143–153.

Lennon, J. E., & Slesinski, C. (1999). Early intervention in reading: Results of a screening and intervention program for kindergarten students. *School Psychology Review, 28*(3), 353–364.

Liberman, I., Shankweiler, D., Fischer, F., & Carter, B. (1974). Explicit syllable and phoneme segmentation in the young child. *Journal of Experimental Child Psychology, 18,* 201–212.

Lipson, M. Y., & Wixson, K. K. (1997). *Assessment and instruction of reading and writing disability: An interactive approach* (2nd ed.). New York: Longman.

Lord, F. M. (1980). *Applications of item response theory to practical testing problems.* Hillsdale, NJ: Erlbaum.

Lovett, M. (1987). A developmental approach to reading disability: Accuracy and speed criteria of normal and deficient reading skill. *Child Development, 58,* 234–260.

Manis, F. R., Szeszulski, P. A., Holt, L. K., & Graves, K. (1988). A developmental perspective on dyslexic subtypes. *Annals of Dyslexia, 38,* 139–153.

Mann, V. A., Cowin, E., & Schoenheimer, J. (1989). Phonological processing, language comprehension, and reading ability. *Journal of Learning Disabilities, 22*(2), 76–89.

Mann, V. A., Liberman, I. Y., & Shankweiler, D. (1980). Children's memory for sentences and word strings in relation to reading ability. *Memory and Cognition, 8*(4), 329–335.

Mann, V. A., Shankweiler, D., & Smith, S. T. (1984). The association between comprehension of spoken sentences and early reading ability: The role of phonetic representation. *Journal of Child Language, 11,* 627–643.

Matarazzo, J. D. (1972). *Wechsler's measurement and appraisal of adult intelligence* (5th ed.). Baltimore: Williams & Wilkins.

Matarazo, J. D. (1990). Psychological assessment versus psychological testing: Validation from Binet to the school, clinic, and courtroom. *American Psychologist, 45*(9), 999–1017.

Moats, L. C. (1995). *Spelling: Development, disabilities, and instruction.* Baltimore, MD: York Press.

Montague, M., & Bos, C. S. (1986). The effect of cognitive strategy training on verbal math problem solving performance of learning disabled adolescents. *Journal of Learning Disabilities, 19*(1), 26–33.

Moran, M. R. (1981). Performance of learning disabled and low achieving secondary students on formal features of a paragraph-writing task. *Learning Disability Quarterly, 4,* 271–280.

Myklebust, H.R. (1973). *Development and disorders of written language: Studies of normal and exceptional children* (vol. two). New York: Grune and Stratton.

Nagy, W. E., Winsor, P., Osborn, J., & O'Flahavan, J. (1994). Structural analysis: Some guidelines for instruction. In F. Lehr & J. Osborn (Eds), *Reading, language, and literacy: Instruction for the twenty–first century* (pp. 45–58). Hillsdale, NJ: Erlbaum.

National Council of Teachers of Mathematics. (2000). *Principles and standards for school mathematics.* Reston, VA: Author.

National Reading Panel. (2000). *Teaching Children to Read: An evidence-based assessment of the scientific research literature on reading and its implications for reading instruction* (NIH Publication No. 00-4754). Washington, DC: National Institute of Child Health and Human Development.

Nunnally, J. (1978). *Psychometric theory* (2nd ed.). New York: McGraw–Hill.

Olson, R., Wise, B., Conners, F., Rack, J., & Fulker, D. (1989). Specific deficits in component reading and language skills: Genetic and environmental influences. *Journal of Learning Disabilities, 22,* 339–348.

Payne, R. W., & Jones, H. G. (1957). Statistics for the investigation of individual cases. *Journal of Clinical Psychology, 13,* 115–121.

Poplin, M.S., Gray, R., Larsen, S. Banikowski, A., & Mehring, T. (1980). A comparison of components of written expression abilities in learning disabled and non-learning disabled students at three grade levels. *Learning Disability Quarterly, 3,* 46–53.

Poteet, J.A. (1978). Characteristics of written expression of learning disabled and non-learning disabled elementary school students (ERIC Document ED159–830). Muncie, IN: Ball State University

Pressley, M., & Wharton–McDonald, R. (1997). Skilled comprehension and its development through instruction. *School Psychology Review, 26*(3), 448–466.

Prifitera, A., & Saklofske, D. H. (1998). *WISC–III clinical use and interpretation. Scientist–practioner perspectives.* San Diego, CA: Academic Press.

Prifitera, A., Weiss, L., & Saklofske, D. (1998). The WISC–III in context. In Prifitera, A., & Saklofske, D. (Eds.), *WISC–III clinical use and interpretation: Scientist–practitioner perspectives* (pp. 1–38). San Diego, CA: Academic Press.

The Psychological Corporation. (1992). *Wechsler Individual Achievement Test.* San Antonio, TX: Author.

Rack, J. P., Snowling, M. J. , & Olson, R. K. (1992). The nonword reading deficit in developmental dyslexia: A review. *Reading Research Quarterly, 27*(1), 29–53.

Rasch, G. (1980). *Probabilistic models for some intelligence and attainment tests.* Chicago: University of Chicago Press. (Original work published 1960, Copenhagen: Danish Institute for Educational Research)

Resnick, L. B. (1987). *Education and learning to think.* Washington, DC: National Academy Press.

Reynolds, C. R. (1985). Critical measurement issues in learning disabilities. *Journal of Special Education, 18*(4), 451–476.

Reynolds, C. R. (1990). Conceptual and technical problems in learning disability diagnosis. In C. R. Reynolds & R. W. Kamphaus (Eds.), *Handbook of psychological and educational assessment of children: Intelligence and achievement* (pp. 571–592). New York: Guilford Press.

Reynolds, C. R., & Kamphaus, R. W. (Eds.). (1990). *Handbook of psychological and educational assessment of children: Intelligence and achievement.* New York: Guilford Press.

Roid, G. H., & Worrall, W. (1997). Replication of the Wechsler Intelligence Scale for Children–third edition four-factor model in the Canadian normative sample. *Psychological Assessment, 9*(4), 512–515.

Salvia, J., & Ysseldyke, J. E. (1991). *Assessment* (5th ed.). Boston: Houghton Mifflin.

Samuels, S. J. (1988). Decoding and automaticity: Helping poor readers become automatic at word recognition. *The Reading Teacher, 48*(8), 756–760.

SAS Institute. (1990). SAS Language: Reference, Version 6 [Computer software]. Cary, NC: Author.

Sattler, J. M. (2001). *Assessment of children: Cognitive applications* (4th ed.). San Diego: Author.

Schoenfeld, A. H. (1988). When good teaching leads to bad results: The disasters of "well taught" mathematics classes. *Educational Psychologist, 23*(2), 145–166.

Shepard, L. (1980). An evaluation of the regression discrepancy method for identifying children with learning disabilities. *Journal of Special Education, 14*(1), 79–91.

Shrout, P., & Fleiss, J. (1979). Intraclass correlations: Uses in assessing rater reliability. *Psychological Bulletin, 86,* 420–428.

Silverstein, A. B. (1981). Reliability and abnormality of test score differences. *Journal of Clinical Psychology, 37*(2), 392–394.

Silverstein, A. B. (1982). Pattern analysis as simultaneous statistical inference. *Journal of Consulting and Clinical Psychology, 50*(2), 234–240.

Smith, S. T., Mann, V. A., & Shankweiler, D. (1986). Spoken sentence comprehension by good and poor readers: A study with the Token Test. *Cortex, 22,* 627–632.

Snowling, M. J. (1981). Phonemic deficits in developmental dyslexia. *Psychological Research, 43*(2), 219–234.

Snyder, T. D., & Hoffman, C. M. (2001). *Digest of education statistics, 2000* (NCES 2001-034). Washington, DC: U.S. Department of Education, National Center for Education Statistics.

SRA/McGraw–Hill. (1992). *Spectrum Dolch Sight Word Activities.* New York: Author.

Stahl, S. A., Heubach, K., & Cramond, B. (1997). Fluency-oriented reading instruction (Reading Research Report No. 79). Athens, GA: National Reading Research Center.

Standards for educational and psychological testing. (1985). Washington, DC: American Psychological Association.

Standards for educational and psychological testing. (1999). Washington, DC: American Psychological Association.

Stanovich, K. E. (1985). Explaining the variance in reading ability in terms of psychological processes: What have we learned? *Annals of Dyslexia, 35,* 67–96.

Steck–Vaughn. (1991). *Developing reading strategies: Insights.* Austin, TX: Author.

Sticht, T. G., & James, J. H. (1984). Listening and reading. In P. D. Pearson (Ed.), *Handbook of reading research* (pp. 293–317). New York: Longman.

Stone, B. J. (1995). Best practices in the use of standardized assessments. In A. Thomas & J. Grimes (Eds.), *Best practices in school psychology–III*. Washington, D.C: The National Association of School Psychologists.

Sunseth, K., & Bowers, P. G. (1996, August). *A double-deficit hypothesis of reading: Phonemic awareness and naming speed*. Poster session presented at the annual meeting of the American Psychological Association, Toronto.

Tallmadge, G. K., & Wood, C. T. (1978). *User's guide: ESEA Title I evaluation and reporting system*. Mountain View, CA: RMC Research Corporation.

Thomas, C. C., Englert, C. S., & Gregg, S. (1987). An analysis of errors and strategies in the expository writing of learning disabled students. *Remedial and Special Education, 8*(1), 21–30.

Thorndike, R. L. (1963). The concepts of over- and underachievement. New York: Columbia University, Teachers College, Bureau of Publications.

Thorndike, R. L., & Hagen, E. P. (1977). *Measurement and evaluation in psychology and education* (4th ed.). New York: Wiley.

Thorndike, R. L., Hagen, E. P., & Sattler, J. M. (1986). *Stanford–Binet Intelligence Scale–Fourth Edition: Technical manual*. Chicago, IL: Riverside.

Torgesen, J. K., Wagner, R. K., & Rashotte, C. A. (1994). Longitudinal studies of phonological processing and reading. *Journal of Learning Disabilities, 27*(5), 276–286.

Trachtenburg, P. (1990). Using children's literature to enhance phonics instruction. *The Reading Teacher, 43*(9), 648–655.

Traweek, D., & Berninger, V. (1997). Comparison of beginning literacy programs: Alternative paths to the same learning outcome. *Learning Disability Quarterly, 20,* 160–168.

U.S. Bureau of the Census. (1998). *Current population survey, October 1998: School enrollment supplement file* [CD-ROM]. Washington, DC: U.S. Bureau of the Census (Producer/Distributor).

Wechsler, D. (1989). *Wechsler Preschool and Primary Scale of Intelligence–Revised*. San Antonio, TX: The Psychological Corporation.

Wechsler, D. (1991). *Wechsler Intelligence Scale for Children–Third Edition*. San Antonio, TX: The Psychological Corporation.

Wechsler, D. (1997). *Wechsler Adult Intelligence Scale–Third Edition*. San Antonio, TX: The Psychological Corporation.

Whitaker, D., Berninger, V., Johnston, J., & Swanson, H. L. (1994). Intraindividual differences in levels of language in intermediate grade writers: Implications for the translating process. *Learning and Individual Differences, 6,* 107–130.

Wilkinson, G. (1993). *Wide Range Achievement Test–Third Edition*. Wilmington, DE: Wide Range.

Wong, B. Y. L. (1991). *Learning about learning disabilities*. San Diego, CA: Academic Press.

Woodcock, R. W., McGrew, K. S., & Mather, N. (2001). *Woodcock–Johnson III*. Itasca, IL: Riverside.

Wright, B. D., & Stone, M. H. (1979). *Best test design*. Chicago: MESA Press.

Yopp, H. K. (1995). Read-aloud books for developing phonemic awareness: An annotated bibliography. *The Reading Teacher, 48*(6), 538–543.